The Field of Geography

General Editors: W. B. Morgan and J. C. Pugh

Regional Industrial Analysis and Development

In the same series

Geoffrey J.D. Hewings

Regional Industrial Analysis and Development

St. Martin's Press   New York

Library of Congress Catalog Card Number: 77-76803

ISBN: 0-312-66910-0

First published in the United States of America in 1977

Contents

The Field of Geography

Progress in modern geography has brought rapid changes in course work. At the same time the considerable increase in students at colleges and universities has brought a heavy and sometimes intolerable demand on library resources. The need for cheap textbooks introducing techniques, concepts and principles in the many divisions of the subject is growing and is likely to continue to do so. Much post-school teaching is hierarchical, treating the subject at progressively more specialized levels. This series provides textbooks to serve the hierarchy and to provide therefore for a variety of needs. In consequence some of the books may appear to overlap, treating in part of similar principles or problems, but at different levels of generalization. However, it is not our intention to produce a series of exclusive works, the collection of which will provide the reader with a 'complete geography', but rather to serve the needs of today's geography students who mostly require some common general basis together with a selection of specialized studies.

Between the 'old' and the 'new' geographies there is no clear division. There is instead a wide spectrum of ideas and opinions concerning the development of teaching in geography. We hope to show something of that spectrum in the series, but necessarily its existence must create differences of treatment as between authors. There is no general series view or theme. Each book is the product of its author's opinions and must stand on its own merits.

University of London
King's College
August, 1971

W. B. Morgan
J. C. Pugh

Acknowledgements

Many parts of this book have benefited from discussions with Drs William Bevers, Peter Cave, Andy Isserman, Lorie Tarshis, Anthony Thirlwall and Morgan Thomas, each of whom is, by tradition, exonerated for remaining errors and omissions. Dr W. B. Morgan, co-editor of this series, and Ms Janice Price of Methuen have been gracious, patient and very cooperative editors.

The author and publishers would like to thank the following for permission to reproduce copyright material:

the Editor of the *Oxford Economic Papers* for fig. 2.1

the Editor of *Social and Economic Studies* for fig. 3.1

Johns Hopkins University Press for fig 4.2 (from Wilbur R. Thomson, *A Preface to Urban Economics*, 1964)

University of California Press for fig. 4.5 (from A. M. Ross, ed., *Employment Policy and the Labor Market*, 1965, copyright © by the Regents of the University of California)

the Administrative Director of the American Economic Association for fig. 5.3

the Editor of the *Bulletin of Economics and Statistics* for fig. 5.5

George Allen & Unwin Ltd for fig. 5.7 (from J. N. Bhagwati and R. S. Eckaus, *Development and Planning*, 1973)

Pergamon Press Ltd for fig. 5.8 (from M. J. Moseley, *Growth Centers in Spatial Planning*, 1974)

Dun and Bradstreet Canada Ltd/Ltée for fig. 5.9

D. C. Heath and Company for fig. 5.10 (from Donald N. Rothblatt, *Regional Planning: The Appalachian Experience*, 1971)

the Editor of the *Annals of Regional Science* for fig. 5.11

Brookings Institution, Washington, D.C., for maps 5.1 and 5.2 (from R. E. Bolton, *Defense Purchases and Regional Growth*, 1966)

Finally, thank you to Jack, Matt, Aaron and especially Anna for your patience, love and understanding.

Champaign, Illinois   G. J. D. H.
May 1977

1 Underlying need for regional analysis and development

Introduction

Assume that one was asked to speculate on the nature of the relationships between the following two sets of variables: (1) real income *per capita* for a nation for each year for the last several hundred years and time itself and (2) some measure of regional disparity (for example, the weighted standard deviation of regional incomes *per capita* or unemployment rates) and time for the same nation. From our own personal experience and observations of the last several decades (and extrapolating backwards through time), we would probably suggest a relationship for the first set of data similar to the one shown in fig. 1.1. Of course, the straight line is indicative only of the trend rather than the exact form of the mathematical relationship between the two variables. The second relationship, between regional disparity and time, is by no means as obvious. It will, in part, depend upon the surrogate measure used for regional disparity since we cannot observe the disparity directly. For example, we should not expect the relationship to look exactly the same in one case in which the disparity was measured using money or current income *per capita* as opposed to another case in which real income *per capita* was used.[1] Similarly, disparity measures using absolute rather than relative deviations from national income *per capita* data might form very different relationships with time. The graph drawn in fig. 1.2. was suggested by Williamson (1965) in an article in which he brought together a large body of diverse literature on this subject and attempted to generalize about regional disparities over time for a large number of countries. His work and previous studies by Myrdal (1957), Hirschman (1958) and Kuznets (1959) among others served to focus attention upon a very important element or

[1] Money or current income *per capita* would represent the actual number of dollars or pounds of income whereas real income *per capita* deflates each year's money income by the rate of increase in the consumer price index. Although there are a number of problems with indexing, it does allow a more useful temporal comparison of incomes. In the literature, such deflated measures are usually referred to as 'constant dollars or pounds'.

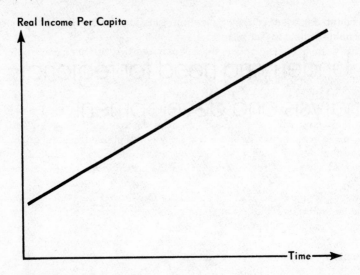

1.1 Hypothetical trend relationship between real income *per capita* in a nation and time.

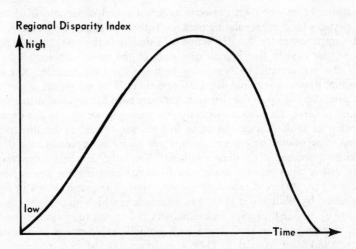

1.2 A possible relationship between an index of regional disparity and time.

dimension in the national growth and development process – namely, that growth in indicators of national prosperity may be only a necessary but not a sufficient condition for ensuring dispersion of this prosperity to all parts of the nation. Regional disparities in levels of welfare, broadly defined, still exist in most countries: whether they have diminished or increased over time remains a major point of debate (see chapter 4).

Fifty years ago, geographers would have regarded the 'regional problem' as an issue related to the core of the discipline. The polemics about regional methodology centred on problems of indentification of regions, regional personality, the 'regional method' in geography and geography's prime concern with regional *qua* areal differentiation. There was little explicit concern with the issues raised in this volume, and while the concerns recounted above are not quite so prominent today in the geographical literature, there is considerable evidence of new initiatives towards fusing once again the theoretical and methodological excursions into partial aspects of regional studies within a more holistic and rigorous framework.

Part of the impetus for this development of a new interest in regional studies can be traced to the development of regional science, a relatively new field of inquiry which first appeared in the United States in the late 1950s. Since its inception, geographers' participation in this field has vacillated from one extreme to the other. This book was written in an attempt to encourage undergraduate geographers to explore the rich offerings of regional science. With current interest in all manner of environmental problems, the concept of Spaceship Earth, the current (1975) energy crises, issues are no longer the sole prerogative of any one individual discipline to solve. While no one is quite ready to proclaim that unanimity exists among practitioners of regional science theory, there is considerable evidence to suggest that there is a move towards looking at regions holistically once again. The interface between the economic and the ecologic system requires understanding of not only the separate components of each system but the way they interact with each other. As an undergraduate, one was told that this was what geographers did in fact, although it was never quite clear how this was to be accomplished since very few usable tools of analysis seemed available. Walter Isard's recent statement of the art of regional science abounds with pleas and suggestions for integrating what has been, to this point, a diverse set of theories in social science into a more general and useful single theory (Isard 1969). The integration with the natural science system still awaits further general development, although there have been some recent pioneering attempts (see Isard *et al.* 1972; Cumberland and Korbach 1973; Laurent and Hite 1972; Miernyk and Seers 1974; Victor 1972).

In this volume only some of the more important techniques of regional analysis are presented as a prelude to a discussion of some of the more important issues in regional development. This book then is in no sense a complete guide: many other excellent volumes are now available which will take the reader into newer and more complicated realms of regional analysis.

This book was written with a clientele of undergraduates in mind, the undergraduates who have already taken a basic course in economic geography, some statistics and simple linear models and intermediate economic theory. As a result, some facility with economic theory is assumed and a knowledge of simple matrix algebra will assist the later discussions.

Approaches to regional industrial analysis

There does not exist one approach to regional industrial analysis which can necessarily claim to be more valuable or more instructive than any other. One could proceed on the basis of detailed case studies of individual industries, an examination in depth of one or two regions, or even at a more macroregional level, emphasizing linkages and interdependence in an interregional system within a country. The approach chosen here is to pursue the interests through discussion and exposition of several sets of methodology and theory. In the final chapter some attempt will be made to tie the theory to some selected case studies.

The scale at which one examines these phenomena is obviously critical. For example, at the county level, one may be able to identify a large number of counties whose unemployment rate has persisted at levels above the national average. If these counties are then grouped into a set of regions, the number of 'problem areas' may fall and, if aggregation proceeds further, one may be able to eliminate all problem areas! Thus, the choice of scale is not one that can comfortably be ignored. However, certain pragmatic considerations relate to any form of analysis, even those forms (of which this volume is not one) claiming to be entirely objective and value-free. Data requirements for any form of empirical analysis set limits on the implementation and testing of models and theories. Thus, regions defined *a priori* will be used without any claim that they represent the optimal division of space.

It is only recently that regional analysis has come to be concerned with not only the more traditional concerns of regional science – what Isard (1969) refers to as situations in which planning and decision-making structures are given and the objective is then one of providing the most efficient operational technique – but also the need to consider whom the recipients of this planning process are liable to be and what input they should make in reaching decisions. For example, Isard (1969) recognizes the linkage between (1) the proper degree of spatial decentralization of decision-making and (2) the efficient allocation of industry and other economic activity among regions. In this sense, there are no 'givens', no fixed institutional or political and administrative structure: the optimal allocation of any industrial capacity is thus a function of the degree of spatial decentralization of decision-making which is, itself, a function of the allocation of industrial capacity. These are issues which require a good deal of systematic understanding of a wide variety of knowledge, and certainly constitute a spectrum of inquiry far broader than the scope of this volume.

Regional issues: a general statement

The renaissance of interest in quality of life indicators, such as pollution and congestion in urban areas, has added a new dimension to the development objectives that have been articulated by a number of national economies. In addition to more traditional concerns with faster rates of growth of GNP, a slow rate of increase of prices and so forth, the environmental issues have created a situation in which unfettered devotion on the part of national governments to the 'growth ethic' is no longer desired by an increasingly vocal minority in many countries.

Concern with regional development has been recast to link it more closely with quality and equity issues: thus, locating new industry, for example, in a less prosperous region is now subject to new air quality constraints such as limitations on air-borne particulate matter emitted and varying standards of water quality control. Very few issues are purely 'regional' in origin – the semantic issues associated with defining regions make it very difficult to assert that there are regional problems *per se* – yet very few issues in contemporary society do not bear directly or indirectly on regional problems.

Regional inequalities (measured in terms of income, employment, growth, outmigration, etc.) in some or all of their various guises have persisted in developed societies even though these societies, considered as nations *in toto*, have experienced long periods of rapid national growth in the last several decades. Paradoxically, to some analysts, these strong periods of national growth have seen some regions become worse rather than better off. The general feeling that convergence of regional differences will result from long periods of national growth is now seriously doubted: the reasons for this are not clear, neither is the theoretical construct suggesting that increasing convergence will be observed over time.

Recent work by King *et al.* (1969, 1972) and Bassett and Haggett (1971) has served to focus attention on regions as sub-systems operating within the larger national economic system. The diffusion of innovations, recessions, booms, leads and lags in business cycles all tend to affect regions in a different fashion: attempts to explore regional problems without reference to interregional and regional-national linkages deny insights into the fundamental structure of the interregional system. As a general statement regions are not capable of truly endogenous growth: neither are they able to shield themselves effectively from expansionary and contractionary trends in other regions, although the degree of interaction among particular regions is uneven over space and time.

Thus by regional issues one really implies interregional issues, by regional growth one implies interregional growth. The frameworks that are to be discussed in this book essentially imply the correct nature of the interregional system but their design usually focuses on only a small subset of that system. The interregional models introduced in chapters 2 and 3 and the discussion of growth and equity issues in the final chapter serve to focus attention once more on the holistic nature of the regional system.

In North America and most western European countries one of the major problems associated with regional development is the issue of unemployment, with its varying spatial and sectoral components. It has received attention, though not always continuous or convincing, since the 1930s because, as Hall (1970) has pointed out, 'It became clear [then] that unemployment was the single most important indicator of economic stress in an industrial economy.' It would be prudent to point out that unemployment statistics are treated somewhat less than reverently by some authors who claim that they either under- or overestimate the 'true' numbers of persons unemployed. But, nevertheless, the statistics do provide some guidance for identifying areas of persistently high unemployment and thereby provide some insights into the workings of these less prosperous areas. Associated with unemployment problems in a region, one may find a declining dominant industry, a narrow economic base, regional growth performance (measured by industry output, labour force, *per capita* productivity, etc.) which is less than that observed nationally and, perhaps, problems associated with outmigration leaving a labour force which is less 'attractive' to entrepreneurs interested in new locations for their plant.

To talk as though there was just one 'regional problem' would understate the complexity of the issues and would further suggest that only one kind of problem exists. The empirical evidence is far from suggesting generality in the sense that *all* regions in *all* countries exhibit similar positive benefits or negative ills. The familiar 'north-south' dichotomy in levels of development across regions within countries and the parallels this has to differentials across countries is well known.

This last point has led to the borrowing and modification of methodology and theory developed for analysis at the national and international level. The feeling was that models of international trade could be modified to describe interregional trade and, similarly, that macro-Keynesian models describing employment and income multipliers could be adapted to describe similar processes at the regional level. In this sense, one can point to very little that is uniquely *regional* theory. However, recently, attempts are in evidence of models designed to integrate national and regional analysis. It is here that some of the ideas developed by Isard and his associates await further refinement and application.

It was noted earlier that the regional problem was, in reality, a composite of many problems, some of which may appear in different guises in any given region or develop in different directions and at different paces over time. It would be foolish to pretend that we may be able to divide a national economy into a set of regions and thereafter assign labels to these regions on the basis of their being 'developed', 'underdeveloped' or 'depressed'. However, we can note the degree to which regional economies have participated in the general national largesse of recent times. This will allow pursuit of two sets of inquiry: (1) an attempt to understand why some regions have benefited more than the general average and (2) to ascertain why other regions experienced less benefit from continuing national growth. In focusing attention on both sets of regions, one is avoiding the danger of concentrating energies solely upon the less prosperous regions. An examination of structure and processes operating in the more prosperous regions may provide the necessary insights into processes and structure in less prosperous regions. For example, we may compare industrial structures in more and less developed regions, noting differences and relating these to growth performances over time. In addition, if the processes operating in less prosperous regions are different, one cannot assume that the sequential development pattern exhibited by the more prosperous regions will be repeated. The implications for policy choice and action should be obvious.

Some regional issues: the examples of unemployment and regional business cycles

As an introduction to the formal analysis, let us examine the spatial and temporal evidence of unemployment in Canada. Table 1.1 lists the average annual unemployment rates by region in Canada for the period 1946 to 1970. The same data are shown in graphed form in fig. 1.3 and transformed to deviations from the annual Canadian average in fig. 1.4 The untransformed data reflect the general trends in regional experience, suggesting a widening of differentials between the 'best' and 'worst' areas in the early 1960s and a tendency towards narrowing of these differentials in the last few years, although the improvement thus exhibited is not quite as great as it may seem at first glance. Clearly, a number of important insights may be gained through transforming the data to deviations from the national average.[1] Of the five regions identified, two have continually experienced unemployment rates below the national average, one region has consistently exhibited a rate 1·5 per cent above the national average, while the rates for the other two regions have fluctuated within 2 per cent of this average. The data suggest that the regions of Canada share periods of growth and decline rather unevenly. The regional response to national business cycles may be gauged by comparing the peaks and the troughs in the cycle (shown in figs 1.3 and 1.4) with peaks and troughs in regional unemployment rates and their deviations from the national average.

A more precise measure of the relationship between regional and national fluctuations may be obtained through regressing the annual regional unemployment rates on the corresponding national rate. Thirlwall (1966) used this method for the UK regions and Denton (1966) has performed a similar analysis for the Canadian regions; the proposition is that the regression coefficients could then be used as a measure of unemployment sensitivity in the regions of Canada. Denton used regressions of the form:

$$Y_t^r = a + b_1 X_t^n + b_2 t \pm e_t, \tag{1.1}$$

where Y_t^r is the rate of unemployment in region r in time t,

        X_t^n is the national unemployment rate in time t,

        t is time $(1946 = 1, 1947 = 2, \ldots)$, and

        e_t is a random disturbance term.

For this analysis, the data were transformed to first differences:

$$Y_t^r - Y_{t-1}^r = \alpha + \beta(X_t^n - X_{t-1}^n) \pm u_t. \tag{1.2}$$

The advantages of using first differences are essentially related to the error specification: time series regression analysis often involves dealing with the problem of serial correlation. It these errors are not random, considerable bias can be introduced into the estimated equation creating suspicion about its validity. By transforming the variables to first differences, we assume that errors of the

---

[1] These deviations are unweighted in the sense that they do not take account of the relative importance of each region in terms of percentage of the labour force resident therein.

Table 1.1   Canadian Unemployment Rates, 1946–1970

Year	Canada	Atlantic	Quebec	Ontario	Prairies	B.C.
1946	3·8	7·7	4·3	2·3	2·4	4·2
1947	2·6	6·5	2·7	1·8	1·8	3·1
1948	2·6	6·2	2·5	1·7	1·7	3·5
1949	3·3	6·9	3·6	2·3	2·2	3·9
1950	3·8	8·4	4·6	2·5	2·2	4·4
1951	2·6	4·7	3·2	1·8	1·8	3·7
1952	3·0	4·6	3·9	2·2	1·9	4·1
1953	3·0	5·5	3·8	2·1	1·9	4·0
1954	4·6	6·6	5·9	3·8	2·5	5·2
1955	4·4	6·5	6·2	3·2	3·1	3·8
1956	3·4	6·0	5·0	2·4	2·2	2·8
1957	4·6	8·4	6·0	3·4	2·6	5·0
1958	7·0	12·5	8·8	5·4	4·1	8·6
1959	6·0	10·9	7·9	4·5	3·2	6·5
1960	7·0	10·7	9·1	5·4	4·2	3·5
1961	7·1	11·2	9·2	5·5	4·6	8·5
1962	5·9	10·7	7·5	4·3	3·9	6·6
1963	5·5	9·5	7·5	3·8	3·7	6·4
1964	4·7	7·8	6·4	3·2	3·1	5·3
1965	3·9	7·4	5·4	2·5	2·5	4·2
1966	3·6	6·4	4·7	2·5	2·1	4·5
1967	4·8	6·7	5·3	3·2	2·4	5·2
1968	4·8	7·4	6·6	3·6	2·9	5·9
1969	4·7	7·5	6·9	3·2	2·9	5·0
1970	5·9	7·6	7·9	4·3	4·4	7·6

Sources: Ostry (1968); Ostry and Zaidi (1972)

original variable will be autocorrelated and therefore largely eliminated by transformation to first differences. Only first difference errors should remain and these are random (see Christ 1966). The results presented in table 1.2 provide a basis for the assessment of regional responses to change in national unemployment rates. The high R^2 values (coefficients of determination[1],) and the 't' values greater than the critical values at 99 per cent confidence level allow one to be able to interpret the regression coefficient with a certain degree of assurance. Regions with a coefficient greater than unity are regions which are cyclically sensitive: a coefficient of less than unity would indicate relative cyclical insensitivity. As one would have expected from the earlier discussion, the Atlantic, Quebec and B.C. regions are cyclically sensitive: for example, using the estimates of the coefficients of X in table 1.2, a one percentage point change in the national unemployment rate would generate a greater than 1·3 per cent change in B.C., 1·12 per cent change in Quebec and 1·08 per cent change in the Atlantic region. In Ontario and the Prairies, a similar national change would result in a regional change of 0·82 per cent and 0·61 per cent respectively.

Having suggested that regional movements, in terms of one indicator, have not necessarily paralleled those of the nation, one now needs to identify some of

[1] The value of R^2 is a measure of the strength of the relationship between X and Y and is the proportion of the variance of Y explained by X.

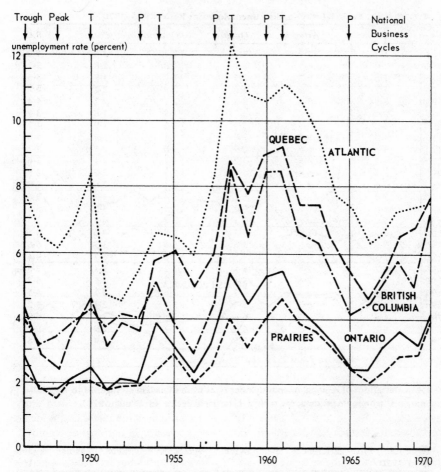

1.3   Regional unemployment rates, Canada, 1946–1970. *Source*: See table 1.1.

the underlying reasons which would cause divergence in individual regional performance *vis-à-vis* the nation. Siegal notes that the explanation is usually sought in industrial structure, in the sense that (1) regions have different industry mixes and (2) as a consequence of the fact that industries at the national level exhibit differing cyclical profiles, a different combination (from the national mix) at the regional level is likely to provide divergent patterns in the regional behaviour of indicators like unemployment (Siegal 1966–7). In addition, leads and lags in regional investment responses to changes in industrial and consumer demands may be reflected in different rates of increases/cutbacks in activity: the applicability of regional investment functions has been explored (Gillen and Guccione 1970, 1972) and will be discussed in later sections.

The divergence between national and regional indicators like unemployment

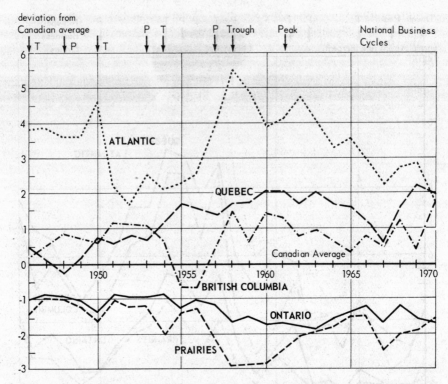

1.4 Deviations of regional unemployment rates from Canadian average, 1946–1970.
Source: Unemployment data, see table 1.1; business cycles, see White (1970).

Table 1.2 First differences unemployment regression equations, Canadian regions, 1946–1970

		R^2	Level of significance
Atlantic	$Y = 0\cdot1198 + 1\cdot2067\ X$ (6·1372)	0·632	1%
Quebec	$Y = 0\cdot0422 + 1\cdot1253\ X$ (12·6181)	0·878	1%
Ontario	$Y = 0\cdot0184 + 0\cdot8438\ X$ (18·7669)	0·941	1%
Prairies	$Y = 0\cdot0263 + 0\cdot5951\ X$ (8·3022)	0·758	1%
British Columbia	$Y = 0\cdot0173 + 1\cdot2978\ X$ (9·4784)	0·802	1%

Notes: The bracketed terms are the 't' values for the regression coefficients: the critical values are 2·07 (95 per cent) and 2·82 (99 per cent).

Since first differences were computed, the period under discussion is really 1946–7 to 1969–70.

may be measured in terms of the duration, amplitude, trend and timing of the regional and national business cycles. With a regional industrial mix more heavily dominated by cyclically sensitive industries, one would expect *a priori* a greater degree of fluctuation in regional activity. However, this may not explain the existing *levels* of unemployment, and for this reason an analysis of industry-by-industry changes in activity in each region may be the only way a solution to this problem will be found. The importance of this information may be suggested as follows. If industry mix is the sole cause of divergence between national and regional business cycles, the policy needs here would be in the direction of changing the regional industrial mixes. On the other hand, if firms in the *same* industry react differently in different regions as a result of structural differences (input–output linkages, product mix, etc.), labour market problems or even the competitive nature of the regional industrial structures, then alternative policies are called for. Siegal attempted to identify and assess the importance of the latter or 'location' influence for a selected number of SMSAs (Standard Metropolitan Statistical Areas) in the US during the period 1949–62 (Siegal 1966–7). He used the Kruskal-Wallis *H*-test (analogous to the analysis of variance but applied to nonparametric data) and his results indicated no significant difference in the average SMSA amplitude for durable goods industries, but a significant difference for nondurable goods industries. Siegal's analysis suggested that other forces were at work but, because of data deficiencies, he was unable to provide an unqualified assessment. What are needed, perhaps, are analyses of individual industries in each region to provide answers to questions of the form: does the fabricated metal industry (for example) in Ontario expand and contract in phase with the industry in the nation as a whole and at the same rate of growth (decline)? The rate of growth will be especially important, as it will affect the rate of recovery in economic activity; *ceteris paribus*, a higher (than national average) rate of growth in a region should allow for a more favourable recovery.

McKee's study of the Southeast of the United States represents one attempt to identify the industry mix contribution to regional cyclical patterns (McKee 1967). Selected income and employment series for the Southeast and for the United States were analysed in an effort to isolate the relative cyclical behaviour of the Southeast. The main differences in the income cycles were in the size of the amplitude. The greater volatility and weight of farm income in the region were suggested as the primary cause of the relative instability of the personal income and income *per capita* in the Southeast. This finding was substantiated by the greater than national instability exhibited in agricultural employment. The aggregate employment series displayed identical national and regional turning points. The agricultural employment series did exhibit differences in amplitudes in the periods of expansion, contraction and the full cycle; on the other hand, the nonagricultural differences were insignificant. McKee suggested that the results indicated greater instability in the Southeast during the post-war period. Apart from the contribution of agriculture noted above, the 'location influences' of the type Siegal alluded to may have been important within the context of firm size. The Southeast region contains a higher proportion of

employment in small firms than does the nation and, as Ferguson has demonstrated, employment in small firms tends to be more variable (Ferguson 1960).
However, employment in nonagricultural sectors in the region tended to greater
stability than the nation – hence the small firm hypothesis may be more applicable in the agricultural sector where a combination of small farms and the
absence of diversification may provide the major source of regional instability.

From the preceding comments, it is obvious that (1) the issues are closely
interrelated (i.e. unemployment fluctuations stem from fluctuations in industrial
activities) and (2) one is able to offer a variety of reasons for any given set of
outcomes. The frameworks one chooses to explore these problems will depend
upon the particular objective in question: regional analysis is still not quite
sophisticated enough to offer the super-model or synthesis that Richardson, for
one, has hoped for (Richardson 1969a) and towards which Isard's *General
Theory* is directed (Isard *et al.* 1969).

Regional-metropolitan problems

The foregoing discussion has treated regions as though they were internally
homogeneous in the sense of levels of unemployment or responses to national
business cycles. In a similar fashion to the problems of generalizing about
regional levels of activity on the basis of national levels, we find it equally difficult to comment meaningfully about intraregional variations on the basis of
activity at the regional level. This dilemma is not a new one in spatial analysis
and while one has no wish to dismiss it as a side issue, a certain amount of pragmatism is in order. Applying some conventional wisdom, we will assume that the
regions we will deal with in this study are sufficiently meaningful to warrant
attention: at times, we will delve below the regional framework and examine
activity at the subregional or urban level. The linkages between urban and
regional analysis are strong – empirically and theoretically: in many situations,
we find a set of urban-metropolitan problems transcending regional boundaries
and affecting cities in all regions irrespective of the degree of development in the
region.

The growth and development of the national urban system has been
approached theoretically and empirically with a view to demonstrating both the
existence and validity of an urban hierarchy. Of particular interest in a regional
analysis context has been the search for city size optima and the associated
positive benefits of achieving optimal city size distributions over size categories
and over space. The issue is extremely relevant in the application of growth pole,
growth centre and industrial complex theory to regional development and is a
topic to which we shall return in later sections. Suffice to comment here that the
underdevelopment of a region's urban system (in terms of size distributions)
may be the main contributor to the region's overall lack of development. At the
other end of the scale, the most prosperous regions contain urban areas which
are experiencing the difficulties of too much or too rapid growth. The dichotomy is not usually quite so clearly defined as is being suggested. However, the
basically urban issues of underprovision of inexpensive urban housing, spatial

discrimination in the housing market, urban congestion and pollution, and the problems of metropolitan government, are issues or externalities associated with prosperity. They are almost necessary conditions for the faster urban growth and problems some municipalities would prefer (perhaps only in the short run) in place of existing problems of no or slow growth. Finally, one notes the continuing urbanization of developed countries, such that it is becoming increasingly difficult to divorce urban from regional problems, especially as the percentage of urban dwellers approaches 70 or 80 per cent of the total population.

Differential growth and stagnation: an overview

The Canadian Prices and Incomes Commission (1972) noted, in June 1972, that

> Although the Canadian economy has been exposed to sufficient intermittent demand pressure since the early 1950s to raise the Consumer Price Index by about 50 percent, the national unemployment rate over the same period has averaged slightly higher than 5 percent of the labour force.

In the search for an explanation of this phenomenon, the Commision suggested the existence of marked regional differentials in unemployment rates, the data series discussed earlier. The regional unemployment rates suggest a nonhomogeneous (spatially) labour market: on the one hand, one has a very sophisticated, efficient market in southern Ontario centred around Toronto, where, for many years a certain degree of 'tightness' has been exhibited as aggregate demand has caused some strain on productive capacity. At the other end of the spectrum and spatially separated from Ontario by over 1000 miles, one finds labour market conditions in the Atlantic provinces which have exhibited all the signs of persistent and often chronic unemployment. Classical equilibrium theory might suggest some market clearing processes whereby unemployed labour would move from the Atlantic region to Ontario and/or firms would relocate in the Atlantic region to take advantage of less expensive labour inputs. However, empirical studies on firm mobility illustrate the complexity of the decision-making calculus of which relative regional factor prices are just one component. Mobility of labour is not without its constraints: job search involves both time and considerable cost in the Canadian context and, apart from the perceived problem of incomplete information, the *de facto* mismatch of vacancies and unemployed by occupation further complicate equilibriating tendencies. The effects of continued high unemployment upon labour force participation and migration behaviour will be explored in later sections. These issues are extremely controversial and bring us right to the forefront of the debate on policy for unemployment, the trade-offs among goals at the national level and their differential impact upon regional economies.

Guide to books and journals in regional analysis

Contributions by geographers to the type of regional analysis contained in this volume have been, until very recently, rather sporadic. The interest of geographers, for the most part, had focused on description and interpretation of the character of various regions. Perhaps spurred by the 'encroachment' of regional science in areas that have been regarded traditionally as those of primary concern to geographers, the more recent contributions by geographers have tended to reflect a broader training in economics and the application of quantitative methods. Thus, it is becoming increasingly difficult to distinguish articles written by geographers, economists or regional planners within the broad field of regional analysis on the basis of methodology, content, interpretation and so forth. If there is any characteristic leaning by geographers, it may well be in the direction of empirical testing and the discussion and evaluation of particular regional development patterns. A comparison of A. J. Brown, *The Framework of Regional Economics in the United Kingdon* (1972), with G. Manners *et al.*, *Regional Development in Britain* (1972), will serve to illustrate that the economists' and geographers' views have not entirely merged, although there is considerable overlap.

For a long time, the serious student of regional analysis had few major sources of material. Perloff *et al.*, *Regions, Resources and Economic Growth* (1960), was one of the first attempts at providing an integration of a diffuse body of theory and empirical testing within the context of the United States. The same year this book was published, Walter Isard's nascent Regional Science Studies series introduced the second volume reflecting the character and rather impressive growth of the new discipline of regional science. *Methods of Regional Analysis* (1960) remains today a valuable reference volume, containing a number of lengthy essays introducing the reader to the various analytical methods of regional analysis. In the fourteen years since this book was published, the field of inquiry has both broadened and deepened. Isard's *General Theory* (1969) attempts to accommodate these changes, but one should be aware that the book is long and, at times, difficult reading since it delves (often simultaneously) into major areas of calculus, linear algebra, decision-making, game theory and behavioural psychology! It is certainly not recommended as a book for the beginning student in this field!

In the interim between the publication of these two books, several alternative texts have appeared as well as collections of readings. John Meyer's article, 'Regional economics: a survey', appraises the state of the art through 1963; A. J. Brown's survey article in 1969 extends the time horizon to that point as well as focusing more heavily on British contributions. Needleman's collection of readings, *Regional Analysis* (1968), provides a useful set of material, none of which was written by geographers. A later collection of readings has been edited by Richardson (*Regional Economics: A Reader*, 1970) essentially to complement his text *Regional Economics* (1969). The latter is concerned with a broad range of issues and has attempted to relate much of regional economics to the theoretical underpinnings of traditional economics. Richardson has also digested some of the more important aspects into two Penguin paperbacks, *The Elements of Regional Economics* (1969) and *Urban Economics* (1971). More recently, he has written a volume dealing entirely with regional and interregional applications of input–output analysis.

Nourse's book *Regional Economics* (1968) was the first with that particular title and frame of reference: although it contains the main elements and is very well written, it attempted to cover a very large field in too short a space. Siebert's *Regional Economic Growth* (1969) is an important theoretical contribution to the field: empirical data are absent from the book but this should not be interpreted to mean the book is dull or turgid. Siebert's book is, in some sense, in the Isard tradition in that the author attempts to generate a number of important theorems about regional structure and regional growth rather than examine the detailed performance of individual regions. A book in a similar vein, although one with some empirical application, is the volume by Borts and Stein, *Economic Growth in a Free Market* (1964). Students without considerable background in economic growth theory will find this book hard going. At an introductory level, Edgar Hoover's *An Introduction to Regional Economics* (1969) is the product of a man whose writing style makes his analysis seem deceptively simple. Those who have read and profited from his earlier book, *The Location of Economic Activity* (1948), will probably derive similar benefits from the later book.

For the most part, geographers' contributions have been in the applied field, and in areas concerned with policy issues. In this category, one would refer to Britton's *Regional Analysis and Economic Geography* (1967), Chisholm and Manners's *Spatial Policy Problems of the British Economy* (1971) and the volume by Manners *et al.* referred to earlier in this section. Other books which are more policy-oriented, although not written by geographers, would include Brewis's *Regional Economic Policies in Canada* (1969), Cameron's *Regional Economic Development: The Federal Role* (1971), Hansen's *Growth Centers in Regional Economic Development* (1972) and a new series published by Mouton under the editorship of Antoni Kuklinski. Books in this series include area studies, for example J. H. Cumberland's *Regional Development: Experiences and Prospects in the U.S.A.* (1971), as well as general studies on growth poles.

Finally, Kain and Meyer's *Essays in Regional Economics* (1971) and McKee, Dean and Leahy's *Regional Economics* (1970) contain some useful papers, the former including many that have not been published before. Perhaps one of the most comprehensive set of readings is found in Friedmann and Alonso's *Regional Policy* (1975). In this collection, theory, issues and case studies are provided in a mix of new and standard articles. The role of public policy is examined in Hansen's *Public Policy and Regional Economic Development* (1974), a collection of analyses of the experiences of nine Western countries.

The serious student should also keep abreast of the major journals in the field, a list of which is given in the appendix. Many of the journals offer appreciable savings to student subscribers, thus providing a favourable cost-benefit ratio to the recipient. Articles in regional analysis do not appear exclusively in these journals; one should also check the major geographical and economic journals and issues of *Environment and Planning, Geographical Analysis* and *Economic Development and Cultural Change*, as well as the *Journal of Economic Literature* issued by the American Economic Association. This last journal provides a list of articles appearing in almost all economic and related journals, the list being classified by both journal and topic: as one of the topics is regional economics, this journal becomes a useful source since it obviates checking a large number of serials (for example, *Journal of Farm Economics*) which only have articles occasionally on regional aspects of study. In addition, abstracts are given of articles in regional economics appearing in some of the major journals.

Organization of the book

We established earlier in this chapter some of the problems that concern us in the field of regional analysis. To assist our understanding of these issues, several analytical tools may be employed. In the next chapter, we begin with a fundamental but essentially simple model, the economic base approach. From there, we extend the analysis to look at regional flows and examine the utility of international trade theory (such as the Hecksher-Ohlin theorem) to interregional trade.

In an attempt to overcome some of the shortcomings of the aggregated base approach, we delve into input–output analysis and evaluate the additional insights this family of models is able to offer us.

Theories of regional economic growth and development are reviewed in the next chapter, followed by some discussion of recent empirical work, especially on the delicate issues of trade-offs between unemployment and inflation at the national and regional levels. This leads us into the problems of implementation of development and an evaluation of some experiments that have been performed. The work is far from complete, as will become readily apparent, but we do seem to be moving in the right direction in terms of the provision and development of analytical techniques.

2 Economic base and trade flows analysis

Introduction

It has become usual in the literature to associate the major development of the economic base concepts with the seminal series of articles by Andrews in *Land Economics* (1953–8). Andrews's work was instrumental in bringing together thoughts and ideas from a wide variety of disciplines and provided a framework in which discussion could take place on the general theme of differential growth and decline exhibited in urban and regional systems. However, one of the most interesting applications of the technique of economic base or spatial multiplier analysis was that provided in an earlier paper by Daly (1940). His concern was with the differential prosperity existing in the UK and with substantiating or refuting certain 'common beliefs' about the reasons for this spatial inequality. Daly divided industry into what he called 'unimpeded' and 'localized', the former characterized by industries 'dealing in easily transportable and imperishable goods' (Daly 1940, p. 249), and the latter by industries affected by 'geographic' rather than 'economic' factors: 'These industries must be located at the point of demand, because the nature of the service they render is personal or perishable or both' (Daly 1940, p. 249). Daly used regression techniques to establish the relationship between the two types of industries:

$$Y = 37,595 + 1 \cdot 042X, \tag{2.1}$$

where Y represented employment in the localized industries and X employment in the geographically unfettered or unimpeded industries. The coefficient b is the multiplier: in this case, for every 100 new jobs created in unimpeded industries an additional 104 new jobs would be created in localized industries. Daly's discussion of the regional variations in this multiplier raised several interesting points about the utility of large-scale transference of firms from the Southeast of the UK to the North. Essentially, his argument rested upon the belief that the indirect effects in the North would be much smaller (i.e., the value of b would be lower) and that

Diverting the newer industries to the distressed areas would, therefore, constitute a vital injury to the future prosperity of the South, make only a negli-
gible contribution to employment in the North, and greatly reduce the potential level of national employment and income . . . (Daly 1940, p. 257)

In later chapters we will explore, in greater detail, the existence of a trade-off
between regional equity and national efficiency: current research would tend to
dispute Daly's findings and, further, there seems evidence to suggest that multipliers in the less prosperous parts of the UK are higher than those in more prosperous regions. However, the issue cannot be reduced simply to who is right or
wrong but, rather, which estimates seem most reasonable. A value-free regional
multiplier does not yet exist.

The economic base model

Interest in the existence of a differential spatial multiplier lay dormant until the
1950s when a profusion of studies of urban areas appeared. The notion of the
multiplier had captivated chambers of commerce eager to share in the national
prosperity and convinced that their communities' salvation and future growth
were a function of the nature and diversity of their 'basic' industries. While
economists like Thompson (1959) and earlier Hildebrand and Mace (1950) were
discussing the local employment multiplier and tracing its linkages to the Kahn
and Keynes employment/income multiplier, geographers (for example,
Alexander 1954) were developing the concept of the economic base and the
cause and effect relationship between two different types of activity in an urban
area or region.

Essentially, the notion of the economic base model is to identify, either in
income or employment terms, that proportion of activity in a region that is
dependent upon markets outside the region and the proportion that is dependent upon intraregional markets. The former has been referred to variously as
basic, autonomous, exogenous or city-forming activity; the latter, as nonbasic,
local, endogenous, city-filling and, occasionally, as residentiary activity
(although this term has a slightly different connotation). The basic activity is
assumed to be the driving mechanism without which the city or region would
not prosper. In a sense, the theory represents an adaptation of the 'export or
die' feeling prevalent in the thinking of some of the international trade literature.
The region thus derives its major stimuli externally and is seen to grow or decline
according to the nature and size of the basic activity. The nonbasic or local
activity is, in turn, dependent upon the basic activity. Nonbasic functions are
thus 'localized' (to use Daly's terminology): their nature and size depend upon
(1) the level of activity in the basic sector and (2) the size of the region. Changes
in the levels of activity in the basic sector will result in changes in the nonbasic
sector: the magnitude of these changes will be determined by the *basic : nonbasic
ratio* and changes in total activity by the *regional multiplier*. As we shall see, the
two concepts are derived from the same assumptions about activity relationships
in a regional setting.

For example, let us assume that there are 750,000 persons employed in the region, of whom 500,000 work in activities we may designate as basic (i.e. the sales of the output from these industries is shipped to markets outside the region). Hence, the remaining employees are occupied in the nonbasic sector. The basic :nonbasic ratio is thus 500,000/250,000 or 2 :1. The theory of the economic base implies that there is a cause–effect relationship between basic and nonbasic activity such that an increase in basic activity, say by 5000 persons, would result in an increase of 2500 persons in nonbasic activity. The ratio thus reads, 'for every two persons employed in basic activity, an additional person will be employed in nonbasic activity'. Hence, the initial increase of 5000 persons will lead to a total increase of 5000 + 2500 or 7500. Thus, as a result of a direct increase of 5000, the regional employment increases by 7500. The multiplier, relating the *total* increase to the *direct* increase, would be 7500/5000 or 1·5. Obviously, we could have obtained this from the basic : nonbasic ratio, since for every two persons employed in basic activity (the direct effect) an additional person would be employed in nonbasic activity (the indirect effect). Therefore, the multiplier would be 3 (total effect)/2 (the direct effect) or 1·5.

The model may be presented in a more formal fashion. Let E_t, E_b and E_{nb} be the total, basic and nonbasic employment in the region. By definition

$$E_t = E_b + E_{nb}, \tag{2.2}$$

and if we define r as the ratio of nonbasic to total employment,

$$E_{nb} = rE_t. \tag{2.3}$$

Let us assume that there has been an increase in the demand for the goods produced by the basic industries, resulting in an increase of basic employment of ΔE_b: what will be the change in non-basic employment, ΔE_{nb}, and total employment, ΔE_t?

Substituting (2.2) into (2.3), we have

$$E_{nb} = r(E_b + E_{nb})$$
$$= rE_b + rE_{nb}.$$

Factoring

$$E_{nb}(1 - r) = rE_b$$

$$E_{nb} = \frac{r}{(1 - r)} \cdot E_b. \tag{2.4}$$

If we may assume that r is constant, then (2.4) may also be written

$$\Delta E_{nb} = \frac{r}{(1 - r)} \cdot \Delta E_b. \tag{2.5}$$

The multiplier k, $\Delta E_t / \Delta E_b$, is

$$k = \frac{\Delta E_b + \Delta E_{nb}}{\Delta E_b}$$

From (2.5) we have

$$k = \frac{\dfrac{r}{(1-r)} \cdot \Delta E_b + \Delta E_b}{\Delta E_b}$$

$$= \frac{\dfrac{r}{(1-r)} + 1}{1}$$

$$= \frac{1}{(1-r)} .$$

From our earlier example, we may derive $r = 250{,}000/750{,}000 = 1/3$. Hence, the multiplier is $1/(1 - 1/3) = 3/2 = 1\cdot5$. Those familiar with the aggregate relationships of introductory macroeconomics will recognize the form of the multiplier derived from equation (2.5) (see, e.g., Samuelson 1976; Lipsey 1969; Rowan 1969). The linkage between economic base, aggregate Keynesian analysis and input–output analysis will form the introduction to chapter 3.

Some problems associated with the economic base model

Before proceeding to a discussion of the applicability and utility of the model, as well as several possible extensions, it should be noted that several authors have expressed doubts about the identification of activity in this fashion. Obviously, with a large research grant, we could survey industrial establishments in a region and ascertain from the firms themselves the proportion of sales made intra-regionally. We could then allocate the proportions to the labour force data and derive our ratios therefrom. The issue of what data are the best to use is import-ant (see Tiebout 1956) although the most popular candidates are employment and income. In the absence of a source of funds to carry out direct survey work, a number of authors have suggested short-cut methods to arrive at estimates of basic:nonbasic ratios for communities and regions.

One of the familiar candidates is the *location quotient*. In this case, employ-ment in a region is compared to national employment in a set of comparable categories. For this, we need access to census data detailing the numbers employed in industries in the region and the nation by some standardized indus-trial classification. Firms are assigned to a classification on the basis of their major product(s): the level of classification may be very broad (at the one-digit level) or very detailed (at the four-digit level). For example,

Slaughtering and meat processors   101 (3-digit)
Slaughtering and meat packaging plants   1011 (4-digit)

Let us assume that we have established comparable categories at the regional and national levels in industry i: the location quotient is derived as follows:

$$LQ_i = [E_i^r / \sum_{i=1}^{i=m} E_i^r] / [E_i^n / \sum_{i=1}^{i=m} E_i^n] \qquad (2.6)$$

where E_i^r and E_i^n are the employment levels in industry i in the region and nation respectively,

$\sum_{i=1}^{i=m} E_i^r$ and $\sum_{i=1}^{i=m} E_i^n$ are the total employment levels in all industries in the region and nation (there being m industries).

The rationale behind the quotient is that a similar proportion of employment in industry i in the region to that of industry i in the nation would indicate a measure of 'self-sufficiency'. In this case, the location quotient would be equal to unity. If the computed quotient was greater than unity, we assume that the region is a net *exporter* of the products manufactured by industry i. Conversely, if the location quotient is less than unity, this would indicate that the region was a net *importer* from industry i. It will be readily apparent that some heroic assumptions underlie these interpretations of the location quotients. We must assume identical production and consumption patterns in *all* regions and, in addition, the product mix within each industrial category i is assumed similar at the regional and national level. Even if we could accept the last assumption, we know that consumption patterns do vary from region to region (especially in North America where the vagaries of the physical environment result in the purchase of different commodities – for example, the market area for snowmobiles is relatively restricted). The open nature of regional economies and the differences in the degree of agglomeration observed in regional space create problems that make uncritical acceptance of spatially homogeneous production patterns rather difficult.

Some years ago, Leven (1964) noted that we need estimates of *gross exports* for multiplier calculations and, by underestimating exports (which the location quotient will do since it assumes regions only export if the quotient is greater than unity and thus denies the possibility of crosshauling), we will overestimate the size of the foreign-trade or regional multiplier. Another but related problem with the location quotient is that it is not independent of the level of aggregation: 'this technique will produce a consistently more downward biased estimate of exports, the greater the degree of aggregation employed in classifying industries' (Leven 1964, p. 133).

Evidence for this assertion may be seen in table 2.1. The greater the degree of disaggregation, the smaller the multiplier. In addition, disaggregation affects estimates of export employment in specific industries.

An alternative method for measuring the economic base has been suggested by Ullman and Dacey (1960). The 'minimum requirements technique' is premised on the assertion that derivation of a region's export or basic activity should not be made with reference to a national average but rather with reference to a *minimum* percentage of employment in each industrial category. It is usual practice to divide cities or regions into groups and, within these groups, to obtain the percentage of employment in each industrial category. Inspection of these data was then made to seek out the minimum such employment in each industrial

Table 2.1   Employment multipliers calculated at various levels of aggregation

| Area | Multiplier | | | |
	Division level data	2-digit level data	3-digit level data	4-digit level data
Georgia	19·01165	6·57299	5·49690	4·84118
Kansas	10·30828	6·51033	4·78054	4·29892
West Virginia	8·32867	4·17737	3·48111	3·14186
Philadelphia SMSA	17·24355	9·10950	6·03754	5·18102
Washington SMSA	3·30660	2·97354	2·81134	2·79792
Ft Monmouth Tri-County New Jersey	15·68284	7·17098	5·18690	4·47776
Monmouth County New Jersey	7·22016	5·16081	3·88481	3·49575

Note: The multipliers were calculated as $E_T/E_B = E_T/\sum_i \{[(LQ_i - 1)/LQ_i]E_i^r\}$ for all $LQ_i > 1$.
Source: Isserman (1976).

category. The sum of these minima was taken to represent the nonbasic portion of total activity. Nonbasic activity so derived varied (in 1950) from 24 per cent in cities of 2500–3000 population to 56 per cent in cities over 1 million population (Ullman and Dacey's study was applied to urban areas but there would appear to be no *a priori* reason why it could not be applied to regions). The variability of the basic: nonbasic ratio with respect to city size supports the earlier empirical observations collected in Alexander's (1954) article. He found that the *proportion* of activity classified as nonbasic increased as city-size increased. The minimum requirements approach has been subject to some criticism but has not yet been rejected convincingly. Pratt (1968) and Ullman (1968) engaged in debate on the issues of the appropriateness of the minima rather than averages (as used in the location quotient derivation) and the question of exactly what was being measured. Subsequently, the method has been used in reference to 1960 Census data and comparisons made with survey-based economic base studies (Ullman, Dacey and Brodsky 1969). The results were inconclusive in the sense that the nonsurvey technique was, at times, both accurate and inaccurate without any apparent consistency.

The variability of the basic: nonbasic ratio over time and over city or regional size presents problems of a different nature. There are few writers who would claim stability for the ratio over different size categories. As noted above, Alexander (1954) was one of the first writers to note the effect increased city size had on the proportion of activity that was nonbasic. This is not altogether surprising since an increase in the size of a city or region results in an increase in the size and buying power of the local market. One then begins to deal with cities and regions exhibiting far more complicated and interrelated industrial structures. Products formerly exported may now find a more convenient market locally. In addition, import substitution may take place. The usual example given is the case of a region with certain level of demand for bottled cola. Initially, the product may be distributed from a warehouse located outside the region. As the population in the region increases, other things being equal, a warehouse may be established in the region and, subsequently, a cola bottling plant. Local glass suppliers may now appear in the region supplying glass bottles and thus further increasing the nonbasic component of regional activity. The issue of the cause-and-effect relationship between the basic and nonbasic activity would seem to become important as the size of the region under consideration becomes very large. In fact, the debates on this particular aspect of economic base theory have been the most contentious particularly when applied to the problem of regional growth. In chapter 4 we will return to this issue, especially the exchange between North (1955, 1956) and Tiebout (1956). Blumenfeld's article of some years ago anticipated some of the criticisms of economic base theory raised by Tiebout (Blumenfeld 1955); however, Blumenfeld's position was rather more extreme in that he found virtually no utility in the concept!

The economic base extended: regional multiplers, the UK experience

One of the universal problems regional science faces continually is the dearth of subnational data. Implementation of even a simple economic base model of the type described earlier requires data inputs that are often too demanding for available resources. In the UK a number of writers have tried to provide estimates of the values of regional multipliers. The policy implications of reliable estimates need to be stressed since the open nature of regional economies may provide some unwanted results from a policy decision premised on a misleading impression of the nature of interregional linkages. Peacock and Dosser's (1959) theoretical exercise is worth reading in this regard. Measurement of the impact of spatially discriminatory government investment programmes becomes crucial if certain policies are to be carried out. Archibald's (1967) technique was designed to estimate the *minimum* value of regional multipliers in the UK, with a view to providing just these sorts of insight in the context of the regional development programmes. The focus of attention was directed to the alternative strategies of encouraging the movement of industry/expenditure or men, alternatives that will be discussed again in the context of strategies for development.

The models of Archibald (1967), Brown (1967), Steele (1969) and others (Wilson 1968) rely heavily on Keynesian macroeconomics. For example, Brown begins with an identity

$$Y^r = C^r + G^r - M^r - T_i^r \qquad (2.7)$$

where Y^r is the change in GNP at factor cost in region r,
C^r is the change in consumption expenditures at market prices,
G^r is the change in government expenditures on value added in region r,
T_i^r is the change in indirect tax payments (net),
M^r is the change in imports for consumption.

Further, the change in consumption is defined as

$$C^r = c(Y^r - T_d^r + R^r) \qquad (2.8)$$

where T_d^r is the change in direct tax payments,
R^r is the change in net transfers to households in the region,

and

$$T_d^r = t_d Y^r \tag{2.9}$$

$$T_i^r = t_i C^r \tag{2.10}$$

$$R^r = -uY^r \tag{2.11}$$

$$M^r = m^r C^r \tag{2.12}$$

and c, t_d, t_i, u and m^r are parameters. Equation (2.10) assumes that all indirect taxation falls on consumption and equation (2.11) assumes that transfers vary inversely with income.

Substituting (2.8), (2.10) and (2.12) into (2.7) we have

$$Y^r = c(Y^r - T_d^r + R^r) + G^r - m^r C^r - t_i C^r. \tag{2.13}$$

Further substitution of (2.8) for C^r in (2.13) yields

$$Y^r = c(Y^r - T_d^r + R^r)(1 - m^r - t_i) + G^r \tag{2.14}$$

and substituting (2.9) and (2.11) for T_d^r and R^r, we have

$$Y^r = c(Y^r - t_d Y^r - uY^r)(1 - m^r - t_i) + G^r \tag{2.15}$$

$$= cY^r(1 - t_d - u)(1 - m^r - t_i) + G^r.$$

Factoring

$$Y^r - cY^r(1 - t_d - u)(1 - m^r - t_i) = G^r$$

$$Y^r = \frac{1}{1 - c(1 - t_d - u)(1 - m^r - t_i)} \cdot G^r \tag{2.16}$$

Conceptually, the formulation is sound: the empirical implementation requires a good deal more attention. Brown, incorporating suggestions from Archibald and Prest, suggests the following values for the parameters:

$c = 0 \cdot 8$ $t_d = 0 \cdot 18$ $u = 0 \cdot 2$ $t_i = 0 \cdot 16$ $m^r = 0 \cdot 4$ (for a development area).

Making the substitution in (2.15) yields a multiplier, k, of

$$k = \frac{1}{1 - 0 \cdot 8(0 \cdot 62)(0 \cdot 44)} = 1 \cdot 28.$$

Brown also provided a feedback version, one that included the repercussions on and from other regions in the UK: we will return to this later in the chapter. Archibald's estimate of a minimum value multiplier was about $1 \cdot 25$ for a development region. Steele, on the other hand, used a slightly different formulation with an assumption that average and marginal savings rates differ in the same relationship as do average and marginal taxes. This assumption allowed him to calculate a single coefficient which simplified the empirical data requirements of the model. Steele's model provided a multiplier of the form

$$k = \frac{1}{1 - [(1 - \alpha S)(1 - t)(1 - m)]} \tag{2.17}$$

where t = proportion of regional consumption paid out in indirect taxes,

α = marginal/average savings coefficient,
S = amalgamated savings, including direct taxes,
m = the marginal propensity to import out of personal consumption.

The results provided estimates ranging from 1·19 (Yorkshire and Humberside) to 1·70 or 1·89 (Scotland), the latter region's high values being explained by a combination of low relative savings and low import coefficients (Steele 1969). Fig. 2.1 shows the important relationship between relative region size and import coefficients. The figure obviously represents a linear extrapolation of the assumptions Steele used in his model; the actual regional estimates for the UK varied somewhat from expectations but the fit seemed reasonable.

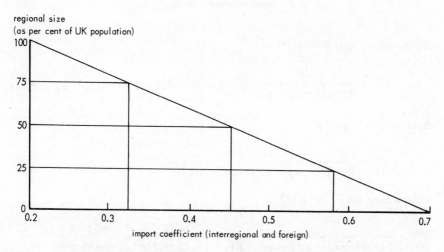

2.1   Regional size and import coefficients. *Source*: Steele (1969).

It was noted earlier that Brown had calculated the importance of the inter-regional feedback effects within a multiplier framework. These effects result from an exogenous change in government expenditures in region *r* creating increased output in region *r*; these effects are then translated into increased imports from region *s* by the industries in region *r*. In order to meet these new import requirements, industries in region *s* will have to expand production and may require imports from region *r* to do this. This latter action would be regarded as the feedback effect: this is shown in fig. 2.2. Thus, if (after Brown 1967) M^s is the change in imports by region *s* (which we will assume to be the rest of the UK), we may ascribe to this

(*a*) M_f^s foreign imports $= m_f C^s$

(*b*) M_r^s imports from $r = m_r^s C^s$

$$= m_r^s Y^s (1 - t_d - u).$$

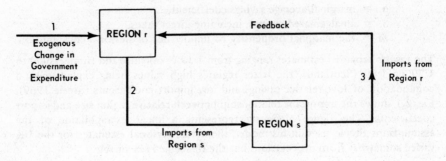

2.2   Interregional feedback effects.

Thus, in the expanded model

$$Y^r = \frac{1}{1 - c(1 - t_d - u)(1 - m^r - t_i)} \cdot G^r + m_r^s Y^s (1 - t_d - u). \quad (2.18)$$

Similarly, for region s

$$Y^s = \frac{1}{1 - c(1 - t_d - u)(1 - m^s - t_i)} \cdot m_s^r Y^r (1 - t_d - u). \quad (2.19)$$

Substituting for Y^s in (2.18)

$$Y^r = \frac{1}{1 - c(1 - t_d - u)(1 - m^r - t_i)} \cdot G^r + \frac{m_r^s (1 - t_d - u) m_s^r Y^r (1 - t_d - u)}{1 - c(1 - t_d - u)(1 - m^s - t_i)}.$$

Factoring

$$Y^r = \frac{G[1 - c(1 - t_d - u)(1 - m^s - t_i)]}{[1 - c(1 - t_d - u)(1 - m^r - t_i)][1 - c(1 - t_d - u)(1 - m^s - t_i)] - [m_r^s(1 - t_d - u)][m_s^r(1 - t_d - u)]}$$

$$(2.20)$$

The additional feedback effects were very small – the multiplier increasing from
1·28 to 1·29! However, Steele's recalculations using his alternative framework
indicated that feedbacks were substantially more important. Table 2.2 provides
the results using the simple multiplier and one with the feedback effects incorporated. These results indicate that, in some regions, feedback effects are
appreciable and cannot be ignored in policy formulation. However, one problem
that occurs when dealing with interregional linkages is that the intensity of linkages may vary between different regions (i.e. instead of aggregating the rest
of the UK into one region, we would calculate the linkages (1) between region r
and t, u, v, etc.) and (2) between different industrial sectors in different regions.
These issues are explored in greater detail in the next chapter on input–output
analysis.

Table 2.2   Simple and feedback multipliers for the UK regions

Region	Simple multiplier (1)	Feedback multiplier (2)	Ratio (2)/(1)
North	1·37	1·42	1·04
Yorks. & Humb.	1·19	1·26	1·06
E. Midland	1·37	1·45	1·06
E. Anglia	1·22	1·33	1·09
Southeast	1·41	1·57	1·11
Southwest	1·37	1·42	1·04
Wales	1·33	1·38	1·04
West Midlands	1·20	1·33	1·11
Northwest	1·27	1·39	1·09
Scotland	1·89 (1)	1·92 (1)	1·02 (1)
	1·70 (2)	1·77 (2)	1·04 (2)

Note: Two estimates were made for Scotland. *Source*: Steele (1969).

Multiplier analysis in an interregional setting: trade flows

Recognizing the importance of the different interregional and interindustrial linkages, Henderson and Krueger (1965) devised a more complicated model to make forecasts of economic activity in the Upper Midwest States (UMW) of the USA. The main thesis of the model was in line with economic base theory – namely, that growth in the UMW was a function of outside changes. To establish the differing impacts that various parts of the 'outside world' might have upon economic activity in the UMW, the rest of the world was divided up into nine regions, seven of which were constituent parts of the USA, the eighth Canada and the last region the rest of the world. The model attempted to specify the linkages the UMW had with each of these regions and the ways in which sales by UMW industries elsewhere would be converted into local income. The basic elements of the income part of the model are described below: it should be noted that this was only one component of a much larger study that included employment estimates among other things.

Total income in state h of the UMW, ($h = 1 \ldots 6$) Y^h, is comprised of the sum of i sector incomes (25 manufacturing and 13 service), Y_j^h, plus exogenous income (dividends, transfer payments, etc.) Y_o^h

$$Y^h = \sum_{j=1}^{38} Y_j^h + Y_o^h. \tag{2.21}$$

The income accruing to each sector may be thought of as some function of each sector's sales

$$Y_j^h = \mu_j^h S_j^h \tag{2.22}$$

where μ_j^h is a parameter,
S_j^h is the total sales of sector j in UMW state h.

Total sales of each sector comprise sales to other states in the UMW and sales to the external regions (6 and 9 respectively)

$$S_j^h = \sum_{l=1}^{7} S_j^{hl}. \tag{2.23}$$

Similarly, total purchases of sector output j by region l will be

$$P_j^k = \sum_{h=1}^{7} S_j^{hl} \qquad \begin{array}{l} b = 1 \dots 6 \text{ are UMW states} \\ b = 7 \text{ is the sum of the external regions} \end{array} \tag{2.24}$$

and these purchases may be specified geographically as the proportion of l's purchases from each b

$$S_j^{hl} = \alpha_j^{hl} P_j^l \tag{2.25}$$

where $\sum_{h=1}^{7} \alpha_j^{hl} = 1$ since the classification is exhaustive. The total state sales in b may be related to total purchases in the 15 regions

$$S_j^h = \sum_{l=1}^{15} \alpha_j^{hl} P_j^l. \tag{2.26}$$

The service sectors (26 to 38) were related to services purchases in the same state

$$S_j^h = t_j^h P_j^h \qquad \begin{array}{l} b = 1 \dots 6 \\ j = 26 \dots 38 \end{array} \tag{2.27}$$

The parameter t specifies sales in b as a proportion of purchases in b. Thus, if t is greater than unity, b is a net exporter of j; if it is less than unity, b is a net importer of j. Demand relationships covered each state's total purchases and income level

$$P_j^h = \beta_j^h Y^h \tag{2.28}$$

where $\beta_j^h = $ purchases of j per dollar of income.

Equations (2.21) through (2.28) represent a system of 690 equations: to avoid piecemeal projection and the chances of inconsistency, the system was reduced to six equations. In the reduced system, income levels were expressed as functions of the parameters, purchase levels by external regions and exogenous income levels. In matrix notation, this system now reads

$$Y = [I - \sum_{j=1}^{25} \mu_j \alpha_j \beta_j - \sum_{j=26}^{38} \mu_j t_j \beta_j]^{-1} \cdot [\sum_{j=1}^{25} \mu_j \alpha_j^* P_j^* + Y_0] \tag{2.29}$$

where Y, Y_0 are six-component column vectors of total and exogenous income levels for the six UMW states,
I is a 6 × 6 identity matrix,
μ_j, β_j, t_j are 6 × 6 diagonal matrices of the corresponding coefficients for the six UMW states,
α_j is a 6 × 6 matrix covering flows between UMW states,
α_j^* is a 6 × 9 matrix covering flows from the six UMW states to the external regions,
P_j^* is a nine-component column vector of total purchases levels by the external regions.

Once total income levels are obtained, sector income levels are derived from

$$Y_j^h = \mu_j^h \sum_{l=1}^{6} \alpha_j^{hl}\beta_j^l Y^l + \mu_j^h \sum_{l=7}^{15} \alpha_j^{hl} P_j^l \qquad (2.30)$$

and for the service sectors

$$Y_j^h = \mu_j^h t_j^h \beta_j^h Y^h. \qquad (2.31)$$

Equation (2.29) is formally analogous to the system derived in equation (2.5). Here we had

$$\Delta E_{nb} = \frac{r}{(1-r)} \cdot \Delta E_b.$$

By definition

$$\Delta E_t = \Delta E_{nb} + \Delta E_b$$

we have

$$\Delta E_t = \frac{r}{(1-r)} \Delta E_b + \Delta E_b$$

$$= \left(\frac{r}{(1-r)} + 1 \right) \Delta E_b$$

$$= \frac{1}{(1-r)} \cdot \Delta E_b = (1-r)^{-1} \cdot \Delta E_b. \qquad (2.32)$$

Instead of one value for r in (2.32), we have a matrix formulation in which any element in the bth row and lth column represents the number of dollars of income generated in state b per dollar of externally generated income in state l. The exogenous part of (2.29) is thus

$$[\sum_{j=1}^{25} \mu_j \alpha_j^* P_j^* + Y_0].$$

The advantage of this system is that different regions can have different impacts upon local (UMW) activity and, thus, projections which accommodate this difference in spatial dependence and sensitivity may be better founded in reality. It should be mentioned that a number of critical assumptions relating to the stability of the parameters were discussed in the study and should be considered before passing judgement upon the validity of the model. For example, the authors did not expect the income multipliers to remain unchanged. Fig. 2.1 discussed earlier provides some clues to answering this question. The point is elaborated in greater detail in Tiebout (1962). As a region grows, several changes may occur: (1) more people may be attracted into the region (*extensive income effect*); (2) the incomes *per capita* of the existing residents may increase (*intensive income effect*) or (3) a combination of (1) and (2) may occur. These issues will become important in the discussion of regional growth, but we will note here that each form of growth will have a different impact on the regional multiplier. For example, increased regional income from population expansion may increase the value of the regional multiplier since the local market will have expanded and the processes of import substitution discussed earlier in the context of the cola plant may operate. The impact on the multiplier will depend to a great extent upon the size of the region and the structure of industry and the nature of interindustry linkages. Growth effect (2) may have the opposite effect on the regional multiplier: as income *per capita* increases, proportionately more consumption may be spent outside the region (for the purchase of more exotic foods, entertainment, foreign travel). Thus the marginal propensity to consume locally may fall as income *per capita* rises. Thus growth effect (3) presents a real problem for estimation and inasmuch as most regions exhibit combinations of both forms of growth, the issue is of more than mere theoretical interest. These issues are taken up again in later chapters.

Regional applications of the Heckscher-Ohlin theorem

Unlike countries, regions are not able to make adjustments to their regional balance of payments accounts through the use of mechanisms such as their 'exchange rate' or 'monetary policy'. For a number of very sound reasons, these mechanisms are controlled by the central governments and thus, as Richardson concedes, 'The adjustment process in interregional payments is much less visible, whether a surplus or deficit exists is very often unknown' (Richardson 1969a). However, Richardson raises an interesting question when he claims that the absence of regularly reported data on chronic regional balance of payments problems does not imply that they never exist: in a sense, one could argue that other indices of malaise may be diagnosed as surrogates for balance of payments problems at the regional level. The issue is clouded by an absence of data and the different ways in which transfers of funds may be made at the interregional level.

The theories of comparative advantage have been tested recently at the regional level by Moroney and Walker (1966), although Estle (1967) has been critical of the testing procedures and the conclusions drawn from the analysis. The more traditional theory of comparative advantage, applied in a regional context, would suggest that regions would tend to specialize in those commodities whose production costs are lower than those in other regions. There is some debate about whether real or money costs should be used and, further, how important capital costs are in the whole analysis. The main emphasis has been to concentrate upon differentials in labour costs. The Heckscher-Ohlin theory of comparative advantage looks at production costs in a broader perspective and views advantages in terms of two sets of criteria: (1) differences in productive factor endowments among countries and (2) different factor intensities of production. Thus a country (or region) with more capital per unit of labour than another area with which it trades would have a comparative advantage in goods which used more capital per unit of output (capital-intensive goods) and consequently would tend to export such goods. On the other hand, the import content of the goods purchased by the country with a relative abundance of capital should reflect relatively higher labour-intensive production. In a very famous test of this hypothesis at the international level, Leontief (1953, 1956) found that, for the United States (a country which would fall into the category of one with a comparative advantage in capital-intensive goods), the exported goods tended to reflect relatively more capital than labour. The 'Leontief Paradox', as this conclusion has come to be known, has generated a great deal of debate. Some of the arguments are reported in Moroney and Walker (1966).

Moroney and Walker provided several suggestions for advancing a regional test of a Heckscher-Ohlin theorem over tests which had used international data. As the theorem depends on the assumption that an individual commodity is produced according to a production function which is of the fixed coefficient type (constant returns-to-scale), it would seem more reasonable to assume that regional production functions for the ith commodity would be more nearly identical when comparison was made across regions within a country. This assertion has not been tested directly, although Gallaway (1963) found that differences in wages across regions could not be explained by differences in regional production functions. At the international level, the possibility of factor-intensity reversal has often clouded the tests of the Heckscher-Ohlin and other theorems of comparative advantage. Such situations would only be permissible if a production function was used such that, with changes in the relative prices of labour and capital, the factor of relative dominance would change. With a fixed coefficient production function it has been shown that factor reversal is not possible. Moroney and Walker applied various tests to demonstrate that the possibility of factor-intensity reversal would not undermine their results. Finally, the authors suggested that the regional test was one concerned with production location rather than regional trade and thus avoided obfuscation caused by regional demand functions being dissimilar for the various commodities that are to be traded.

The latter point is important since it represents a departure from the tests of the Heckscher-Ohlin theorem applied at the international level. In a sense, they concentrated on the side of *production* rather than attempting to predict flows. Thus, their general thesis would be that regions would tend to produce more of a commodity that uses a factor in which the region has a relative abundance. Using location quotients, Moroney and Walker (1966) attempted to test the hypothesis that industries with relatively low capital-labour ratios were concentrated in the South (of the United States). It was not assumed that such industries should have a location quotient in excess of unity but rather that the ranking of industries with respect to their capital-labour ratios should reflect regional comparative advantage. Hence, industries with a low capital-labour ratio should be ranked highly and hence the correlation between rank and capital-labour ratio should reveal a negative sign. However, the rank correlation test revealed a relationship with the wrong sign, although the relationship was shown to be not significantly different from zero (i.e. no relationship). A further test was adopted – namely, that industries with the greatest comparative advantage should be the ones developing more rapidly in the region. The indicator of development was taken to be the percentage change in location quotients (between 1949 and 1957); this was correlated with the rank ordering of capital-labour ratios. An inverse relationship again was expected, and the one obtained was also significantly different from zero.

The conclusions to be drawn from this analysis were that 'initial endowment of natural resources may be more important than relative abundance of material capital or labour in determining the *initial* structure of comparative advantage' (Moroney and Walker 1966). This conclusion was drawn from the zero correlation between ranking of industries in terms of capital-labour ratios and location quotients. Once development is initiated, the relative endowments of material capital and labour would influence the pattern of development. The initial endowment may be totally different from that exhibited after development has been under way for several decades and thus continual modification of regional comparative advantage could be expected over time.

Estle (1967) suggested that the Moroney and Walker data indicated that the South was relatively abundant in capital and it was the non-South that should have exhibited relatively labour-intensive industries. Using data from New England states, Estle showed that for this region there was an inverse relationship between capital-labour ratios and location quotients, and further that there was also a significant inverse relationship between the ranking of capital-labour ratios and percentage changes in location quotients. This indicated that New England was a region relatively abundant in labour and one that was tending to attract industries which were relatively labour-intensive. Moroney (1970) retorted that Estle's results still did not deny that the South was an overall labour-abundant region; Moroney claimed that the capital-intensive industries only produced 13 per cent of the South's output, and further that the higher capital intensity of the South in these industries was due largely to regional differences in the time period of investment.

The real source of disagreement appears to centre around the nature of the data rather than the assumptions and constructs of the Heckscher-Ohlin theorem. For example, the nature of the data used in constructing the capital estimates may have biased the construction of the capital-labour ratios. Construction of location quotients, as has been suggested in this chapter, is not a procedure without problems: minor changes in the location of industries may result in major changes in the quotients obtained. In addition, ranking data assumes equal weight to differences in rank – that is, the difference between rank 6 and rank 7 is assumed to be as great as the difference in rank between numbers 1 and 2. Referring to the sensitive nature of the location quotients again, it does not seem reasonable to use percentage changes in these quotients as a developmental measure of changing comparative advantage. In Moroney and Walker's study, the two-digit SIC Industry Instruments' location quotient changed from 0·0240 to 0·0600 between 1949 and 1957 in the South. By most standards, this would be interpreted as a very modest or even a minor change, but, in percentage terms, it represented an increase of 150 per cent!

It is clear that a more conclusive test of this important theorem awaits analysis at the regional level. The ambiguity that has resulted in the applications of a number of models, such as the Heckscher-Ohlin model, at the regional level may reflect a dearth of adequate data as much as the need to consider substantial modifications in the conceptual frameworks of these models.

3 Regional and interregional structure: interindustry models

Relationship of aggregate Keynesian, economic base and input–output models

The notion of the multiplier, introduced in the preceding chapter, is usually associated with the work of Keynes and subsequently with Kahn and others at Cambridge, England, and Cambridge, Massachusetts. In this brief introductory section, we will review the relationship of aggregate Keynesian analysis and economic base analysis to input–output methodology.[1]

The usual Keynesian identity for a closed economy is

$$Y = C + I \tag{3.1}$$

where Y is gross national product, C gross domestic consumption and I gross investment. If we include transactions on foreign account, where X is exports and M imports,

$$Y = C + I + X - M. \tag{3.2}$$

This may also be written as

$$Y + M = C + I + X \tag{3.3}$$

and, in this particular formulation, it is referred to as the input–output approach by Kennedy (1966a). With this arrangement, the output (supply) terms are collected on the left-hand side and the expenditure (demand) terms are grouped on the right-hand side. The input–output label has been attached to this formulation because, if we combine $C + I$ as an expenditure item, E,

$$Y + M = E + X \tag{3.4}$$

and the four terms are, in fact, the row and column totals of a two-sector input–output table, comprising a home and a foreign sector. Such a model is shown in table 3.1. The entries V_{hh} and V_{hf} represent the distribution of home sales to

[1] The ideas of Charles Kennedy in describing the first relationship are here acknowledged (Kennedy 1966a, 1966b).

Table 3.1   Two-sector macro input–output model (Kennedy 1966a)

Producing sectors	Spending sectors		Total
	Home	*Foreign*	
Home	V_{hh}	V_{hf}	Y
Foreign	V_{fh}	V_{ff}	M
Total	E	X	T

the home and foreign markets respectively, while V_{fh} and V_{ff} are foreign sales to the home and foreign market. Graphical analysis can be employed to assist in illustrating the impact that changes in the autonomous sectors would have upon Y, the national product (fig. 3.1). Since, from the two-sector model, total expenditures = total output = T, the 45° dotted line represents such equilibrium conditions. The second dotted line, from a to r relates exports to imports: in this particular situation, there is a deficit on balance of payments of Pr. Kennedy (1966a) claimed that the most important relationship was that between M and T: in the diagram we may see that an import coefficient, m, may be defined as equal to tan α, i.e. $m = M/(X + E)$. This coefficient is different from the usual marginal propensity to import which relates M to Y rather than M to T in the case of the import coefficient. The utility of the coefficient will become apparent when a multiplier formulation is desired.

Let us assume that E has been disaggregated again into its components C and I: let us further assume that I and X are autonomous and that there has been an autonomous change of ΔI and ΔX. What effect will this have on Y, i.e. what will be the magnitude of ΔY? Will it be equal to $\Delta I + \Delta X$ or greater? By definition of M

$$\Delta M = m\Delta T \qquad (3.5)$$

and since $Y + M = T$

$$\Delta Y + \Delta M = \Delta T, \qquad (3.6)$$

therefore

$$\Delta Y = \Delta T - \Delta M$$
$$= \overline{(1 - m)}\Delta T. \qquad (3.7)$$

Let us define c as the marginal propensity to consume and thus

$$\Delta C = c\Delta Y \qquad (3.8)$$
$$= c(1 - m)\Delta T. \qquad (3.9)$$

Restoration of equilibrium implies

$$\Delta I + \Delta X = \Delta T - \Delta C$$
$$= [1 - c(1 - m)]\Delta T. \qquad (3.10)$$

Dividing (3.7) by (3.10)

$$\frac{\Delta Y}{\Delta I + \Delta X} = \frac{(1 - m)}{[1 - c(1 - m)]}. \qquad (3.11)$$

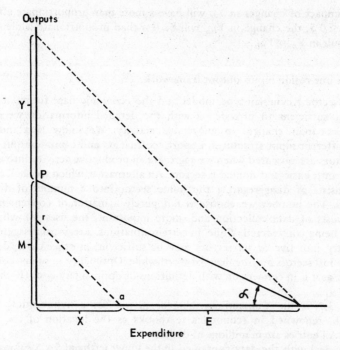

3.1   The components of output and expenditure. *Source:* Kennedy (1966a).

The numerator of (3.11) takes account of the fact that only a proportion of the *initial* increase in expenditures on I and X will lead to an increase in domestic incomes. The denominator takes account of the increase in Y resulting from an increase in C in the usual multiplier fashion.

Similarly, using a two-sector economic base model,[1]

$$Y_t = Y_b + Y_{nb} \tag{3.12}$$

where Y_t, Y_b and Y_{nb} are the total, basic and non-basic (or local) components of regional output (or income). We may define r as the ratio of non-basic to total output and thus

$$Y_{nb} = rY_t. \tag{3.13}$$

Hence

$$Y_{nb} = r(Y_b + Y_{nb})$$

$$= rY_b + rY_{nb}$$

$$= \frac{r}{(1-r)} Y_b. \tag{3.14}$$

Assuming that Y_b may be projected exogenously, we will be able to determine

[1] In this chapter, the economic base is described in income (Y) rather than employment terms (E). The accounting system is identical.

that the impact of changes in Y_b will have a more than proportionate effect on Y_{nb}: if $r < 0.5$, the change in Y_{nb} will be less than proportionate while $r = 0.5$ would result in $Y_b = Y_{nb}$.

The static one-region input–output framework

The two-sector Keynesian-type model and the economic base formulation are often not sufficient to provide us with the detailed information we require consequent upon changes in exogenous activity. We know that industries exhibit different input structures, import coefficients and capital-output ratios; these factors are obscured when we aggregate all productive activity into a home sector or into basic and nonbasic sectors. An alternative, which we shall explore now, consists of disaggregating the home sector into a number of different industries. The number we choose is not purely a matter of convenience but reflects costs of data collection and, more important, the uses for which the model is being constructed. While, in certain situations, a regional disaggregation of industry into five or six sectors may be sufficient, in other cases, disaggregation to 350 sectors may be deemed worthwhile. Optimality in such a context is as elusive as it is in connection with definitions of optimal city size! (Richardson 1972).

Table 3.2 is the transactions table or matrix for a hypothetical region, Fforeggub, renowned in economics textbooks as the location of the Widget Factory. All entries are in millions of dollars.

Let us deal with the data contained in the upper lefthand 5 × 5 submatrix of the transactions table. Note that the five industry sectors identified at the left, as rows, are similarly identified as columns. What are these industrial sectors? Basically, there are groups of firms producing similar products although certain assumptions have to be made in the case of firms producing more than one major product. In some input–output accounting systems, secondary products are allocated to other sectors, if appropriate, so that one firm's inputs may appear in the input vectors of two or more sectors. In other accounting systems, the whole of the firm's input vector is allocated to the sector in which the major product is identified. This lack of consistency in designing regional and national accounts has often prohibited useful comparison of regional and national industry structures and where such comparisons have been made considerable caution has been advised for the interpretation of the results (see Goldman 1969).

If we may assume that we have resolved the problem of allocation of a firm's input and outputs, how do we interpret the data contained in the 5 × 5 sub-matrix? If we examine row 3, Electrical Engineering, we may note that the industry's output is allocated to other industries in the region as follows: $3 million to Agriculture (row 3, column 1), $20 million to Mining (row 3, column 2), no sales to Electrical Engineering, $50 million to Business Services (row 3, column 4) and $7 million to Transportation (row 3, column 5). Similarly, we may examine the sales pattern of each of the industries at the left to each of the other industries in the region at the head of each column.

If we look down the columns, we may discover how much each industry at

Table 3.2 Transactions table, Fforeggub, 1972 ($ millions (current), producers' prices)

From \ To	1 Agriculture	2 Mining	3 Electrical engineering	4 Business services	5 Transportation	6 Total intermediate sales	7 Households	8 Local authorities	9 Defence	10 Non-Defence	11 Interregional exports	12 Foreign exports	13 Total Final Demand	14 Total output
1 Agriculture	21	—	9	3	—	33	30	10	5	—	20	2	67	100
2 Mining	1	8	7	29	—	45	25	5	2	—	15	8	55	100
3 Electrical engineering	3	20	—	50	7	80	5	1	4	4	3	3	20	100
4 Business services	31	2	38	—	3	74	12	2	—	11	1	—	26	100
5 Transportation	10	25	26	1	4	66	9	6	—	13	4	2	34	100
6 Total intermediate purchases	66	55	80	83	14	298	81	24	11	28	—	—	—	—
7 Value added	20	40	10	17	40	—	2	49	4	9	—	—	—	—
8 Interregional imports	7	4	4	—	30	—	47	18	—	21	—	—	—	—
9 Foreign imports	7	1	6	—	16	—	30	2	—	14	—	—	—	—
10 Total input	100	100	100	100	100	—	160	93	15	72	—	—	—	—

the top of the column purchases from the other industries at the left; for example, Electrical Engineering purchases $7 million from Mining (column 3, row 2), Transportation purchases $3 million from Business Services (column 5, row 4). These flows, purchases and sales between industries in the region are known as the *interindustry transactions* and are sales and purchases on current account. Industry output is also allocated to other sectors, collectively known as *Final Demand*: these are the sectors shown in columns 7 through 12 and summed in column 13. Sector 7, Households, represents local consumption; sales from industries at the left are shown in this column. In reality, households make purchases from retail outlets, which in turn make purchases from wholesalers who usually deal directly with the firms in the various industries. However, in input–output accounting systems, sales from firms to wholesalers-retailers-households are shown as direct sales to households. The retailers' and wholesalers' mark ups are shown as purchases by households from the trade sector, although in our region a trade sector is not identified separately. In this model, the exports' sectors of final demand are differentiated into sales to other regions and foreign exports. The Non-Defence component of final demand includes investment sales: this is usually shown separately and occasionally, as we will see later, in even more detail as a matrix of sales on capital account. Summing across each row, we may arrive at the total output for each industry, and this is shown in column 14.

Thus far, inputs into industries have consisted solely of goods and material from other industries in the region. Labour inputs are shown in row 7 (value added) and inputs from other regions and other countries are shown in rows 8 and 9. Summing down each column, the entries denote Total Input (row 10). Total Inputs equal Total Outputs for each industry: balance is achieved through the inclusion of non-income value added, such as profits, dividends, in the value-added row.

If X_{ij} denotes the flow of output from industry i to industry j, Y_{ik} the flow of output from industry i to final demand sector k, and X_i the total output of industry i, we may write

$$\sum_{j=1}^{j=n} X_{ij} + \sum_{k=1}^{k=m} Y_{ik} = X_i \tag{3.15}$$

for each industry, i.

In place of X_{ij}, we may define r_{ij}

$$r_{ij} = \frac{X_{ij}}{X_j} \tag{3.16}$$

r_{ij} is the regional input or requirement coefficient and is the cents worth of i needed per unit output of j.

Table 3.3 shows the input coefficient matrix. Equation (3.15) may be rewritten

$$\sum_{j=1}^{j=n} r_{ij} X_j + \sum_{k=1}^{k=m} Y_{ik} = X_i. \tag{3.17}$$

What do the entries in table 3.3 mean? If we look at column 3, we will see that

Table 3.3 Regional input coefficient matrix

| Sectors | Sectors | | | | |
	1	2	3	4	5
1	0·21	——	0·99	0·43	——
2	0·01	0·08	0·07	0·29	——
3	0·03	0·20	——	0·50	0·07
4	0·31	0·02	0·38	——	0·03
5	0·10	0·25	0·26	0·01	0·04

for every $1 output in that sector, $0·09 of inputs are purchased from Agriculture, $0·07 from mining and so forth. We may use this table, and, with the assistance of a computer, determine the impacts on the region of changes in purchases by the components of the final demand sectors.

Let us define a square matrix, R, a typical entry of which is r_{ij}, and a column vector, X, of total outputs (inputs). If we collapse the final demand sectors into one, we may define a column vector, Y, of final demand. Thus instead of writing i equations of the form (3.17), we may now write

$$RX + Y = X. \tag{3.18}$$

Factoring

$$X - RX = Y$$

$$[I - R]X = Y$$

$$X = [I - R]^{-1}Y \tag{3.19}$$

The matrix formulation thus allows the solution of the i simultaneous equations. The term $[I - R]^{-1}$ is known as the Leontief inverse matrix: the I matrix is the identity matrix whose elements are

$$\begin{cases} i_{ij} = 0 & i \neq j \\ i_{ij} = 1 & i = j \end{cases}$$

In other words, it is a matrix with the value 1 on the principal diagonal and zeros elsewhere.

The elements of the inverse matrix are shown in table 3.4.

Table 3.4 Leontief inverse matrix

| | Sectors | | | | |
	1	2	3	4	5
1	1·33	0·05	0·18	0·15	0·02
2	0·23	1·17	0·30	0·50	0·04
3	0·40	0·36	1·41	0·82	0·13
4	0·58	0·19	0·61	1·38	0·09
5	0·31	0·41	0·48	0·38	1·09
Multiplier	2·85	2·18	2·98	3·23	1·37

Each entry in the inverse matrix represents the *direct* and *indirect* impact of a $1 change in final demand for the output of the industry at the top of the column on all the other industries at the left. What is the indirect effect? Let us examine column 3 of table 3.5.

Table 3.5   (column 3 of table 3.3)

	1	2	3	4	5
1			0·09		
2			0·07		
3			——		
4			0·38		
5			0·26		

These are the direct inputs required from the other industries by Electrical Engineering: if there is a unit increase in final demand for Electrical Engineering, we know that output in other industries will increase according to the schedule shown above. It will be apparent that some restrictive assumptions are embodied in this procedure – fixed coefficient production functions,[1] no economies of scale and similar product mixes within each industry as output increases. Now if Electrical Engineering is going to purchase an additional $0·09 worth of output from Agriculture, the latter industry in turn will have to increase its output, and thus its inputs to meet this new demand. Thus, agricultural output would be increased as shown in table 3.6.

Table 3.6

0·21 X 0·09	or	0·0189
0·01 X 0·09		0·0009
0·03 X 0·09		0·0027
0·31 X 0·09		0·0279
0·10 X 0·09		0·0090

In turn, other industries supplying inputs to Agriculture will have to increase their output to meet the new demands placed upon them by Agriculture, demands which originated in an increase in Final Demand for Electrical Engineering. One of the industries supplying inputs to Agriculture is Electrical Engineering – $0·03 for $1 of output or $0·0027 for a 0·09¢ increase. Thus, we know that Electrical Engineering output will have to increase at least $1·0027 to meet an additional Final Demand of $1.

Rather than work through these linkages many times, since there will be many rounds of purchasing, we may approximate the impact via the expansion of the R matrix

$$\sum_{k=0}^{k=\infty} R^k = I + R + R^2 + R^3 \ldots \tag{3.20}$$

[1]Production functions in an input–output sense, since the open nature of the regional economy may result in large imports of inputs.

This rapidly converges and is known as the power series expansion of the $[I - R]^{-1}$ matrix.

The inverse matrix captures the indirect as well as the direct inputs of these many rounds of purchasing. Summing down each column of table 3.4, we may ascertain the total impact on all industries in the region of a $1 change in final demand for each of the regional industries. This summation is shown in the row labelled 'Multiplier'. This multiplier is not the same as the Keynesian multiplier since the latter was related to income change. The multipliers in table 3.4 are column output multipliers and are simply the total direct and indirect change in output in industry *i* divided by the initial change in output in industry *i* (the $1 of Final Demand). This matrix enables us to examine the more sophisticated indirect linkages of industries to each other. With reference to table 3.7 the direct, direct and indirect and indirect inputs are shown for Electrical Engineering. Here we may note that the indirect impact of a $1 change in final demand on Electrical Engineering is $1·41, of which $1 is the change in final demand. Thus an additional $0·41 is required to meet the change in final demand, although no direct impacts, in the form of direct input coefficients, were recorded in table 3.3. A comparison of entries in tables 3.3 and 3.4 will reveal that a number of industries are often very highly linked *indirectly* whereas there are no *direct* linkages: in other cases, the indirect impacts are larger than the direct impacts.

Table 3.7   Direct, direct and indirect, and indirect inputs for industry 3

	(1)	*(2)*	*(3)*
1	0·09	0·18	0·09
2	0·07	0·30	0·23
3	—	1·41	1·41
4	0·38	0·61	0·23
5	0·26	0·48	0·22

Notes: Column (1) is Column (3) from Table 3.3
Column (2) is Column (3) from Table 3.4
Column (3) is (2)−(1)

Table 3.6 details the impact of exogenous change upon the regional economy. We may see that industry 4 generates the greatest *regional* impact from a $1 increase in Final Demand. Why are the multipliers in some industries larger than others? Essentially, for two reasons: (1) industries exhibit different interindustry linkages as a result of differences in quantities and types of inputs required per unit of output and (2) some industries are more highly linked *intra*regionally whereas other industries have greater *inter*regional linkages. Thus, if we transformed rows 8 and 9 of table 3.2 to coefficients (the cents worth of foreign or interregional inputs per dollar of input) to table 3.8, we may derive some idea of the intensity of the leakages in the regional economy. Industry 4 is unusual in that it is able to satisfy its requirements purely from local sources, whereas industry 5 expends $0·46 per $1 of output on extraregional sources of inputs. These factors are reflected in the low regional output multiplier for industry 5

Table 3.8   Import coefficients

	Sector				
	1	2	3	4	5
Interregional	0·07	0·04	0·04	–	0·30
Foreign	0·07	0·01	0·06	–	0·16
Total	0·14	0·05	0·10	–	0·46

and the high multiplier for industry 4. A word of caution here: one must not assume from this that industry 4 is more 'valuable' to the regional economy and industry 5 less so. We have mentioned nothing about the income or employment effects each industry generates; also, the whole notion of the input–output approach is the stress upon linkages and interdependencies. While industry 5 may not be highly linked directly to other industries in its purchases, $65 million worth of its output is sold to other industries in the region. Hence, we must beware of sweeping assumptions based solely on the size of the regional column output multiplier.

If we transform row 7 of table 3.2 into coefficient form, this will give us an indication of the income generated per $1 of input. While the value added entry includes non-income value added, let us assume for the time being, that all the value added is local income. These value added coefficients are shown in row (1) of table 3.9. To obtain the direct and indirect income change (row (2) of table 3.9) we multiply the inverse matrix by the row vector of value added coefficients

$$C = V[I-A]^{-1} \tag{3.21}$$

where C is a row vector of direct and indirect income changes, and V the value-added coefficients row vector. The indirect income effects are derived through simple subtractions and the multiplier in this case, known as Type I Multiplier (see Miernyk 1965) is obtained by dividing the direct and indirect income change by the direct income change, e.g. for agriculture, the Type I multiplier is $0·62/0·20$ or $3·1$. This multiplier provides the potential impact on incomes of changes in final demand: it is greater than unity because the industry output increases resulting from changes in final demand are greater than unity. Again, differences in magnitude of the multiplier reflect differential utilization of labour inputs and the indirect inputs of labour in industries supplying any particular sector. Thus, a high value-added coefficient, the direct income change, will not suggest a large income multiplier, since the indirect income generated may not be large – e.g. in sector 5, the indirect income generated is only $0·08.

Additional income earned in the region, as a result of changes in Final Demand, will itself have a further impact upon the economy. This is known as the induced impact. There are two ways we can go about measuring this impact: one way requires an expansion of the R matrix, the other the calculation of a scalar using data we have already assembled. While the latter method is more convenient, heuristically it may be of value to detail the more involved methodology.

First of all, we expand the matrix by making the Household column of Final

Table 3.9   Derivation Type I multiplier

	Sectors				
	1	2	3	4	5
(1)	0·20	0·40	0·10	0·17	0·40
(2)	0·62	0·72	0·59	0·69	0·48
(3)	0·42	0·31	0·49	0·52	0·08
(4)	3·1	1·78	5·9	4·1	1·20

Notes: Row (1) The value-added entry of table 3.2 shown as a coefficient
(*V/X*).
(2) The direct and indirect income change.
(3) The indirect income change (2) — (1).
(4) Type I mulitplier, (2) ÷ (1).

Demand endogenous. To balance the matrix, the value added row is now
included: we may do this if we assume that value added is, essentially, local
value added (more sophisticated models, to be described later, differentiate
types of value added; see Tiebout 1969). The expanded matrix is shown in table
3.10.

Table 3.10   Expanded *R* matrix

	Sectors					HH
	1	2	3	4	5	6
1	0·21	——	0·09	0·03	——	0·18
2	0·01	0·08	0·07	0·29	——	0·15
3	0·03	0·20	——	0·50	0·07	0·03
4	0·31	0·02	0·38	——	0·03	0·07
5	0·10	0·25	0·26	0·01	0·04	0·05
HH 6	0·20	0·40	0·10	0·17	0·40	0·01

What is the *HH* column (6) of table 3.10? Essentially, it is the regional consumption function, disaggregated by industry. In similar fashion to the column
vector of input coefficients, it provides us information on average propensities to
consume the output of the industries at the left per dollar of income. Thus, 18¢
could be expanded on Agriculture products and only 3¢ on Engineering and 1¢
on Households (domestic help and the like). If we designate this 6 × 6 matrix as
R^*, we may derive a new equation of the form of

$$X = [I - R^*]^{-1} Y^* \qquad (3.22)$$

Y^* is the new vector of final demand (sectors 8 through 12 in place of sectors 7
through 12 since column 7 is now part of the R^* matrix). The new Leontief
inverse matrix is shown in table 3.11.

From table 3.11 we may derive a new set of multipliers. These are shown in
table 3.12.

As one would expect, the Type II multiplier is much larger than the Type I
multiplier, reflecting the induced impacts of additional rounds of consumer
expenditure upon the local economy. A point may be raised that one is dealing
with *additions* to consumer incomes and thus it may be inappropriate to consider

Table 3.11   Leontief inverse matrix with Households endogenous

Sectors	1	2	3	4	5	HH 6
1	1·59	0·34	0·43	0·43	0·21	0·41
2	0·48	1·46	0·54	0·78	0·23	0·41
3	0·62	0·61	1·62	1·07	0·30	0·36
4	0·82	0·47	0·84	1·65	0·28	0·39
5	0·52	0·65	0·68	0·62	1·25	0·34
HH 6	0·3	1·07	0·89	1·05	0·72	1·50

Table 3.12   Derivation of Type II multipliers and comparison with Type I

	1	2	3	4	5
(1)	0·20	0·40	0·10	0·17	0·40
(2)	0·93	1·07	0·89	1·05	0·72
(3)	4·67	2·68	8·99	6·19	1·89
(4)	3·1	1·78	5·9	4·1	1·20

Notes: Row (1) Value added coefficient derived from table 3.2.
(2) Household row of table 3.11 — the direct, indirect and induced income change.
(3) Type II multiplier, column (2) — (1).
(4) Type I multiplier, from table 3.9.

them in terms of being spent according to a schedule of average consumption patterns. More appropriately, one would relate changes in consumer incomes to a schedule of marginal propensities to consume. Hence, if we know the income elasticities of demand for each industry we may derive the marginal propensities to consume. If ϵ_y^1 is the income elasticity of demand for sector 1 (Agriculture), then we know that it is the percentage change in consumption of agriculture per percentage change in income, i.e.

$$(\Delta C^1/C^1)/(\Delta Y/Y) \qquad (3.23)$$

where C^1 refers to consumption of Agriculture and Y to income. The average propensity to consume Agriculture is C^1/Y; however, the marginal propensity to consume, $\Delta C^1/\Delta Y$, is the average propensity multiplied by the income elasticity of demand

$$mpc^1 = \Delta C^1/\Delta Y = \frac{C^1}{Y} \cdot (\Delta C^1/C^1) \frac{Y}{\Delta Y} = apc^1 \cdot \epsilon_y^1. \qquad (3.24)$$

Knowing this, we will examine the effect of allocating changes in consumer income to the schedule of marginal propensities to consume upon the regional economy, and the sensitivity of the regional economy to changes in the allocation of final demand among the various sectors of final demand.

While the input–output framework we have detailed thus far can be immensely useful in a regional planning framework, the model can be applied to assist in the solution of a number of different problems. A glance through the list of papers read at the two most recent Geneva Conferences on Input–Output Analysis will reveal the breadth and increasing sophistication of the methodology (Carter and Brody 1970, 1972). One recurring question that we may wish to provide some assistance in answering is: what are the likely direct, indirect and induced impacts of changes in foreign and national markets upon activity in the region? Let us assume that Defence spending is cut in the region by $10 million. The government may now redistribute these 'savings' in many ways: for example, (1) to other regions, to promote faster industrial growth therein, (2) to Non-Defence forms of final demand (e.g. health and welfare services) or (3) to Households, through a reduction in direct taxation. While the administrative mechanics of such a redistribution are neither costless nor as smooth as we are implying here, the interest is more in the sensitivity of the regional economy to changes in allocation of exogenous expenditure.

Table 3.13   Reallocation of Final Demand consequent upon a reduction in Defence spending

		(1)	(2)	(3)	(4)	(5)	(6)
		HH	ΔHH	Defence	ΔD	Non-Defence	ΔND
	1	30	0	1	− 4	—	——
	2	25	0	0	− 2	—	——
	3	7	+ 2	2	− 2	6	+ 2
	4	15	+ 3	–	——	13	+ 2
	5	10	+ 1	–	——	16	+ 3
HH	6	3	+ 1	2	− 2	12	+ 3
Imports	7	80	+ 3	–	——	—	——
Total		170	+ 10	5	− 10	47	+ 10

Note: The Imports rows of table 3.2 have been combined.

In table 3.13, three effects are shown: column (1) is the Household column from table 3.2. Rather than allocating the $10 million from Defence to Households in a similar fashion to the average expenditures, we have made use of income elasticities of demand for each of the industries and assumed that, for example, no additional income will be allocated to Agriculture or Mining. Rather, Households will use the additions to disposable income to buy more from sectors 3, 4 and 5 and more imports. The changes in expenditure are shown in column (2) of table 3.13. The new reduced vector of Final Demand for Defence is shown as column (3), the changes in column (4). Similarly, the new vector of Non-Defence Final Demand is given in column (5); the changes among the sectors are noted in column (6). If the reallocation of expenditures had been similar, i.e. the $4 million Defence cut in Agriculture reallocated to a $4 million increase in Non-Defence spending on Agriculture, then the net change in the regional economy would have been zero, *ceteris paribus*.[1] We know that readjustments in

[1] By this we imply that the products demanded by Defence from Agriculture would now be allocated to Non-Defence. If different products are demanded the results would not be identical but this would involve changing assumptions about the constancy of product mix over changes in output.

productive capabilities are not instantaneous: firms are not able to shift from making swords to ploughshares overnight. Thus we would expect some disruptive effects in the short to medium run. Some firms would experience expansionary effects from this reallocation: in these cases we assume that spare or unused capacity exists in each industry such that increases in demand may be met merely by increasing output in a linear fashion. What we are interested in testing is the advocacy of the prophets of doom from the military-industrial complex who claim that a cut in defence spending would be bad business. This exercise follows a more sophisticated procedure adopted by Leon (1965) and Rosenbluth (1968a) for the USA and Canada respectively. The works in Benoit and Boulding (1965) and a symposium edited by Tiebout (1965) are worth consulting.

Table 3.14 denotes the employment needed per $1 million of output (input) in each sector. These figures make little real sense in that there may be more flexibility in employment inputs than that suggested by a dogmatic ratio of employment to output. However, let us adopt some necessary conventional wisdom and assume that in the absence of other information these data accurately reflect conditions in the industry. Thus a change (positive or negative) of $1 million in industry 3 will result in an increase or decrease of 300 employees.

There are several points we can make here: not only can we obtain data for the total impact of these changes upon the regional economy, we are also able to see which industrial sectors would be affected the most, both in a positive and negative sense. By including Households endogenously, a similar analysis could be performed to measure the impacts of these changes in final demands in terms of the induced, as well as the direct and indirect impacts.

While the reallocation of Final Demand from Defence to other sectors results in an aggregate net loss of employment and output, some industries gain under both reallocations, e.g., sectors 4 and 5, while Electrical Engineering gains from a reallocation to Households but not from a reallocation to Non-Defence. The other two sectors suffer net losses in both cases, although the losses are less severe in the reallocation to Households.

The particular choice of numbers in table 3.14 obviously would influence the outcome on the employment totals, but the general sophistication of the input–output model over the economic base formulation may be appreciated. With more detailed information, about employment/output sensitivity, the existing utilization of capacity, the time and reaction paths of expansion and cutback, a considerable degree of accuracy may be applied to experiments of this type.

We have talked occasionally about leakages and the degrees of intraregional and interregional linkages. We have accepted the fact that our region is part of a national economy: it seems logical to explore what happens in other regions when output is expanded in Fforeggub, or whether activity changes in other regions have any impact upon Fforeggub.

Table 3.14   Employment per $1 million output

Sector	
1	200
2	500
3	300
4	500
5	400

Table 3.15   Employment and output effects of changes in Final Demand

Sectors	Decrease output	Defence employment	Increase output	Non-Defence employment	Increase output	Household employment
1	− 5·78	− 1056	+ 0·72	+ 154	+ 0·83	+ 166
2	− 3·86	− 1930	+ 1·72	+ 860	+ 2·14	+ 1070
3	− 5·14	− 1542	+ 4·85	+ 1455	+ 5·41	+ 1623
4	− 3·90	− 1950	+ 4·25	+ 2125	+ 5·45	+ 2725
5	− 3·02	− 1208	+ 4·99	+ 1996	+ 3·19	+ 1276
Total	$ − 21·70	− 7686	$ + 16·53	+ 6590	$ + 17·02	+ 6860

Table 3.16   Net gains (losses) from reallocation of Final Demand

Sectors	Defence to Non-Defence		Defence to Household	
	Output	Employment	Output	Employment
1	− 5·06	− 902	− 4·95	− 890
2	− 2·14	− 1070	− 1·72	− 860
3	− 0·29	− 87	+ 0·27	+ 81
4	+ 0·35	+ 175	+ 1·55	+ 775
5	+ 1·97	+ 788	+ 0·17	+ 68
Total	$ − 5·17	− 1096	$ − 4·68	− 826

The interregional input–output framework

Over a decade ago, Peacock and Dosser (1959) suggested that, in planning the allocation of government expenditures, consideration should be given to what are now generally termed the *feedback effects* of expenditures in region *r* on another region *s* and back to *r*. They suggested that some of these interregional linkages may be so strong that the total direct and indirect effect of an expenditure made directly in region *s* may be greater on region *r*'s economy than if the expenditure had been made directly in *r* in the first instance. Although their model has never been conclusively tested empirically, their use of highly aggregated data for Scotland caused them to conclude that such impacts could occur in the UK context.

Miller's work on the magnitude of these interregional feedbacks has produced some rather confusing and conflicting results (Miller 1966, 1969). In dealing with a two-region economy, the magnitude of the feedbacks can become quite important, especially in the context of the influence of feedbacks on regional income multipliers (see the work of Brown (1967) and Steele (1969) and the discussion in chapter 2).

In the one-region framework, sales to other regions in the nation were shown as a separate vector of final demand (column 12 of table 3.3); interregional purchases are usually shown as a separate row or aggregated with foreign imports. In our case, we showed them separately as row 7 to table 3.3. Rather than defining an interregional import coefficient of the type m_j^r, the cents worth of imports needed per dollar of output j in region r, we seek to show m_{ij}^{sr}, the cents worth of i from region s required per dollar of output of j in region r. In a two-region framework, the R matrix is subdivided into four partitions:

$$R = \begin{bmatrix} R_{11} & R_{12} \\ R_{21} & R_{22} \end{bmatrix} \tag{3.25}$$

where R_{11} is the intraregional flows matrix (analogous to the 5×5 section of table 3.3) for region 1 and R_{22} the intraregional flows matrix for region 2. R_{21} may be interpreted in two ways. It is the interregional export flows matrix for region 2 (to region 1) and the interregional import flows matrix for region 1 (from region 2). Similarly, R_{12} is the interregional export flows matrix for region 1 (to region 2) and the import flows matrix of output into region 2 from region 1. The interindustry flows for this system are shown in table 3.17.

Table 3.17 Interindustry transactions matrix: two-region case

From	To	Region 1					Region 2				
		1	2	3	4	5	1	2	3	4	5
Region 1	1	21	—	9	3	—	10	—	5	5	—
	2	1	8	7	29	—	—	—	10	5	—
	3	3	20	—	50	7	—	—	—	3	—
	4	31	2	38	—	3	—	—	1	—	—
	5	10	25	26	1	4	—	4	—	—	—
Region 2	1	2	—	—	—	—	17	1	8	—	—
	2	—	—	—	—	—	1	6	1	31	—
	3	—	4	—	—	15	4	16	—	57	45
	4	—	—	1	—	6	36	1	60	—	19
	5	5	—	3	—	9	18	20	45	1	28

If the final demand (less sales to region 1) vector and Total Output (Input) vector for the five sections in region 2 are as shown in table 3.18 we may develop in equation (3.26) a system of equations analogous to (3.18).

$$\begin{bmatrix} R_{11} & R_{12} \\ R_{21} & R_{22} \end{bmatrix} \begin{bmatrix} X_1 \\ X_2 \end{bmatrix} + \begin{bmatrix} Y_1 \\ Y_2 \end{bmatrix} = \begin{bmatrix} X_1 \\ X_2 \end{bmatrix} \tag{3.26}$$

where the divided vectors of final demand (Y) and output (X) in (3.26) reflect allocation to region 1 or 2. Solving for X, we have

$$\begin{bmatrix} X_1 \\ X_2 \end{bmatrix} = \begin{bmatrix} B_{11} & B_{12} \\ B_{21} & B_{22} \end{bmatrix} \begin{bmatrix} Y_1 \\ Y_2 \end{bmatrix} \tag{3.27}$$

Table 3.18

Sector	Final Demand	Total Output
1	87	120
2	37	80
3	34	150
4	4	120
5	68	210

where submatrices B_{11}, B_{12}, B_{21} and B_{22} are the partitioned constituents of matrix B, the Leontief inverse matrix corresponding to $[I - R]^{-1}$ of equation (3.19).

If the equation system is expanded from (3.27), we have the following solution for X_1 (see Leontief 1965, Miller 1966).

$$X_1 = B_{11} Y_1 + B_{12} Y_2 \tag{3.28}$$

$$= [(I - R_{11}) - (I - R_{22})^{-1} R_{12} R_{21}]^{-1} Y_1$$

$$+ [(I - R_{11}) - (I - R_{22})^{-1} R_{12} R_{21}]^{-1} R_{12} (I - R_{22})^{-1} Y_2 \tag{3.29}$$

The terms in the second part of the right-hand side of the equation represent the additional demands placed upon output in region 1 as a result of increases in region 2's final demand. Of the terms in the first part of the equations, $(I - R_{11})^{-1}$ is the usual intraregional matrix of equation (3.19), while the additional entries represent the increases in output in region 1 due to feedback effects. Miller (1966) defined these as the increases in output in region 1 caused by increased demands in region 2 which were themselves the result of expansion in region 1. Obviously, the nature of the interindustry relationships, both sectorally and interregionally, will condition the magnitude of these feedback effects. In a multiregional framework, equation (3.28) would be expanded and take on the form

$$X_1 = B_{11} Y_1 + B_{12} Y_2 + B_{13} Y_3 \ldots B_{in} Y_n \tag{3.30}$$

where n is the number of regions.

Using the data from tables 3.17 and 3.18 (pp. 48 and 49), equation (3.28) was solved for X_1. It was assumed for ease of computation that the ΔY_1 was \$10 million in each sector and the $\Delta Y_2 = 0$. Hence the second term of the equation reduces to zero and ΔX_1 is obtained from

$$\Delta X_1 = [(I - R_{11}) - (I - R_{22})^{-1} R_{12} R_{21}]^{-1} \cdot \Delta Y_1. \tag{3.31}$$

For purposes of comparison, to evaluate the magnitude of the feedback effects, the ΔX_1 was also calculated from the single-region system.

$$\Delta X_1 = (I - R_{11})^{-1} \cdot \Delta Y_1. \tag{3.32}$$

Table 3.19 Regional and interregional models compared: Change in Total Ouptut associated with $10 million change in Final Demand in each sector

	(1) *Regional model* *Eq. (3.32)*	(2) *Interregional model* *Eq. (3.31)*	(3) *Feedback* *(2) — (1)*	(4) *Feedback as* *% of (1)*
1	17·277	18·456	1·179	6·824
2	22·378	23·946	1·568	7·006
3	31·074	32·139	1·065	3·427
4	28·414	29·321	0·907	3·192
5	26·756	27·704	0·948	3·543

Other interregional frameworks

The Isard and Moses frameworks

The full information framework described above is rarely available. In fact, the empirical implementation of the interregional framework presents a daunting problem of data collection and manipulation. Isard's (1951) framework was only partially tested empirically in a later study: the data were so poor that little confidence could be placed in the results. The Isard framework was analogous to the one described in the earlier section, with interregional trade matrices containing as much detail as the interregional matrices. Inasmuch as few countries publish interregional trade statistics in such detail, the application of models of this kind, although conceptually satisfying and rewarding, is precluded by empirical obstacles. Moses (1955) employed an ingenious extension of Isard's framework, utilizing trade coefficients based on US census data and ICC (Interstate Commerce Commission) waybill samples. These trade coefficients, t_i^{rs} described the proportion of purchase in region s of industry i's output which originated in region r. In the Moses system, the coefficients were represented as a diagonal block matrix. From them Moses was able to estimate the regional input coefficients, b_{ij}^{rs} where

$$b_{ij}^{rs} = a_{ij}^s(t_i^{rs}) \tag{3.33}$$

and a_{ij}^s is the total technical input coefficient. As these coefficients were not available locally, 1947 national (US) data were used for all regional a_{ij}'s. In the empirical test of the model, Moses aggregated spatially into three regions and sectorally into eleven industries, and 1947 interregional shipments were predicted using 1949 trade coefficients. The many assumptions necessary for the implementation of this model suggest that the good results claimed by Moses should be viewed with caution.

The Leontief-Strout gravity trade model

By far the most useful model developed to date has been the Leontief and Strout gravity formulation[1] (1963). The structural equations of the multiregional system take the following form

[1] Hereafter referred to as the Leontief-Strout model.

$$X_i^{rs} = \frac{X_i^{ro} \cdot X_i^{os}}{X_i^{oo}} \cdot Q_i^{rs} \qquad \begin{aligned} i &= 1 \ldots m \\ r &= 1 \ldots n \\ s &= 1 \ldots n \\ r &\neq s \end{aligned} \qquad (3.34)$$

where X_i^{ro} represents the supply pool of good i in region r,

X_i^{os} represents the demand pool of good i in region s,

X_i^{rs} represents the total shipment of good i from supply pool in region r to demand pool in region s,

X_i^{oo} is the aggregate amount of the commodity (industry output) i produced in all regions

Q is an empirical coefficient.

The Leontief-Strout system has many advantages over the earlier multiregional formulations: (1) the equation permits use of the gravity concept, since Q_i^{rs} reflects transfer costs of commodity i from region r to region s; (2) if X_i^{ro} and X_i^{os} or X_i^{so} and X_i^{or} are not equal to zero and Q_i^{rs} and Q_i^{sr} are positive, then both X_i^{rs} and X_i^{sr} will be positive too, and thus cross-hauling (exchange of good or industry output i in both directions between two regions) will be possible. Leontief-Strout described two procedures for the estimation of the Q_i^{rs}'s, one in which certain trade data were available for a base year and another for cases where no interregional flows data were available. For the solution of the system in the latter case, information is required on total regional inputs and outputs together with supplementary data on interregional distances (or unit transportation costs).

For a particular good i,

$$Q_i^{rs} = (C_i^r + K_i^s)d_i^{rs} \qquad r, s = 1 \ldots n \qquad (3.35)$$

where d_i^{rs} is a measure of the reciprocal of the distance between r and s, measured in miles or per unit transportation costs, and C and K are empirical constants. Note, however, that d_i^{rs} does not necessarily equal d_i^{sr}, reflecting the fact that certain back-hauling possibilities or the like may exist say between r and s for good i but not between s and r. By definition

$$X_i^{ro} = \sum_{s=1}^{n} X_i^{rs} \qquad (3.36)$$

$$X_i^{os} = \sum_{r=1}^{n} X_i^{rs} \qquad (3.37)$$

that is, the supply pool of good i in region r will be the sum of all flows from r to s ($s = 1 \ldots n$) and the demand pool of good i in region s will be the sum of all shipments of i from r ($r = 1 \ldots n$) to s. X_i^{rs} is the shipment of good i from r to s.

By substituting (3.34) into (3.36)

$$X_i^{ro} = \frac{X_i^{ro} \sum\limits_{s=1}^{n} (X_i^{os} Q_i^{rs})}{X_i^{oo}} + X_i^{rr} \qquad (3.38)$$

The term X_i^{rr} is the internally absorbed part of the output of i in region r. Since $Q_i^{rr} = 0$, the term $X_i^{or} \cdot Q_i^{rr}$ reduces to zero.

A similar substitution of (3.34) into (3.37) yields

$$X_i^{os} = \frac{X_i^{os} \sum\limits_{r=1}^{n} (X_i^{ro} Q_i^{rs})}{X_i^{oo}} + X_i^{ss}. \tag{3.39}$$

Incorporating (3.35) in (3.38) and (3.39) we have, for each i,

$$X^{ro} \sum_{s=1}^{n} [X^{os}(C^r + K^s)d^{rs}] = (X^{ro} - X^{rr})X^{oo} \tag{3.40}$$

$$X^{os} \sum_{r=1}^{n} [X^{ro}(C^r + K^s)d^{rs}] = (X^{os} - X^{ss})X^{oo}. \tag{3.41}$$

Since the values of the X's are known, the combined system (3.40) and (3.41) represents a system of $2n$ simultaneous linear equations with $2n$ variables, the unknown parameters C^r and K^s. Leontief-Strout claimed that since total regional inputs and outputs were equal, the system would balance if $2n - 1$ of the equations could be satisfied: in other words, the arbitrary fixing of one of the unknowns would allow estimation of all the other. An additional modification could be made, if we know, for example, that good i is not shipped to all regions from a particular region and that in some cases there will be no cross-hauling. Thus, we can assign a value of 1 or 0 to δ_i^{rs} as appropriate. The δ_i^{rs}'s are included in equation (3.38) as follows:

$$X^{ro} \sum_{s=1}^{n} [X^{os}(C^r + K^s)d^{rs}\delta^{rs}] = (X^{ro} - X^{rr})X^{oo} \tag{3.42}$$

and similarly in equation (3.41).

Other models

A number of alternative suggestions have been proposed for dealing with the problem of limited regional and interregional trade data. One suggestion by Hewings (1970a) involved the use of nonsurvey techniques to derive a set of interregional flows matrices from national data, using only regional gross outputs and various reduction techniques of the type discussed in Czamanski and Malizia (1969), Schaffer and Chu (1969) and Hewings (1969). In this model aggregate interregional imports and exports, which are derived as residuals, are allocated through the use of the transportation programme of linear programming analysis. A modification of the Leontief-Strout system has been suggested by Polenske (1966) and tested with two simpler alternative models on the much more detailed interregional trade flow for Japan (Polenske 1970a, 1970b).

To date, only the Polenske (1966), Leontief and Strout (1963) and Moses (1955) models have been tested empirically. As noted above, Moses's model suffered serious deficiences, particularly as a result of the data that were employed. The Leontief-Strout system has been tested for a small number of commodities over a limited number of regions. Polenske (1966) used fruit and vegetable interregional flows, while Leontief-Strout used only four goods – bituminous coal and lignite, portland cement, soybean oil and steel shapes. Finally, Polenske (1970a, 1970b) implemented a model for the Japanese and US economy. For the Japanese model, 1960 base year data on interregional flows and 1963 regional final demands were used to predict 1963 regional outputs. It was assumed that 1960 trading coefficients were applicable to 1963. All the results were better with the gravity type models; in the Japanese economy model, the column coefficient model performed almost as well, whereas in the fruit and vegetable application in the USA the row coefficient and gravity models provided the better estimates and the modified gravity model predicted best of all.

Regional forecasting using input–output models[1]

The use of regional input–output models for forecasting purposes has not been a striking characteristic of the majority of the studies completed thus far. As one would have expected, the major emphasis in the earlier studies was the completion of the accounting framework *per se*, although there were attempts to make use of the framework in developing forecasts (see O'Donnell *et al.* 1960). The projection methods used thus far have displayed considerable ingenuity of technique applied to scarce and incomplete data. In this section, two of the techniques, the *comparative static* and the *dynamic*, will be discussed.

The comparative static approach

In its simplest form, the accounting framework for the base year t is

$$X_t = [I - R_t]^{-1} \cdot Y_t \qquad (3.43)$$

in most cases, the stability of R, the regional input coefficient matrix over time was assumed, i.e. $R_t = R_{t+1} = R_{t+2} \ldots$. Estimates of X or Y were usually made independently of the model, through the use of time series analysis of trends, or relationships with state or national income statistics or even national projections of final demand. Thus for the period $t + 1$, assuming Y_{t+1} has been estimated,

$$X_{t+1} = [I - R_t]^{-1} \cdot Y_{t+1}. \qquad (3.44)$$

Theil (1967) and Tilanus (1966) have used slightly modified procedures for prediction purposes at a national level. Their objective was the forecast of intermediate demand at time $t + 1$.

For time t,

$$Z_t = [(I - R_t)^{-1} - I] \cdot Y_t \qquad (3.45)$$

where

$$Z = [Z_i] = [\sum_j z_{ij}] \qquad (3.46)$$

and

$$z_{ij} = a_{ij} X_j.$$

Z_i is thus the row sum of all the interindustry flows for industry i. Y again was

[1]This section draws heavily on Hewings (1971a).

projected to $t + 1$ and the system solved in similar fashion to (3.44), only using (3.46) to obtain the estimate of Z_{t+1}. The R matrix remained constant for the projection period in this method as well. The procedure outlined in (3.45) made use of the very detailed Dutch input–output tables and was compared to a method known as the final demand 'blow-up', an analysis which, in effect, ignores the interindustry matrix. Thus

$$Z_{i(t+1)} = \frac{Z_{i(t)}}{Y_{i(t)}} \cdot Y_{i(t+1)}. \tag{3.47}$$

The ratio $Z_{i(t)}/Y_{i(t)}$ is the base year ratio of intermediate and final demand. In matrix notation (3.47) may be written

$$Z_{t+1} = \hat{Z}_t(\hat{Y}_t)^{-1} \cdot Y_{t+1} \tag{3.48}$$

where ^ denotes the transformation of a vector into a diagonal matrix. This method compared less favourably with the interindustry projections (of the type shown in (3.45)) on the basis of mean square prediction error. In addition, the assumption of stability of R over an extended time period may not seem justifiable. The earlier projection attempts using regional models incorporated elements from the very simple techniques described above. In the Puget Sound and Adjacent Waters Study (Tiebout 1968) and the Washington State projections (Tiebout 1969) an empirical approach was used that differed somewhat from the Dutch experiments. Given the following framework for the State of Washington for 1963 (obtained from the state input–output tables: Bourque *et al.* 1967),

$$_rX_i^{63} = \sum_{j=1}^{57} r_{ij}X_j^{63} + Y_{ip}^{63} \quad \begin{array}{l} i = 1 \ldots 57 \\ p = 1 \ldots 4 \end{array} \tag{3.49}$$

several modifications were made to project $_rX_i$ to 1980. In this system $i = 1 \ldots 54$ are the normal input–output industries, and sectors 55 through 57 are special features of the model, termed 'local final demand'. These will be discussed later. The 1980 system was solved for total output

$$_rX_i^{80} = [I - R]^{-1} \cdot Y_i^{80} \quad i = 1 \ldots 57. \tag{3.50}$$

The R matrix represents the regional input coefficients for 1980 and, as will be explained below, it is not the same as the R matrix for 1963. Before equation (3.50) could be solved, the projection system was modified; thirteen industries had their outputs projected separately. These were mainly industries which were 'supply constrained' such as Agriculture and Forest products and those which may be regarded as 'special cases', such as Aluminum and Petroleum and the Aerospace industry (94 per cent of which was represented by the Boeing Company). In the case of the supply constrained industries, it did not seem reasonable to assume that they had the capacity to supply necessary increases in inputs to other industries *and* final demand consequent upon changes in final demand over such a long time horizon. For the special case industries, there were problems of identification of just what would be produced in 1980: the current (1970–1972) difficulties in the Aerospace industry are further testimony to the wisdom of isolating such industries. For these thirteen industries, final demand fell as a residual after interindustry demands were satisfied. The remaining forty-four sectors were projected

$$_rX_h^{80} = [I - R]^{-1} \cdot [Y_h^{80} + \sum_{m=1}^{13} Z_{hm}] \quad b = 1 \ldots 44 \quad (3.51)$$

The term $\sum_{m=1}^{13} Z_{hm}$ of (3.51) represents the intermediate flows needed as inputs by the thirteen output-projected industries from the other forty-four. Thus

$$\sum_{m=1}^{13} Z_{hm} = \sum_{m=1}^{13} r_{hm} \cdot {}_rX_m^{80} \quad b = 1 \ldots 44 \quad (3.52)$$

sales to final demand in 1980 were estimated on the basis of trade coefficients, incorporating an analysis similar to the one employed by Moses (1955) in an earlier formulation of an interregional accounting system discussed in the section on interregional models. These estimates (of final demand) were used for the solution of equation (3.51); sales to final demand from the thirteen industries projected separately were then calculated and equation (3.50) was solved.

In making the projections, Tiebout maintained that certain constituents of final demand should be considered endogenous, these were columns 55 through 57 – the *local* final demand. They comprised average and marginal propensities to consume out of regional personal income disaggregated by industry and a vector combining the average propensity to invest and state and local government spending in the region. These three columns were made endogenous through the inclusion of three rows of disaggregated value added: extensive income value added, intensive income value added and nonpersonal income value added, the latter including items such as federal, state and local taxes and depreciation. The theoretical validity for the separation of marginal and average propensities to consume was discussed earlier. While this is an issue to which we will return in the sections on regional growth, we may mention that the rationale behind this separation in an input–output framework is to differentiate the expansionary effects of additions to consumer spending caused by immigration and those resulting from additions to *per capita* income of existing residents. In any regional economy, there will probably be some mix of the two effects; it is assumed that immigrants would consume approximately according to a schedule of average propensities, while increases in income would be spent by local residents via a schedule of marginal propensities to consume. The effects on the local economy for a similar aggregate increase in regional personal income will not be the same in each case: hence the need to differentiate them.

In projecting the R matrix Tiebout used Almon's (1966) projections to 1975 of changes in national *technical* coefficients, the a_{ij}^n's. The next step involved the allocation of the coefficient between local and nonlocal requirements, i.e. if we assume equality of national and regional technical coefficients,

$$a_{ij}^r = a_{ij}^n \quad (r \text{ refers to region } n \text{ to the nation}) \quad (3.53)$$

how do we allocate the a_{ij}^r between r_{ij}^r and m_{ij}^r, the regional input coefficient and the import coefficient, since

$$a_{ij}^r = r_{ij}^r + m_{ij}^r. \tag{3.54}$$

The allocation was made with the help of an import matrix developed for the state for 1963 (Bourque and Weeks 1969) and a California–Washington interregional matrix for the same year (Riefler and Tiebout 1970). Thus base year information was available for (3.54); by assumption (3.53) $^{80}a_{ij}^r$ was known (Almon provided some private projections to 1980 from his original 1975 estimates) since $^{80}a_{ij}^n$ was known. To facilitate the allocation between local and import inputs, some attempt was made to compare input structures for the San Francisco Bay area industries that were also represented in Washington State. The rationale was that, by 1980, the Washington economy would approach in size that of the Bay region in 1964. Of course, this was not possible in the case of every industry and the adjustments were made only as a first approximation as to the possible direction of future regional import substitution. For a number of industries, whose size and structure were markedly different from their counterparts in the Bay area, this analysis was rather meaningless but the idea has considerable appeal, especially with the growth in the number and variety of studies being produced (see Bourque and Hansen 1967; Bourque and Cox 1970, Hewings 1970b, for bibliographies of regional input–output studies in North America). The results of a rather detailed investigation of the printing and publishing industries in Boston and Philadelphia (Isard and Romanoff 1968) revealed many problems attendant upon this type of 'borrowing' but the comparison of one set of regional coefficients with another set would perhaps provide greater insights into comparability of structures of regions of similar size.

An alternative comparative static projection was made by Miernyk *et al.* (1969) for West Virginia. The R matrix was modified in a rather ingenious fashion, the idea being developed by Leontief and used as a basis for the Colorado River Basin input–output study (Miernyk 1965, pp. 118 ff.). From the original sample of firms that were surveyed, a subsample of firms was made. Four ratios were computed using values of employment, wages, profits and depreciation in an attempt to identify 'best practice' firms. The latter's technologies were presumed to be those of the average in the projection year of 1975. As in the case of the Washington study, an attempt was made to consider changes in trading patterns: this was effected by assuming that the best practice firms' trading patterns would be those of the average in 1975. The projections of input coefficients were compared to those made by the United States Bureau of Labor Statistics (1966) on the presumption that while there may be differences in the national and regional coefficients, there would be less difference in the *rates of change* of these coefficients.

While one may find considerable satisfaction in the notion of the 'best practice' projection, the application problem is rather more difficult in that one has to determine the time horizon over which it is felt the best practice technology will transfer itself from the margin to the industry average. In this connection, the work of Carter (1966, 1967, 1970) with national (US) coefficient change proved valuable as a basis for comparison. In most cases, it was assumed that the diffusion process would take about ten years.

Final demand projections were made using time series and comparisons with national trends. These estimates were then used in the prediction of 1975 levels of output in the various regional industries. Some of the results, especially the increases in general inputs (such as electricity, communications and printing and publishing) tied in with Carter's findings at the national level.

The dynamic model

In addition to making projections with a comparative static model, a dynamic system was developed for the West Virginia economy. The basic equation for the model was

$$X_i - \sum_{j=1}^{n} X_{ij} - \sum_{j=1}^{n} D_{ij} - \sum_{j=1}^{n} \dot{S}_{ij} = Y_i \qquad (3.55)$$

when X_i is the total output of industry i,

X_{ij} total current input requirements $= a_{ij}X_j$,

D_{ij} capital required by industry j from industry i to maintain stocks at current levels,

$= d_{ij}X_j$ i.e. sales *replacement* capital by industry i depend on output level of industry j,

$\dot{S}_{ij}$ expansion in the stock of capital goods produced by industry i and and held by industry j and equals $b_{ij}\dot{X}_j$, i.e. the changes in the stock of industry i's capital held by industry j depend upon the rate of changes of output of industry j.

In matrix notation, the system is

$$X - RX - DX - B\dot{X} = Y. \qquad (3.56)$$

There are a number of problems with this analysis, not only empirical implementations, but also conceptualization. Capital coefficients relate additions to capital stock required to increase capacity over time: the term 'capacity' involves three problems: (*a*) the concept itself, (*b*) its measurement, and (*c*) the stability of the relationship between capital requirements and expansion over time. The NBER study (1957) provides many early insights into this problem: Carter's paper in this volume deals with the assumption of unchanging capital coefficients over time. It was noted that interindustry (current account) coefficients are rendered somewhat less variable by the moving average effect generated through the inclusion and dampening effect of old capital stocks. Capital coefficients, on the other hand, represent prospective rather than sunk investment and are therefore that much more sensitive to change

Miernyk (1969) describes the method of estimation of the b_j's and the reader is referred to this excellent study for the details. The $\dot{X}$ matrix was obtained by assuming

$$\dot{X} = X_t - X_{t-1}. \qquad (3.57)$$

Substituting in (3.56), we have

$$X_t - R_t X_t - DX_t - B(X_t - X_{t-1}) = Y_t. \qquad (3.58)$$

The values in the matrix R_t were obtained through linear interpolation between base year (1965) observations and the 1975 forecast (using the 'best practice' coefficients). Thus equation (3.58) could be solved for X_t as follows

$$X_t = (I - R_t - D - B)^{-1} \cdot (Y_t - BX_{t-1}). \tag{3.59}$$

A recursive process, on a yearly basis, was followed to obtain final projections to 1975.

The aggregate differences between the two projections (comparative static and dynamic) was only 1 per cent but the sector by sector differences were much larger – indicating the strategic importance of investment. The importance of the dynamic model lies in its use in simulating the *process* of structural change in a regional economy, a topic which will be discussed in later sections.

Linkages between national and regional input–output models

The methods of constructing regional input–output tables may be summarized into three broad categories: (1) the use of unaltered national coefficients; (2) the use of adjusted national coefficients; and (3) the use of direct survey information. The methods which may be ascribed to categories (1) and (2) are generally features of earlier models, especially in the United States, while category (3) is most definitely a feature of models constructed within the last decade. In recent years, however, the upsurge in interest in the development of regional input–output models by various national and local government authorities has generated an interest once again in utilizing the more readily available national input–output data.

The observed differences in regional and national input–output technical structures may be attributed to (1) differences in regional and national input–output production functions in similar industries which may be a function of industry mix differences and (2) different accounting practices, especially in the treatment of secondary products.[1] Even if we could assume that the national and regional input structures were the same for all industries in a region, there still remains the problem of assigning the proportion of each input between regional and interregional purchases. Thus

$$a_{ij}^r = r_{ij} + m_{ij}$$

where a_{ij}^r is the regional technical coefficient,
r_{ij} is the regional requirement coefficient (cents unit of i purchased in region per unit of output of j),
m_{ij} is the interregional input of i per unit of j.

A number of nonsurvey techniques have been proposed for the purpose of estimating the r_{ij}'s – Czamanski and Malizia (1969) and Schaffer and Chu (1969) in the USA, and Nevin, Roe and Round (1966), Round (1972) and Hewings

---

[1] In assigning a firm producing more than one major product to a single industrial sector one may be biasing the input structure for that industry especially if the firm's products fall into two or more input–output sectors. In US national accounts, secondary products are treated as fictitious flows between sectors whereas most survey-based regional input–output tables ignore this problem.

(1971b) in the UK have explored many of these techniques, although adequate testing has not been carried out. Su (1970) has proposed a slightly different approach. Through estimating the m_{ij}'s and by assuming equality of the national a_{ij}'s and the regional a_{ij}^r's, the estimation of the matrix of regional requirement coefficients is facilitated. In other contexts, linear programming techniques have been applied to update input–output matrices using only minimal information for the year of projection. These techniques would seem to have some utility in the context of generating regional tables from national data (see Matuszewski, Pitts and Sawyer 1964). In addition the RAS technique developed by Stone *et al.* (1963) and its further development by Bacharach (1970) are suggestive of the utility of the biproportional methodology. One of the difficulties appears to be not so much in the applicability of a technique as in its economic interpretation.

Table 3.20 shows the results of estimation of 1963 Washington State gross outputs using the unadjusted national (US) input coefficient matrix for that year and three nonsurvey state matrices which were derived from the national table. It is obvious that the use of unadjusted national coefficients provides estimates of state outputs that are much too large in the majority of cases, reflecting the relatively open nature of the regional economy *vis-à-vis* the nation. However, the success of the nonsurvey methods is not as apparent as the earlier results obtained by Schaffer and Chu (1969) would have led us to believe. A detailed examination of these results is not appropriate here, but it is apparent that nonsurvey techniques leave much to be desired in their ability to replicate regional structure from more complete national data.

Alternative forms of input–output and linkage models

In our discussion of regional input structures and their possible divergence from national structure, it was noted that differences in product mix may cause considerable problems. There are very rare instances in which we come across an industry producing just one commodity; concomitantly, many commodities are produced in more than one industry. Thus, interindustry coefficients rarely represent commodity inputs in the productive process and certainly do not represent inputs into processes producing single commodities. To paraphrase Rosenbluth (1968b), one cannot escape from these issues through refining the industry classification (i.e. through aggregation or disaggregation). With more disaggregation one would be able to demonstrate greater homogeneity in output, but the probability of a commodity being produced in more than one industry will increase. If one attempts to aggregate so that each commodity is specific to one aggregated industry, one will correspondingly increase the heterogeneity of the industry output.

These and other dissatisfactions with standard interindustry analysis have led a number of Canadian economists to develop commodity-by-industry analysis, building upon some earlier ideas developed by Stone and his associates at Cambridge (1963). The reader is referred to Gigantes (1970) and Matuszewski *et al.* (1967) for a description of these models. The methodology has been used recently by Victor (1972) in a study of air pollution in Canada.

Table 3.20   Simulated Washington state sectoral ouputs, 1963 ($ millions)

	Using unadjusted* national coefficients		Using adjusted** national coefficients		Observed outputs
	(1)	(2)	(3)	(4)	(5)
Field Crops, vegetables, other agriculture	630·1	550·0	496·2	537·1	422·9
Livestock	454·9	293·7	275·6	403·3	235·4
Forestry, fishing	122·7	106·0	81·4	119·5	118·3
Meat products	261·9	257·2	250·0	255·7	222·5
Dairy products	205·8	204·7	203·3	203·9	177·3
Canning	296·4	295·3	294·9	294·6	264·4
Grain mills	182·6	157·1	145·9	151·5	124·8
Beverages	161·5	160·6	158·8	160·3	150·0
Other foods	271·1	226·1	221·4	243·2	174·0
Textiles	110·8	19·5	21·9	39·5	12·3
Apparel	76·4	60·1	58·7	69·0	60·2
Mining	411·5	80·3	76·3	304·8	53·4
Logging	271·4	266·8	254·2	265·0	256·8
Sawmills	358·4	352·3	343·4	350·1	327·2
Plywood	238·9	237·1	235·6	236·2	196·1
Other wood	177·3	169·6	155·8	167·1	135·5
Furniture	55·5	46·5	44·5	51·3	40·1
Pulpmills	119·2	115·6	113·4	114·2	96·5
Paper mills	434·4	419·9	408·7	411·8	357·5
Paperboard mills	401·3	367·3	314·6	357·5	235·1
Printing & publishing	190·7	137·3	126·4	148·2	122·8
Indus. chemicals	425·1	357·7	330·3	343·1	251·2
Other chemicals	244·3	73·6	62·1	157·5	58·1
Petroleum ref.	406·7	355·6	316·9	365·3	265·5
Glass and stone	94·5	33·4	30·2	67·1	22·9
Cement, clay prod.	105·9	96·7	93·2	95·1	108·3
Iron and steel	398·7	111·7	109·5	197·1	68·3
Nonferr. metals	365·9	121·7	11·35	203·7	49·4
Aluminum	636·2	598·4	595·9	592·1	368·6
Heavy metal	147·3	125·5	119·2	136·0	86·7
Light metal	308·3	94·8	84·1	220·0	67·9
Non-elec. motive	122·7	79·4	76·4	97·5	56·6
Machine tools	260·1	50·9	43·6	210·9	32·6
Non-elec. ind.	17·49	95·2	92·8	124·7	66·7
Elec. mach.	308·1	70·9	72·7	210·4	50·5
Aerospace	1558·4	1550·7	1549·3	1548·9	1210·1
Motor vehicles	180·1	136·1	138·5	117·7	91·2
Shipbuilding	227·8	226·5	225·6	226·4	218·0
Other mfg.	239·8	63·1	63·1	162·1	45·7
Transport	744·0	669·4	565·5	652·8	527·5
Utilities	571·9	513·4	435·7	496·8	416·7
Communications	260·4	238·4	210·7	228·9	215·2
Construction	1108·3	1051·8	1024·0	1041·3	1033·5
Trade	2039·1	1933·3	1833·7	1904·9	1753·7
Finance	295·9	275·5	263·5	270·9	260·4
Insurance	270·3	251·5	235·9	247·2	270·5
Real estate	505·0	115·0	112·1	379·7	126·1
Bus. & pers. services	1381·1	1179·2	1068·7	1240·9	998·3

The linkages expressed in interindustry analysis represent technological relationships. An alternative approach to the study of interindustry relationships has been developed by Pred (1974) who has examined the growing importance and dominance of what he refers to as major job-providing organizations. Table 3.17 and 3.18 show the headquarters location of leading manufacturing and non-manufacturing organizations in the United States. It is evident that there appear to be strong concentrations of these organizational headquarters in a small number of metropolitan regions. What impact might this have upon regional economic activity? Obviously, the concentration in a small number of cities provides attraction for all kinds of support and peripheral service activities to administer to the needs of these large corporations. These activities, in turn, increase the attractiveness of the larger cities for future locations of headquarters establishments – thereby exacerbating the trends towards metropolitan dominance and control. In addition to these impacts, the headquarters establishments, through their horizontal and vertical linkages, are able to exert a very pervasive influence upon activity levels in smaller cities. A corporate decision made in New York may affect the future viability of inumerable communities in the rest of the United States. At the international level, the influences of these large corporations are equally apparent although the post energy crisis era has seen the dominance shift somewhat from the United States to the Middle East.

In the next chapter, various theories of regional growth and development will be presented. It will become evident that industrial linkages assume an important role in these discussions, although the technological rather than the ownership aspects have tended to receive greater attention. However, many of the ideas will bear transfer to more general concepts of linkages without too much disturbance.

Notes: (Table 3.20)
*These estimates are obtained from

$$\hat{X}^r = [I - A^n]^{-1} \cdot Y^r$$

where $\hat{X}^r$ is the vector of estimated Washington state outputs,
   A^n is the matrix of national input coefficients,
   Y^r is the observed vector of Washington state final demands.
**The methods used to generate columns (2), (3) and (4) are given in the appendix to Hewings (1971b). The observed output (column (5)) are derived from Bourque and Weeks (1969).

Table 3.21 Headquarters location of leading US manufacturing organizations, 1960 and 1972

Located by metropolitan complex	1970 population	500 largest 1960	Top 500	1000 largest, 1972 Second 500	Total
New York[a]	16,894,371	156	147	108	255
Los Angeles[b]	8,452,461	18	20	26	46
Chicago[c]	7,612,314	52	55	44	99
Philadelphia[d]	5,317,407	22	15	18	33
Detroit SMSA	4,199,931	16	13	7	20
San Fran-Oklnd-S José[e]	4,174,235	16	15	12	27
Boston[f]	3,388,795	8	6	16	22
Washington, D.C. SMSA	2,861,123	0	1	0	1
Cleveland-Akron[g]	2,743,433	21	21	20	41
Pittsburgh SMSA	2,401,245	24	15	9	24
St Louis SMSA	2,363,017	14	10	9	19
Dallas-Fort Worth[h]	2,318,036	7	8	14	22
Baltimore SMSA	2,070,670	1	2	6	8
Houston SMSA	1,985,031	2	6	10	16
Seatle-Tacoma[j]	1,832,896	3	3	0	3
Minn.-St Paul SMSA	1,813,647	3	12	10	22
Cincinnati[k]	1,611,058	5	5	4	9
Milwaukee[l]	1,574,526	9	11	9	20
Atlanta SMSA	1,390,164	0	4	6	10
San Diego SMSA	1,357,854	2	1	1	2
Buffalo SMSA	1,349,211	5	3	2	5
Miami SMSA	1,267,792	0	1	3	4
Kansas City SMSA	1,253,916	3	2	4	6
Denver SMSA	1,227,529	4	2	3	5
Indianapolis SMSA	1,109,882	4	3	1	4
New Orleans SMSA	1,045,809	0	1	1	2
Tampa-St Ptrsbrg SMSA	1,012,594	0	1	1	2
Portland SMSA	1,009,129	1	4	5	9
Phoenix SMSA	967,522	0	3	1	4
Columbus SMSA	916,228	0	0	3	3

Table 3.21 (continued)

Located by metropolitan complex	1970 population	500 largest 1960	Top 500	1000 largest, 1972 Second 500	Total
Providence SMSA	910,781	2	1	3	4
Rochester SMSA	882,667	2	3	4	7
San Antonio SMSA	864,014	0	1	2	3
Dayton SMSA	850,266	3	4	4	8
Louisville SMSA	826,533	0	1	4	5
Hartford[m]	809,160	2	4	3	7
Memphis SMSA	770,120	0	1	3	4
Birmingham SMSA	739,274	1	1	0	1
Albany-Schen.-Troy SMSA	721,910	0	0	1	1
Toledo SMSA	692,571	6	7	1	8
Oklahoma City SMSA	640,889	2	1	2	3
Syracuse SMSA	636,507	1	2	1	3
Honolulu SMSA	629,176	1	1	1	2
Grnsbr.-Winston Salem SMSA	603,895	3	5	1	6
Salt Lake City SMSA	557,635	0	0	1	1
Allentown-Bethlehem-Easton SMSA	543,551	2	2	1	3
Nashville SMSA	541,108	1	2	1	3
Omaha SMSA	540,142	2	3	1	4
Grand Rapids SMSA	539,225	0	0	2	2
Youngstown-Warren SMSA	536,003	1	0	2	2
Springfield-Holyoke SMSA	529,922	1	0	3	3
Jacksonville SMSA	528,865	0	0	0	0
Richmond SMSA	518,319	3	3	3	6
Other lesser metropolitan centres (< 500,000)		43	43	64	107
Smaller cities and towns (≤ 45,288)		24	25	39	64

Notes to table 3.21 overleaf

Source: Pred (1974).

a New York-New Jersey SCA + Stamford SMSA + Bridgeport SMSA + Norwalk SMSA. This and all other combined metropolitan areas contained in subsequent tables are based on overlapping commuting patterns and the sharing of major airport facilities.

b Los Angeles-Long Beach SMSA + Anaheim-Santa Ana-Garden Grove SMSA.

c Chicago-Northwestern Indiana SCA.

d Philadelphia SMSA + Wilmington, Del., SMSA.

e San Francisco-Oakland SMSA + San José SMSA.

f Boston SMSA + Brockton SMSA + Lawrence-Haverhill SMSA + Lowell SMSA.

g Cleveland SMSA + Akron SMSA.

h Dallas SMSA + Fort Worth SMSA.

j Seattle-Everett SMSA + Tacoma SMSA.

k Cincinnati SMSA + Hamilton-Middletown SMSA.

l Milwaukee SMSA + Racine SMSA.

m Hartford SMSA + New Britain SMSA.

Table 3.22 Headquarters location of leading US nonindustrial organizations, 1972

Location by metropolitan complex (in order of population as given in table 3.21)	50 largest retailing	50 largest utilities	50 largest transportation	50 largest commercial banking	50 largest life insurance	50 largest diversified financial	Total non-industrial	Total manufacturing + nonindustrial
New York[a]	17	12	8	11	9	15	72	327
Los Angeles[b]	3	2	5	4	2	6	22	68
Chicago[c]	7	2	7	4	3	4	27	126
Philadelphia[d]	3	3	2	4	3	2	17	50
Detroit SMSA	3	1		4			7	27
San Fran.-Oklnd-S. José[e]	2	1	3	3		1	10	37
Boston[f]	3	1		1	2		7	29
Washington, D.C. SMSA	1	2	2		1		6	7
Cleveland-Akron[g]	2	1	3	2		1	9	50
Pittsburg SMSA		1		2			3	27
St Louis SMSA	1	1	2		1	1	6	25
Dallas-Forth Worth[h]	1	1	1	2	2	1	8	30
Baltimore SMSA		1				1	2	10
Houston SMSA		5		1		1	7	23
Seattle-Tacoma[j]				1		1	2	5
Minn.-St Paul SMSA	2	1	4	2	2	2	13	35
Cincinnati[k]	2				2	2	6	15
Milwaukee[l]		1		1	1		3	23
Atlanta SMSA	1	1	1	1			4	14
San Diego SMSA	1	1	1				3	5
Buffalo SMSA				1			1	6
Miami SMSA		1	1				2	6
Kansas City SMSA		1	2		1	1	5	11
Denver SMSA			2				2	7
Indianapolis SMSA							0	4
New Orleans SMSA							0	2
Tampa-St Ptrsbrg SMSA							0	2
Portland SMSA		1		1			2	11
Phoenix SMSA				1		1	2	6
Columbus SMSA				1	1		2	5

Table 3.22 (continued)

Location by metropolitan complex (in order of population as given in table 3.21)	50 largest retailing	50 largest utilities	50 largest transportation	50 largest commercial banking	50 largest life insurance	50 largest diversified financial	Total non-industrial	Total manufacturing + nonindustrial
Providence SMSA							0	4
Rochester SMSA				1			1	8
San Antonio SMSA							0	4
Dayton SMSA							0	8
Louisville SMSA						1	1	6
Hartford^m		1			5	3	9	16
Memphis SMSA							0	4
Birmingham SMSA					1		1	2
Albany-Schen.-Troy SMSA							0	1
Toledo SMSA							0	8
Oklahoma City SMSA							0	3
Syracuse SMSA		1					1	4
Honolulu SMSA							0	2
Grnsbr.-Winston Salem SMSA			2	1	1	1	5	11
Salt Lake City SMSA							0	1
Allentown-Bthm. SMSA		1					1	4
Nashville SMSA					1	1	2	5
Omaha SMSA		1			1		2	6
Grand Rapids SMSA							0	2
Youngstown-Warren SMSA							0	2
Springfield-Holyoke SMSA	1						1	4
Jacksonville SMSA	1		1				2	2
Richmond SMSA		1			1	2	4	10
Other lesser metropolitan centres (< 500,000)	1	5	3	1	8	1	19	126
Smaller cities and towns (≤ 45,288)					1		1	65

Source: Pred (1974)

a-m See corresponding letters in table 3.21.

4 Theories of regional economic growth and development

Introduction

In this chapter an attempt will be made to expand upon some of the ideas and methodology introduced in earlier chapters in terms of a growth and development framework. From the beginning, it will be apparent that considerable borrowing from national and international literature has dominated the essential theoretical bases of regional development theory. It is within this sphere of inquiry that some of the most fascinating controversies have arisen: their resolution is still not within striking distance and while for long periods interest in them may flag, new flurries of activity occasionally appear in the literature.

The issues of regional growth and development are somewhat clouded by the nature of a society's objectives and the ways in which these objectives may be met. There are few universal regional objectives: the unique character of the feedback process between national–regional growth and development results in a continual process of modification and rearticulation of objectives, new policy initiatives and so forth. The precise formulation of societal objectives will provide the main focus of the final chapter; in this chapter our objective will be an evaluation of theories that have been proposed to explain regional growth and development.

Development stages and base theories

The exchange between Tiebout and North some years ago brought to the surface some long-held opposing beliefs about the way regions grow (Tiebout 1956; North 1955, 1956). To some extent, Tiebout (1956) and later Thomas (1964) were able to offer some avenues of reconciliation between the two opposing schools of thought. However, in the meantime, certain 'side issues' have become more interesting and the overall broad debate has lost its initial perspective.

In the 1930s Fisher (1933) and later Clark (1957) articulated a sequential path of development through which it was maintained all societies would progress. The theory has generally become known as the *development stages theory of growth*. Societies were assumed to experience changes in the dominant occupation of the labour force: Fisher and Clark referred to these stages as primary, secondary and tertiary while, as Katouzian (1970) reminds us, Kuznets's terms were agricultural, mining and service (Kuznets 1959). The crucial variables in this sequential development process were (1) changes in comparative costs and (2) changes in income elasticities of demand. In fact, Thomas regards the latter as the strategic variable in an economy where *per capita* income is rising (Thomas 1964).

During the initial stages in the development of an economy, the society is fragmented in the sense that there is little investment or trade and agricultural occupations provide the vast majority of the job opportunities. As a result one would tend to find a certain degree of self-sufficiency exhibited in all the regions in the national economy. Intraregional dependence would be reduced as increases in transportation facilities, among other things, enabled trade and hence local specialization. In a sense, we are arguing for an intranational application of the general theory of comparative advantage. With this increasing interregional trade, cottage industries were established and, later, a movement from dependence upon subsistence to commercial and specialized agriculture. It is at this stage that the comparative cost issue becomes important: increases in population, in conjunction with diminishing returns in agriculture, provide conditions conducive to the slow progress of industrialization. In the earlier stages, the industry would reveal a structure of dependence upon agriculture and the extraction and pi_ cessing of raw materials (e.g. forest products and mining). With continued growth, regional industrial specialization would take place associated with a rise in *per capita* incomes. Finally, a service sector would develop and eventually this sector would come to dominate the employment structure of the labour force. The sketch of the theory just presented represents the general drift of the arguments rather than the statements of any one of the major proponents.

An alternative theory of regional growth was first articulated by North (1955): he maintains that the earlier writings of Harold Innis and his concept of the importance of the *export staple* in shaping new economies have considerable relevance to the quest for an explanation for differential regional growth (Innis 1933). It should be clear, with the *caveat* that the staple theory of Innis was modified, that the idea of the importance of the export sector has considerable relevance to the theory of the regional economic base discussed in chapter 2. Growth in a regional economy is considered to be dependent upon the export base: hence, this particular theory has become known as the *export base theory*. The export base is seen as the medium through which exogenous changes in activity levels in other regions are translated into changes in activity in the region in question. Thus, increases (decreases) in demand for the products comprising the export base will lead, *ceteris paribus*, to an increase (decrease) in total activity within the region. The total impact will be greater than the initial increase because of the indirect effects (recall the non-basis component of the economic base) and the magnitude of the total effects will be a function of the size of the multiplier. North and others have looked at the role of the export base in terms of the cyclical sensitivity of the region – a topic we introduced in chapter 1. A region with a narrow economic base will thus be prone to more disturbing ramifications resulting from changes in income levels (and thus demand) from other regions. The narrowness of the economic base is not, in itself, a sufficient condition for a region to be the recipient of more violent fluctuations. Of greater importance will be the income elasticity of demand for these export 'staples'.

Evaluation of these theories

The underlying explanatory variable in both theories is the income elasticity of demand. In the development stages theory, rising *per capita* income eventually results in a shift in emphasis away from primary production to manufacturing and eventually to service industries. Table 4.1 illustrates the changes that have taken place in Ontario from 1931 until 1972.

Table 4.1   Percentage distribution of employment by aggregate sector, Ontario, 1931–72

Sector	1931	1941	1951	1961	1972[1]
Primary[2]	24·7	21·5	13·0	8·9	4·8
Manufacturing[3]	38·3	38·9	41·0	37·4	35·8
Service[4]	36·9	39·3	45·0	53·5	59·4
Total[5]	100·0	100·0	100·0	100·0	100·0

Notes: (1) 1972 data relate to employment by occupation: the earlier data relate to occupational distributions of the labour force.
(2) Includes agriculture, fishing, hunting, trapping, logging, mining and fishing.
(3) Includes construction, transportation and communications.
(4) Includes personal service and white collar occupations.
(5) Totals may not add up due to rounding.
Source: Smiley (1973).

What has caused these shifts? One could envisage aggregate regional Engel curves of the form shown in fig. 4.1 The nature of the curves is somewhat arbitrary. In a sense, and the Ontario evidence points in that direction, we would expect the manufacturing curve to begin to exhibit a relationship to income *per capita* similar to that of the primary sectors at some level of income *per capita* since we would not expect the income elasticity of demand for manufacturing products to remain greater than unity over all ranges of income *per capita*. What may happen, though, is that through the process of technological innovation, we would need to disaggregate the manufacturing sector and examine the income elasticity of demand for a range of constituent products. Thus, for some products, we would expect to find this elasticity to be greater than unity, whereas for other products the values may be unity or less.

While the conceptual analysis is credible, it somewhat begs the question as to how the rise in income *per capita* is achieved and, if it is achieved, how each region and why each region should progress through this deterministic sequence of stages. North (1955) maintains, and the evidence of Thomas (1964) and Katouzian (1970) would seem to substantiate, that this theoretical sequence

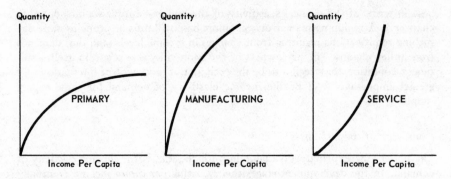

4.1 The relationship between income *per capita* and consumption of primary, manufacturing and service goods.

bears little or no resemblance to the actual development of regions – or even nations for that matter. North suggests that regional growth may take place in a number of ways, through improvement in the terms of trade (i.e. exports of one region being more competitive *vis-à-vis* those of competing regions), or through the development of new exports which may reflect improvements in technology which are then translated into changes in regional production functions. In this way, he claims that industrialization is not a necessary condition for regional growth and that an agriculturally based region may indeed support a substantial service sector. Thus, the sequential pattern may be bypassed in the sense that certain service functions may arise with the shift from subsistence to commercially based agriculture. Katouzian's (1970) research amply illustrates this particular point: he argues that the service sector is characterized by greater heterogeneity than either agriculture or manufacturing. By subdividing the service activity into three categories – (1) New Services (2) Old Services and (3) Complementary Services – he was able to show that each category had a different relationship to a supposed demand stage theory of growth. For example, the demand of New Services 'is highly sensitive to the growth of *per capita* incomes, and it is also an increasing function of the amount of *per capita* leisure time (especially if the community curve of the distribution of leisure time is not lopsided)' (Katouzian 1970, p. 366). These particular services would be the ones we would associate with Rostow's Age of High Mass Consumption, services such as education, medical, specialized entertainment and the like (Rostow 1960). Complementary Services, on the other hand, are ones associated with the rise of the importance of the manufacturing sector – services such as transportation, finance, wholesale and retail trade. In a sense, Katouzian's Complementary Services are part of the component of the economic base we would call nonbasic (they are only part because some manufacturing may be nonbasic as well).

The final category, Old Services, includes items such as domestic service: some of these services have now been substituted by taxi drivers and mass transit workers. However, as a group, these services decline with increasing industrial development as they are substituted by New or Complementary Services.

Katouzian's findings substantiate some earlier results of Bauer and Yamey reported in Thomas (1964, p. 425). At the regional level, we would expect a certain amount of tertiary and even secondary activity associated with the development of the export base sector during the stage of primary dominance. North maintained that the sequential path of development was very much a theoretical construct, whereas in reality it was the basic sector that was the driving force behind regional growth.

Tiebout (1956) responded that the economic base concept of regional growth may be applicable to smaller, less developed regions, but was certainly not true of regional growth in larger regions. In this context, the discussion in chapter 2 about the *stability* of the basic: nonbasic ratio is relevant. It was noted then that as a city or region grew in size, the proportion of activity that was classified as basic (export) declined. Further, if the size of the region is extended through nations, to groups of nations and finally to the world economy, the proportion of basic activity would decline to zero. Yet nations and regions survive and prosper without recourse to volume exporting. How then are we able to explain regional growth outside the context of export base? Tiebout offers a number of suggestions: many other components, apart from export activity, will determine regional income – business investment, government expenditures, the volume of residential construction and, further, 'the larger the region, the more the dynamic forces causing income change will be found inside the borders' (Tiebout 1956). Thus, the size of the region seems to be a critical determinant in ascertaining the sources of regional growth. Other things being equal, the multiplier effect should be greater in a larger region but the determination of a region's income may be explained only in part by the success of the export base sector. In this sense, Tiebout maintains that the concept of the export base growth theory is essentially short run. Responding, North (1956) agreed with Tiebout's analysis although he claimed that his own concern was with the longer-run issue and, while the export base was not the sole determinant of regional growth, it was the most important. In addition, North offered some qualifications to his analysis, but this did not completely satisfy Tiebout who responded: 'For long-run growth, merely to look at exports as the key factor in explaining regional growth is no more adequate than merely looking at investment at the national level'.

In Thomas's evaluation of the two theories discussed thus far, he pondered whether a regional economy could grow while experiencing a net decline in the size of its export sector (Thomas 1964). Three alternatives were suggested: (1) outside investment to compensate for the contraction of exports, (2) increase in internal trade and (3) improvement in the region's terms of trade. Pfister, in two papers (1961, 1963), attempted to explore alternatives (2) and (3) in the context of the Pacific Northwest of the USA. In the earlier paper, he explored the utility of the terms of trade tool as a method of regional analysis. However, as Pfister points out, the introduction of new products distorts the computation of price indices and, in addition, unlike a national economy, the value of exports does not automatically result in regional income because of high import leakages. This factor complicates the measurement of the effects of changes in the terms of trade upon regional income although, intuitively, it is possible to trace a linkage from improvement in the terms of trade to increases in regional income. Pfister's other analysis was more far reaching than a simple inquiry into the proportion of exports and local consumption as a region grew. He attempted to test the applicability of a number of national growth hypotheses to regional growth; of interest in the context of this discussion is the test of the hypothesis that foreign trade decreases as a proportion of total product or output as economic growth takes place. The reasons given for this are that services are traded among nations much less than goods, while the income elasticity of demand for services is generally greater than that for goods (see fig. 4.1). As a consequence, services grow and imports and/or exports decrease as a percentage of income as economic growth occurs. Using data for the Pacific Northwest for 1929–55, Pfister found that there was a positive correlation between *net* exports and personal income in the region. However, it should be noted that Pfister used *net* rather than gross exports: thus, this should not be taken as a measure of cause and effect relationship between the export base of the region and total income.

Tiebout and Lane took up this issue, in a broader context, by focusing on the local service (nonbasic) sector in relationship to economic growth in a region. (Tiebout and Lane 1966). The authors postulated that if we equate manufacturing employment with the export base, we may note that although income originating in manufacturing has increased, it is a relatively smaller component of national income than in the past. Does this mean that regions are losing their export base? While it could be argued that the assumption equating manufacturing and export base is a gross oversimplification, it seems more probable to look for these changes in terms of the increasing importance of export-linked activities and the corresponding importance of intraregional trade. Tiebout and Lane maintained that interregional trade is a much smaller percentage of regional income than a decade before (i.e. in 1955). However, there were no data available to substantiate their interpretation of trends in manufacturing activity in relationship to economic base theory.

Summary

Interpretation of data and the consideration of the time horizon in question (whether we are dealing with short-run or long-run growth) make it difficult to marshal arguments in favour of one or other of the two theories presented thus far. Most authors are agreed that the export base has some utility in determining the *initial* growth of a region: in the longer run, especially as the complexity of the region increases, divergence of opinion is clearly apparent. In this context, indirect effects – both interindustry and induced (via the income multiplier) – will complicate the picture and lend credence to notions that regions may be capable of truly endogenous growth.

Alternative theories of regional growth

Thompson's model

One of the seriously limiting factors with the two theories presented thus far is the orientation almost exclusively to demand considerations. Little, if any, attention is paid to problems of supply of factors of production, entrepreneurial ability, technological innovations and adaptability to change. Wilbur Thompson attempted to broaden the scope of inquiry by looking at the growth of urban economies within this larger framework (Thompson 1965, 1966, 1968). His analysis, although focused upon urban economies, is equally applicable in a regional context and will serve in addition as a useful introduction to the problems of goal formulation and policy.

Thompson, like a number of writers before him, had great difficulty in reconciling the arbitrary division of regional economies into export and local. While the direction of money flows may be from export to local, when we deal with interregional competition, comparative cost considerations become important. For the most part, these are a function of the supply and efficiency of *local* services (e.g. the transportation system, public utilities, educational systems) (Thompson 1968, p. 44). In a sense, when we look at the process of regional development, the performance of the local sector may be more or at least as crucial as that of the export base. However, the tendency to 'lean' on one side or another is unnecessary since, as Tiebout (1956) pointed out earlier, the issues of regional size and level of development will condition which of the two divisions of the economy is more important.

In his earlier model of regional/urban growth, Thompson attempted to describe various stages in the growth process not in a rigid sequential framework but rather in terms of the importance of (1) interindustry linkages and (2) the crucial interaction between supply and demand factors (Thompson 1965).* Assume a region with an agricultural base dominated by the raising of beef cattle; further assume that this encourages the location of a number of meat products and meat packaging plants in the region (Reference 1 on fig. 4.2). The output of these firms is exported to other regions and part of the revenues so earned will become local income to the local labour pool (Reference 2). Eventually, two additional linkages are established: the existence of the meat firms encourages a firm producing meat-cutting tools to locate in the region (Reference 3) since the joint demand by the three meat firms is above the minimum threshold level of demand required by the cutting tool firm. The meat byproducts represent a valuable source of inputs and, to take advantage of these, a number of shoe firms are located in the region (4). The existence of a growing industrial complex will further encourage the development of a business sector (5) and, eventually as the region grows, this may involve the creation of some specialized services, some of which may be exported. The wages and salaries obtained by employees in the export-linked firms (6) will now be spent on local consumer goods (7). The incomes of employees in the local consumer firms as well as part of the incomes

*This section is derived and modified from Thompson (1965).

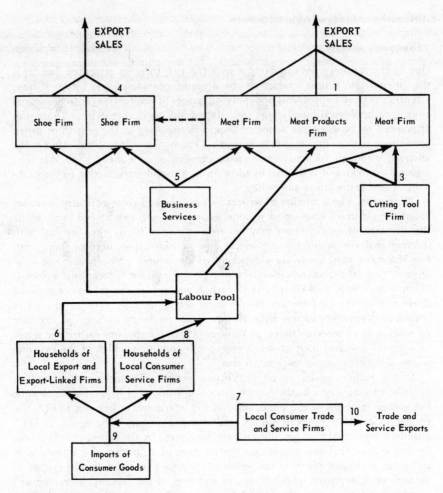

4.2 A schematic view of regional growth. *Source*: Simplified and modified from Thompson (1965).

of employees in export-linked industries will be spent on imported goods (9). As The region grows, a number of trade and service exports may result (10).

From this simplified overview, Thompson was able to identify four general levels in the urban/regional growth process: (1) export specialization (Reference 1 on fig. 4.2), (2) export complex (2, 3 and 4), (3) economic maturation (5, 6, 7, 8 and 9), and (4) regional metropolis (10). The earlier experience would be one of a local economy dominated by a single firm or firms in a particular industry. As the growth process evolves, through horizontal and vertical integration, the local productive sector would have broadened and the forward and backward linkages strengthened. Then, we would expect a gradual improvement in local business and consumer services and perhaps the beginnings of import substitution. Finally, the regional economy would evolve to a stage where services may be exported.

However, we note that not all regions have reached this final level of development: that some regions have exhibited a growth path that has been characterized by different structural dominance over time. One useful notion introduced by Thompson was the idea of an urban size ratchet, which may be fruitfully applied in a regional context. There will probably be some size, expressed in population terms or the degree of sophistication of the interindustry linkages beyond which growth is assured. This does not mean that there will be no reversals in economic growth; rather, that the degree of contraction will be much smaller and less inhibiting to recovery. If we accept this view, then the composition and integration of the local industry mix will be the prime determinant of growth not the export base *per se*. Thus, the supply of labour, managerial ability, capital and land will assume a greater role in directing the future regional growth path. In this fashion, the interaction between national and regional changes, especially in the context of factor mobility, becomes more crucial. The interaction between the supply and demand for labour in a regional context will be examined in a latter section with a view to demonstrating the importance of supply factors.

Accelerator and multiplier theories of regional growth

Having borrowed the Keynesian-Kahn multiplier analysis from aggregate macro-economics, regional scientists have now been exploring the utility of dynamic models of the type pioneered by Harrod and Domar (Harrod 1949; Domar 1957). Hartman and Seckler (1967) explored their potential in the context of a question raised earlier: is a region, within a larger economy, capable of strictly endogenous, self-sustained growth? Their objective was to determine the rate of investment necessary to bring supply and demand into equality. However, the closed economy rate of investment specified by Harrod and Domar and the specification of an equilibrium rate of growth was not possible because of import and export leakages comprising such a significant part of local income.

For any particular time period t in region r

$$Y_t^r = C_t^r + I_t^r + E_t^r - M_{ct}^r - M_{kt}^r \qquad (4.1)$$

where Y, C and I refer to regional income consumption and investment,

$\quad E^r$ represents autonomous exports net of imports used in production of exports (i.e. local value added),

$\quad M_{kt}^r$ represents the import of capital goods used in the production of regionally purchased output,

$\quad M_{ct}^r$ represents the import of consumption goods.

Further define

$$C_t^r = b Y_{t-1}^r, \qquad (4.2)$$

consumption is some function of income in the previous time period, and

$$M_{ct}^r = c C_t^r, \qquad (4.3)$$

the import of consumption goods is a constant fraction of present consumption, and

$$E_t^r = \text{autonomous.} \tag{4.4}$$

Domestic investment is assumed induced by changes in consumption net of imported goods and changes in exports. Hence

$$I_t^r = K[(C_t^r - C_{t-1}^r - M_{ct}^r + M_{ct-1}^r) + (E_t^r - E_{t-1}^r)] \tag{4.5}$$

where K is a constant.

From (4.2), we may rewrite (4.3) as

$$M_{ct}^r = cbY_{t-1}^r. \tag{4.6}$$

Substituting (4.2) and (4.6) into (4.5), we have

$$I_t^r = K[bY_{t-1}^r - bY_{t-2}^r - cbY_{t-1}^r + cbY_{t-2}^r) + (E_t^r - E_{t-1}^r)]$$

$$= K[b(1-c)Y_{t-1}^r - b(1-c)Y_{t-2}^r) + (E_t^r - E_{t-1}^r)]. \tag{4.7}$$

If it is further assumed that imports of capital goods are a constant fraction of investment, then,

$$M_{kt}^r = mI_t^r. \tag{4.8}$$

Substituting (4.2), (4.6), (4.7) and (4.8) into (4.1), we have

$$I_t^r = bY_{t-1}^r + K[b(1-c)Y_{t-1}^r - b(1-c)Y_{t-2}^r + (E_t^r - E_{t-1})] + E_t^r - cbY_{t-1}^r$$

$$- m[K(b(1-c)Y_{t-1}^r - b(1-c)Y_{t-2}) + (E_t^r - E_{t-1}^r)]$$

$$= b(1-c)Y_{t-1}^r + (1-m)K[b(1-c)Y_{t-1}^r - b(1-c)Y_{t-2}^r)$$

$$+ (E_t^r - E_{t-1}^r)] + E_t$$

$$= b(1-c)[1 + (1-m)K]Y_{t-1}^r - [b(1-c)(1-m)K]Y_{t-2}^r$$

$$+ (1-m)K(E_t - E_{t-1}) + E_t. \tag{4.9}$$

Equation (4.9) is a second-order difference equation and yields the solution (see Baumol 1970, pp. 171 ff.):

$$Y_t^r = \frac{E_t}{1-b(1-c)} + \frac{K(1-m)}{1-b(1-c)}(E_t^r - E_{t-1}^r) + a_1(x_1)^t + a_2(x_2)^t. \tag{4.10}$$

Of the terms in equation (4.10)

$$\frac{E_t^r}{1-b(1-c)}$$

is the multiplier

$$\frac{K(1-m)}{1-b(1-c)}$$

is the accelerator–multiplier effect on income. This additional term reflects the effect that changes in income from previous time periods and changes in autonomous exports have upon investment (equation 4.7). K is the accelerator coefficient. The last two terms in equation (4.10), $a_1(x_1)^t$ and $a_2(x_2)^t$, are in general form and are the roots of the quadratic equation obtained from the general solution of (4.9). The magnitude of the a's will be a function of the various parameters in the equation (i.e. b, K, c and m) and the initial conditions of Y^r (Y^r at time t_0, t_1, etc.) Hartman and Seckler thus make a distinction between the path of growth desired by the multiplier and accelerator terms of (4.10) which is autonomous and the endogenous or self-sustaining path which is given by the last two terms of (4.10). They show, through substitution of parameter values, that because of high import leakages, it is highly unlikely that a region would be able to achieve truly endogenous or self-sustained growth (Hartman and Seckler 1967). The external impulses it receives from other regions will still be important determinations of its growth path while, in turn, it will have some bearing on the growth paths of other regions. Models describing these sorts of interactions have been developed by Airov (1963, 1967) and earlier by Metzler (1950). Richardson has attempted to summarize the main elements and to develop, in a more explicit fashion, a regional form of the Harrod-Domar model (Richardson 1969a, pp. 323–36). Parallel and in some cases more extensive regional econometric models have been discussed by Bell (1967) and Klein (1968); in this direction, two papers by Gillen and Guccione (1970, 1972) have explored the developments of regional consumption and investment functions. Their papers report a partial analysis framework of investment and consumption determination since a full Airov-type model would be necessary to understand the full implications of, for example, regional investment behaviour. Models of this sort have other added advantages, especially in the sense that they are formally similar to national models of this type and thus would facilitate integration of national and regional forecasting. The main drawback preventing their full implementation is the lack of data on regional macro-accounts, especially data series developed which are consistent with national accounting practices. There is no doubt, however, that this is one important direction in which models of regional growth will be taking over the next several years.

Shift and share analysis

The more sophisticated models described above have approached regional growth within the context of a macroeconomic framework. Earlier regional science endeavours were much more modest and operated at a much more disaggregated level: one such set of methodologies has come to be known as *shift and share analysis*. In this context, the growth of an industry in a region was considered (1) in relation to the growth of that industry in the nation as a whole, (2) in relation to the growth of all industries in the nation and (3) in relation to the growth performance of all industries in the region. The analytical framework for dealing with these growth components was suggested by Dunn (1960) and developed by Perloff and others (Perloff *et al.* 1960). Thus, for a region, we may consider the growth of all industries to be some function of (after Stilwell 1969):

    (1) Regional share component (RS): This would be the growth in employment or output that we would have expected if the industry in the region grew at the same rate as *total* industrial growth in the nation.

(2) Proportionality shift or industry mix component (PS): If the region under consideration contained a higher proportion of industries with above average growth rates, we would expect higher than national average growth in the region than in the nation. In this case, the proportionality shift will be positive: on the other hand, for a region with an industrial composition biased toward slower than average growth industries, this shift will be negative.

(3) Differential shift (DS): Extra growth may occur in the region because employment or output in the region grew faster than the national average. Thus, from the national industrial mix, we expect a certain growth rate: if the regional growth rate is higher, there will be a positive shift, if it grew less rapidly, there will be a negative shift.

Total regional growth is the sum of (1), (2) and (3). Assume E_o^r and E_t^r are total regional employment in region r at time o and t:

$E_{i.o}^r, E_{i.t}^r$ are employment in the ith industry in region r at time o and t

hence, $\sum_i E_{i.o}^r, \sum_i E_{i.t}^r$ are the total employment in all i industries in region r in the two time periods

$\sum_r E_{i.o}^r, \sum_r E_{i.t}^r$ is the total employment in the ith industry in all regions

$\sum_{ri} E_{i.o}^r, \sum_{ri} E_{i.t}^r$ is the total employment in all industries in all regions in the two time periods.

Total regional growth from time o to t is

$$G = \sum_i E_{i.t}^r - \sum_i E_{i.o}. \tag{4.11}$$

By definition

$$G = RS + PS + DS \tag{4.12}$$

and

$$RS = \sum_r E_{i.o}^r \sum_{ri} E_{i.t}^r / \sum_{ri} E_{i.o}^r - \sum_i E_{i.o}^r \tag{4.13}$$

$$PS = \sum_i E_{i.o}^r \sum_r E_{i.t}^r / \sum_r E_{i.o}^r - \sum_{ri} E_{i.t}^r / \sum_{ri} E_{i.o}^r \tag{4.14}$$

$$DS = \sum_i [E_{i.t}^r - E_{i.o}^r (\sum_r E_{i.t}^r / \sum_r E_{i.o}^r)] \tag{4.15}$$

The total shift components, *PS* and *DS*, are thus equal to

$$TS = \sum_i E_{i.o}^r [\sum_r E_{i.t}^r / \sum_r E_{i.o}^r - \sum_{ri} E_{i.t}^r / \sum_{ri} E_{i.o}^r]$$

$$+ \sum_i [E_{i.t}^r - E_{i.o}^r (\sum_r E_{i.t}^r / \sum_r E_{i.o}^r)]$$

$$= \sum_i E_{i.t}^r - \sum_i E_{i.o}^r [\sum_{ri} E_{i.t}^r / \sum_{ri} E_{i.o}^r] \tag{4.16}$$

The analysis may be pursued in two ways: (1) comparison of sectoral growth within any one region or (2) a comparison of one sector's performance across all regions. Perloff *et al.* commented upon the usefulness of the technique as follows:

The differential effect arises out of the fact that some regions gain, over time, a differential advantage (*vis-à-vis* other regions) in their access to important markets and inputs for each of one or more specific activities .... The proportionality effect arises out of the fact that the various regions start with a different industry mix or composition – that some regions claim a larger (or smaller) proportion of the nation's rapid-growth (or slow-growth) industries. (Perloff *et al.* 1960, p. 74)

It should be noted here that while we may be able to 'explain' differential regional growth with this technique, it does not of course provide any insights into the even more basic issue of why the national growth rates of some industries were greater or smaller than others. Stilwell (1969, p. 165) adds, too, that one cannot apply any statistical tests to establish whether the differential shifts are significantly different from zero. Houston (1967) has claimed that shift and share analysis does not provide a theory of regional differential growth: one doubts that such a claim was made explicitly for this technique. In fact, Perloff *et al.* (1960, p. 74) go to great lengths to point to directions in theory (for example, location theory, income elasticity of demand, regional input–output analysis) to which one must turn to *understand* the differential shift effects.

The data reported in table 4.2 represents the results of a shift and share analysis of Ontario's manufacturing employment between 1963 and 1967. In computing the various growth components, reference was made to the growth performance of comparable industries in the whole of Canada. In column (4) of table 4.2, the regional shares are indicated: these figures describe the growth that would have occurred if each industry in Ontario had grown at the same rate as total industrial growth in Canada: obviously, as total Canadian growth was positive during this period, all the entries are positive. The differences between the entries in column (4) and (5) (the observed growth in employment) reflect the effect of the two shift components. The total shift (column 3) is comprised of (1) a differential shift, reflecting the fact that aggregate regional growth may have been greater or less than growth in that particular industry and (2) the proportionality shift reflecting differences in industry mix between the region and the nation. For the province as a whole, the regional share component of growth is less than observed aggregate growth indicating that the province contained (1) industries that grew faster than the average for industry as a whole in the nation and (2) industries whose growth performance was better than their counterparts in the nation as a whole. Thus, both the differential and proportionality shift are positive in aggregate, although the performance of individual industries varied appreciably. In table 4.3, we may classify the industries' growth performance in the province on the basis of the signs of the various growth components.

Interpretation of the entries in table 4.3 may be illustrated as follows: a negative proportionality shift indicates that the growth rate in the industry as a whole was less than the growth rate in all industries. A negative differential shift implies that the growth rate in the industry in the region is less than the growth rate in that industry in the nation as a whole. Thus, the growth rates in the knitting and food and beverages industries in the nation as a whole were less than the

Table 4.2 Shift and share analysis of Ontario manufacturing employment growth, 1963–1967

Industrial sector	Differential shift (1)	Proportionality shift (2)	Total shift (3)	Regional share (4)	Observed growth (5)
Food & beverages	− 1458	− 5,880	− 7,338	13,425	6,087
Tobacco products	71	− 722	− 650	572	− 78
Rubber	968	− 716	251	2,531	2,786
Leather	− 165	− 2,826	− 2,992	2,311	− 681
Textile	2040	− 1,429	611	3,880	4,492
Knitting	− 961	− 1,350	− 2,312	1,448	− 864
Clothing	− 51	− 2,182	− 2,234	3,653	1,419
Wood	2180	− 1,983	196	2,534	2,731
Furniture & fixtures	487	1,060	1,547	2,618	4,166
Paper & Allied	− 528	222	− 305	6,107	5,802
Printing & publishing	626	− 2,387	− 1,761	6,198	4,437
Primary metal	295	2,321	2,616	9,084	11,701
Metal fabricating	− 439	4,651	4,211	10,281	14,493
Machinery (non-elec.)	− 250	7,528	7,278	6,409	13,688
Transportation equipment	− 735	13,452	12,717	11,342	24,060
Electrical products	− 3062	6,937	3,875	10,783	14,659
Nonmetallic	613	− 1,203	− 589	3,615	3,026
Petroleum	1586	− 943	643	1,057	1,701
Chemicals	960	− 1,423	− 462	5,656	5,194
Miscellaneous	1232	2,471	3,703	5,614	9,318
Total	3411	15,598	19,009	109,128	128,137

Notes: Numbers may not add due to rounding. Column (3) is the sum of (1) and (2). Column (5) is the sum of (3) and (4).

Source: Statistics Canada (formerly Dominion Bureau of Statistics), *Manufacturing Industries of Canada*: Section A, Summary for Canada 1963, 1967; Section D, Ontario, 1963, 1967 (Ottawa, 1966, 1971).

aggregate industrial growth rate: in addition, the growth performance of these industries in Ontario was less rapid than for the comparable industry in the nation as a whole. In the case of knitting this is not hard to see since the provincial growth rate was negative. However, the food and beverage industry grew by 8·8 per cent in the nation and by 7·2 per cent in Ontario in comparison with an aggregate industrial growth rate of 15·8 per cent in the nation and 18·5 per cent in Ontario. Thus, although the growth rate for the food and beverage industry in Ontario was positive, its performance in comparison with the province and the nation resulted in a negative differential and proportionality shift. A word of caution here: negative entries in the differential and proportionality shift columns should not be taken to mean that jobs were lost. Actual job creation and losses are shown in column (5) of table 4.2. The entries in the other columns are measures of 'what would have happened if . . .'; this is pointed out to avoid the possibility of an absurd interpretation of an industry 'releasing' employees

Table 4.3   Classification of industry growth performance in Ontario, 1963–1967, on the basis of the signs of the various growth components

Differential shift	Proportionality shift	Total shift	Growth rate	Example
−	−	−	−	Knitting
−	−	−	+	Food and beverages
−	+	−	+	Paper and allied
−	+	+	+	Metal fabricating
+	−	−	−	Tobacco
+	−	−	+	Printing and publishing
+	−	+	+	Wood
+	+	+	+	Primary metal

Source: Derived from table 4.2.

because of negative differential shift and 'hiring' others to accomplish the positive proportionality shift (e.g. in the metal fabricating industry).

Other problems with the technique have been discussed by MacKay (1968): one, in particular seems to be a recurring theme in the evaluation of these techniques, the problems posed by aggregation. The shift and share technique implicitly assumes that industrial mix within each industry group *i* is the same in all regions and the nation. If this is not the case, then questions of comparability become important. MacKay commented upon the absence of concern by practitioners of the technique for the importance of industrial structure, especially changes in the structure in the region during the initial and final time periods under consideration. Thus, MacKay states that even if the problem of aggregation could be solved, the technique takes no account of interindustry effects, that is, changes in industrial structure in one sector and their effects upon other sectors (MacKay 1968, p. 135). Later Stilwell (1969, p. 168) recognized this and attempted to modify the technique: he noted that the weights used to relate industrial composition to employment were those of the start of the time period (time *o*) and that no account was taken of modification of structure between time *o* and *t*. To compensate for these changes, Stilwell proposed a reversed proportionality shift (RPS) as follows:

$$RPS = \sum_i E^r_{i.t} [(\sum_{ri} E^r_{i.o} / \sum_{ri} E^r_{i.t}) - \sum_r E^r_{i.o} / \sum_r E^r_{i.t}). \qquad (4.17)$$

In this formulation, employment growth associated with industry mix at the start of the period is subtracted from employment growth associated with industry mix at the end of the period. Stilwell claims this to be the net shift in employment one would have expected in view of the region's final industrial structure. The difference between RPS and PS is the net shift associated with a difference in initial and final conditions in the industrial structure in the region. Stilwell refers to this as the proportionality modification shift (PMS):

$$PMS = \sum_i [E_{i.t}^r [(\sum_{ri} \sum E_{i.o}^r / \sum_{ri} \sum E_{i.t}^r) - (\sum_r E_{i.o}^r / \sum_r E_{i.t}^r)]$$

$$- \sum_i E_{i.o}^r [(\sum_r E_{i.t}^r / \sum_r E_{i.o}^r - (\sum_{ri} \sum E_{i.t}^r / \sum_{ri} \sum E_{i.o}^r)]]. \qquad (4.18)$$

Interpretation is as follows: a positive PMS implies a modification of the regional industrial structure so as to specialize in industries which are experiencing faster than average growth rates and less specialization in industries which are growing more slowly. All of these shifts are in relative (to the nation) and not absolute terms. However, in a footnote, Stilwell concedes that increases in productivity may give a perverse result: industries which may have been relatively labour saving in the region *vis-à-vis* the nation may experience less rapid employment growth although productivity may have increased (Stilwell 1969, p. 168). Finally, the PMS is removed from the DS to obtain the residual differential shift (RDS):

$$RDS = DS - PMS. \qquad (4.19)$$

Ashby (1970), in a response to Stilwell's article, notes that changing the base from the initial to the final time period does not *solve* the problem of changing industrial structure. He suggests the use of base weights of the general form $b_{ir}(\alpha, (1 - \alpha))$ where b is the data cell indexed by industry and region and $(\alpha, (1 - \alpha))$ are weights that can be attached to the data cell at the initial and concluding time period. Stilwell, in Ashby's terminology, objected to reliance on initial conditions (i.e. weights $(1 \cdot 0, 0 \cdot 0)$) and proposed $(0 \cdot 0, 1 \cdot 0)$. Ashby contends that Stilwell's change in base is arbitrary, since of the three components (the share and two shifts) only one has been changed, one slightly modified and the share component left unchanged. Ashby provides some results from his experiments using different weights.

Chalmers (1971, p. 289) contends that both Ashby's corrections and Stilwell's methods 'can provide perverse results under a broad range of conditions'. He relates it to the problem of differentiating between changes over an interval and what is happening at different points within the interval. The problem, as he sees it, is that positive shifts may hide the fact that there is a relative deterioration in industry mix and that in the long run the shifts may be negative. On the other hand, negative shifts may not reflect changes in industrial mix in a favourable direction leading to positive changes in the long run. Thirlwall (1967) attempted to avoid this problem by looking at changes in subperiods. Chalmers suggested a relative mix modification (RMM). The DS is modified by a term reflecting difference between the rate of growth of the industry at the national level and the rate of growth of all industries:

$$RMM = \sum \left[DS_i^r \left(\frac{\sum_r E_{i.t}^r}{\sum_r E_{i.o}^r} - \frac{\sum_{ri} E_{i.t}^r}{\sum_{ri} E_{i.o}^r} \right) \right] \qquad (4.20)$$

The RMM components summed across regions for a given industry are zero and hence for all industries across all regions. Chalmers (1971, p. 291) contends that the measure allows the determination of 'whether the net effect of the PS and DS shifts is to generate an improvement in the industrial structure of the region relative to that occurring in other regions'.

In addition to the use of shift and share analysis in the description of the various components of regional growth in a historical sense, some authors have claimed the technique to be useful as a predictive tool. One of the first to test the technique in this fashion was Brown (1969): his conclusions were generally negative, namely that the shift or competitive component was unstable when compared for two successive periods (e.g. 1947–54 and 1954–8). This conclusion has been challenged by Floyd and Sirmans (1973, 1975) whose research indicated that the shift component was not unstable – at least not for twenty-three of the twenty-nine individual industries that comprised their data set. They did, however, discover that the shift component was unstable at the substate level. James and Hughes (1973) found that the model was appropriate for short-run projections but inappropriate for long-run projections. Numerous refinements to the general shift–share model have been proposed by Esteban-Marquillas (1972), Klassen and Paelinck (1972), Paraskevopoulos (1974), Sakashita (1973) and Zimmerman (1975). For the OBERS (1972) projections of regional economic activity in the United States, an extrapolated share technique was employed in which the shift component was calculated implicitly. To date, adequate and consistent testing of the basic methodology has not been conducted. Recently, some naive shift–share and constant share models were among a set of models which were used to step down multicounty employment estimates to counties in the state of Illinois (Hewings 1976). Although the overall results were not favourable, the shift–share models generally provided better results than models based on linear or exponential trends of average or regression growth rates. One of the major problems with shift–share analysis is that, in its simple form, it ignores the nature of interindustrial and spatial interdependencies. The former issue has been explored by Chalmers and Beckhelm (1974) in an attempt to relate shift–share analysis to traditional location theory. Hewings and Schranz (1976) have attempted to examine the influences of spatial autocorrelation and spatial aggregation on employment estimation using shift–share models. The work of Cliff and Ord (1973) has provided considerable impetus for research design which includes explicit consideration of spatial interdependence. Shift and share analysis, like economic base analysis, occasionally experiences a renaissance of interest as new extensions and ideas are grafted on to the existing theoretical stock. The extensions, noted above, to shift and share analysis are being paralleled by the work of Mathur and Rosen (1974) and Isserman (1975) in applying a bracketed econometric estimate of regional economic base multipliers.

Some problems associated with regional growth

Many models, not necessarily those used by regional scientists, are premised on the understanding that their partial nature requires considerable faith in the adoption of certain assumptions or conditions that other things remain equal or constant over time. In regional growth, some of these changes are too significant to be overlooked. The following section does not attempt an exhaustive classification of these problems: two critical ones have been chosen with a view to illustrating some of the issues involved.

Import substitution

There has been considerable argument in the literature about the role of import substitution in assisting the promotion of economic development in less developed countries, in efforts to increase the real rate of growth and, at the same time, to reduce balance of payments difficulties. While this may be true, there exists some doubt about the contribution, in real terms, that import substitution makes to growth. For example, if we assume that a country commences production of widgets rather than importing them, this move may require substantial imports of raw materials and intermediate products so that local value added comprises a very small percentage of the finished product. However, in the long run, import substitution of intermediate products and other raw materials may take place and, coupled with the expansion of the local consumer industry combine to decrease consumer leakages and thus increase the internal multiplier. It has been suggested that a large investment is needed before domestic production of a previously imported good can commence and, if not available, this may result in a high import of capital requirements. In addition, one may have to take into account the loss of external revenue from goods (especially raw materials) formerly exported that are now consumed locally.

At the regional level, the real issue, in the context of a Hartman-Seckler type model is that reduction of imports may merely raise the *level* of income, whereas increase in the rate of growth of export activities may raise the *rate of growth* of income. In this context, is import substitution important, and, further, does it occur in a significant fashion at the region level? Hirschman (1958) has discussed this concept in terms of the effects on backward and forward linkages. Import substitution will take place when local demand reaches a threshold such that it may be profitable for a new form to locate in the region to take advantage of this local demand.

It will be recalled from the discussion in chapter 3 on regional forecasting that Tiebout and Miernyk implicitly tried to take this process into account in formulating their projections. Tiebout (1969) used another regional structure for comparison whereas Miernyk (1969) assumed that the trading patterns of the 'best practice' firms would be those of the average for the projection year. On this latter modifcation, it may be claimed that the technologically more advanced firm may have a higher propensity to *import* inputs as a result of its more specialized needs, and that as the innovation diffuses to other firms in the industry they too will have to seek these inputs from outside the region. In the longer run, the existence of high local demand may (in the context of a Thompson-type model) encourage the location of a supplier of imported goods within the region. Thus, it is conceivable that, in the short run, there may be an increase in imports as a region grows: this seems to be borne out by some empirical work by Beyers (1972) using the survey-based 1963 and 1967 Washington State input–output tables. As Beyers noted, the period 1965–7 was one of relatively rapid growth compared to the period 1961–3. Beyers applied a Carter type analysis to measure the changes in (*a*) technical coefficients and (*b*) changes in the import requirements (m_{ij}'s) *vis-à-vis* the regional requirements (r_{ij}'s)

(Carter 1970). Beyers found three main changes: (1) regional and import coefficient changes moved in opposite directions, (2) in the same direction and (3) in cases where either the regional or import requirement was zero, there was a change in one of these coefficients. However, the overall tendency was for the import coefficients to rise and the regional ones to fall (Beyers 1972, p. 373). In addition, he found that the technical structure (a_{ij}'s) was somewhat more stable than the regional interindustry structure (r_{ij}'s). Our earlier comments about the possibilities of import substitution applying in the long run will have to await empirical substantiation when the Washington State 1972 input–output study is made available.

A quasi form of import substitution, what Thomas (1969) calls a quality multiplier, may occur in the form of technological spin-offs. Local suppliers may be forced to upgrade the quality of their output, in the face of import competition, to maintain their share of the local market. In determining future import substitution, one is concerned with the growth of the sector or sectors *in toto*, although rapid technological innovation and diffusion of ideas could stimulate changes in the trading patterns of an entirely different kind. The implementation of ideas about this process of substitution appears more difficult at the regional level, especially in regions undergoing considerable structural changes. The author of the Idaho interindustry study suggested that some notions about future possibilities for import substitution may be ascertained from 'weak interdependencies' in the regional industrial structure. The absence of certain intraregional linkages may be indicative of a number of factors and not at all suggestive of growth-sensitive lines of development. One obvious factor may be the small size of the industrial sector (and thus total intraregional demand): in this case, it would not be feasible to locate in the region in the hope of achieving the necessary economies of scale to make production feasible (unless markets can be found in other regions as well). Finally, of course, accessibility to suppliers in adjacent regions may dampen the possibilities of import substitution.

Regional factor supply, demand and mobility: the case of labour

Several issues will be explored here: (1) the existence and utility of regional labour markets, (2) the failure of a classical equilibrium adjustment process to allocate factor (labour) resources, and (3) some of the effects that factor mobility has on regional growth. In chapter 1, as an introduction to the 'regional problem', an examination was made of the behaviour of regional unemployment rates *vis-à-vis* the national average for the Canadian economy. The different relationships exhibited there partially reflect differences in the ability of each region to adjust to equilibrium conditions in the supply and demand for labour. This inability to adjust may be a function of:

(1) Difference in labour force participation
(2) Differences in skill mix, age–sex differences, etc.
(3) Differences in money wages
(4) Differences in the relationship between unemployment rates and vacancy rates

If we can explain these phenomena, we may be able to shed some light on the regional variations noted in chapter 1. However, the issue is further complicated by the fact that there is often considerable variation *within* urban and regional labour markets and, secondly, we do not have data for true labour markets, even if we knew what they were! (Archibald 1972, p. 226).

Labour economists have long been in dispute over the reaction of the labour force to cyclical changes in the unemployment rate. Two general schools of thought prevail, although there is some contention that the division between these schools is not mutually exclusive. The *discouraged worker hypothesis* contends that high and persistent periods of unemployment will be characterized by withdrawals from the labour force of workers who feel there is little prospect of their obtaining work in the near future. These 'discouraged workers' may only re-enter the labour force when conditions improve markedly (i.e. the unemployment rate begins to fall). The alternative hypothesis suggests a positive relationship between increases in the unemployment rate and increases in labour force participation. The *additional worker hypothesis* indicates that increasing unemployment rates will result in new entrants into the labour force, especially from what is termed the secondary labour force.* The argument proceeds in the following fashion: the head of the household becomes unemployed and, in an attempt to maintain the household standard of living, other members of the household are thus forced to seek work. Clearly, it is conceivable that both hypotheses could be observed during any period in which the unemployment rate increased, especially if the labour force was disaggregated by (1) sex and (2) age groups. Officer and Anderson (1969), employing equations of the form

$$LF_i = a + b_1 U_i + b_2 t, \tag{4.21}$$

where LF_i is the labour force participation rate for age–sex group i,
U_i is the unemployment rate for age–sex group i,
t is time,

found that for Canada as a whole the discouraged worker effect dominated the male age groups (the sign of b_1 was negative) while the additional worker hypothesis characterized the female age groups, except for teenagers. Obviously, many other factors can and do influence labour force participation: specifically, one could consider, as Officer and Anderson did, a 'standard of living effect' to see whether labour force participation is effected by the level of real *per capita* income. Other authors, for example Wachter (1972), have attempted to examine the influence of real wage rates on the participation of the secondary labour force.

Using Canadian regional data for the period 1953–68, Davis (1971) fitted an equation of the form

$$LF_i = a + b_1 C + b_2 D + b_3 t \tag{4.22}$$

where LF_i and t are defined as for equation (4.21),

---

*The secondary labour force is usually defined as males age groups 14–19 and over 65 and all female age groups. The precise definition, however, varies with almost each study.

C is a measure of cumulative demand for labour over the time period of
data observation,
D an indicator of labour demand in any given time period (in this study,
an imputed vacancy rate was calculated).

The Canadian regional experience revealed strong and marked differences, not
only in the cyclical response of labour force participation rates to changes in
demand variable but also in the trends in participation rates over time. In both
the Atlantic and Quebec regions, there was a pronounced negative coefficient for
variable t (time) for the aggregate male group and, although in Canada as a whole
the trend in male labour force participation has been one of decline, the effect in
these two regions has been much more pronounced. On the other hand, there is
no evidence of significant responses to changing labour market conditions on the
part of females as an aggregate group or for each of the age subgroups 14–19,
20–24, 25–44, 45–64, and 65 and over. In fact, variation in female labour force
participation is almost entirely explained by the time variable, exhibiting a positive trend. Davis (1971) suggests that in the Atlantic and Quebec regions persistent structural deficiencies have hardened the response of the secondary labour
force to short-run changes in labour market conditions. In the Atlantic region,
there is some evidence to indicate an additional worker effect – that is, in
response to downturns in the level of labour market conditions, males are drawn
into the labour force. However, there appeared to be a discouraged effect pre-
dominating when conditions became very bad. *A priori*, this is what one would
have expected: during the initial period of cyclical decline (rising unemployment),
one would anticipate an influx of males into the labour force but persistence of
high unemployment should reverse this trend and thus result in a net discouraged
worker effect. In Quebec there was a strong discouraged worker effect among
male age groups 14–19, over 65 and, surprisingly, in the group 45–64. It is in
this latter group that one would expect the strongest attachment to the labour
force, but here again persistently high unemployment levels and depressed labour
market conditions may have combined to produce this result. One may ask why
such an occurrence was not observed in the Atlantic region where conditions
have been shown to be inferior to those in Quebec in terms of unemployment
rates? Davis (1971) suggests that the large outmigration in the region observed
over the time period of observations (1953–68) may have reduced the presence
of any discouraged worker effect in the comparable male age group in the
Atlantic region.

The picture in Ontario was far more complicated with one effect dominating
in one age group and the other effect dominating in another age group with the
result that no one effect dominated overall. For example, for males, a net discouraged worker effect was observed for the 14–19 age group while a net
additional worker effect dominated the 25–44 group. Similar results were found
with female age groups. The Prairies behaved in a fashion unlike any other region.
No one age group seemed to be influenced by labour market conditions; this
may be explained by the nature of the industrial mix in the region and the
relative dominance of agricultural occupations. The industrial structure here may
be such that the cyclical tendencies are not in phase with those observed

elsewhere and thus responses to changing labour market conditions may not work in a manner that was observed in other regions in Canada. The considerable outmigration from the region may have dampened some of the potential responses that would have been observed. Finally, in British Columbia it was observed that a cumulative discouraged effect dominated mainly influenced by the strength of this effect in the over 65 age group. For example, in the 20–24 male group an additional worker effect was observed but all groups aggregated revealed a discouraged worker effect.

In examining the trends in labour force participation over time, Tandan (1969) employed a measure of underutilization of manpower in the regions of Canada for the period 1953–67. The approach was to compare each region's participation rate with that which would have been obtained with an unemployment rate the same as that in Ontario in 1952–3 (a low rate) and a participation rate equivalent to the trends observed in Ontario from 1952–3 to 1966–7. One of the most striking results was the fact that the underutilization of female participation was 35 per cent in the Atlantic region in 1953 and it dropped to only 22 per cent in 1967. In aggregate, Tandan suggested that if the levels of labour force participation observed in Ontario are regarded as attainable goals for each of the provinces or regions, then something of the order of 80 per cent of the underutilized males and females are found in Quebec and the Atlantic region.

Fig. 4.3 shows the differences between the standardized trend participation rates (obtained by regressing participation rates against a trend variable) for each of the five regions and the Canadian national average for the period 1953–72. The regional differences are striking and parallel those observed in fig. 1.2. Note the relative deterioration in participation rates in Quebec, a factor emphasized by the strong discouraged worker effect noted in the 25–44 males age group. Participation rates in British Columbia and the Prairies have shown a tendency to increase relative to the national average while, in Ontario, there has been a slight downward trend. The Atlantic provinces continue to experience a relative worsening of their position *vis-à-vis* the nation.

One final point must be noted in connection with the Canadian results described above. Davis (1971) and the present writer have observed how minor changes in the time periods over which equations are fitted can often cause significant changes in the results. As an example, in Davis's study, the standardized trend participation rate line for the Atlantic provinces computed for the period 1953–68 shows a very slight upward trend, whereas the one shown in fig. 4.2 has a very definite negative trend. The problem of what is the 'best period' is obviously an elusive one to deal with especially in the context of a linear regression framework.

The analysis of unemployment rates in chapter 1 and participation rates above suggest very clearly that spatial sensitivity to national changes in employment levels is far from uniform in Canada. The results are suggestive of a market which is definitely nonhomogeneous especially in terms of the relationship between the number of vacancies and numbers unemployed. Thus, in Ontario, where the labour market has been relatively tight, we would expect a different relationship between unemployment and vacancies than in the Atlantic region

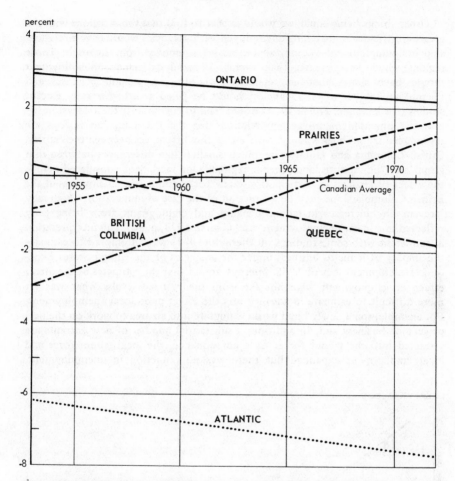

4.3 Differences between standardized trend participation rates in the regions and the Canadian national average, 1953–1972.

where labour market conditions reflect a situation of almost chronic unemployment. A major problem arises, in dealing with labour markets, when one attempts to impute the reasons for unemployment levels varying over space. Lipsey's (1965) admonition that an examination of the unemployed will not provide useful inferences about the *causes* of unemployment is not always heeded. The lively discussions about whether high unemployment results from deficient demand or structural imbalances form an issue of considerable relevance to regional labour market efficiency. Essentially, the issue is one very closely related to policy prescriptions. If regional unemployment is caused by structural imbalances (a mismatching of the skills available (unemployed) and the skills required (vacancies)), national fiscal policies designed to alleviate this problem through expansion of aggregate demand may be counter-productive. This is an issue to which we shall return in the final chapter.

Other things being equal, we would expect to find that those regions with the greatest difficulty in matching unemployed with vacancies would have a relationship in unemployment–vacancy space that is far removed from the origin. Those regions which have greater than average demand deficiency unemployment should have slopes that are shallower, because, as demand increases and unemployment decreases, vacancies should be filled at a higher rate. Recent studies (for example, Thirsk 1973) would tend to corroborate these ideas. In fig. 4.4, the unemployment–vacancy relations for the five Canadian regions are reproduced from Thirsk's study. Notice that the differences between the Prairies, British Columbia and Ontario are much smaller than differences between that group and the Atlantic and Quebec regions. One factor not considered here is the effect of changes in participation rates: for example, the shallowness of the British Columbia slope may be a function of the ease of inmigration which may 'prevent any increases in labour demand and employment from being fully reflected in a lower unemployment rate' (Thirsk 1973, p. 90). This interpretation is consistent with some findings of Miernyk (1971) who attempted to estimate the impact of loans to business under the auspicies of the United States Economic Development Act of 1965. Miernyk found that the estimates of the *direct* effect on employment were not far from the realized levels. What was far more difficult to estimate in advance was the effect upon local unemployment. For example, some newly hired workers migrate into an area to work on the new project or business and, in addition, a substantial number of new entrants are attracted into the labour force. As a consequence, the local labour force and local employment expanded but there was no reduction in unemployment.

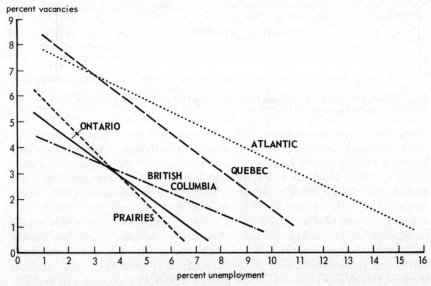

4.4 Canadian regional vacancy–unemployment curves, 1953–1966. *Source*: Thirsk (1973).

Returning to the data presented in figs. 1.4 and 4.3 and 4.4, we may suggest that a spatial version of classical equilibrium theory would provide a solution to this problem of spatial imbalances in regional labour market supply and demand. A market clearing process would effectively reallocate labour from 'surplus' areas of eastern Canada to the more 'labour deficient' areas of central Canada, or firms would take advantage of the 'surplus' labour in Quebec and the Atlantic region and move their plants to those areas. However, we have not observed this happening to the degree that the spatial disparities are being reduced; in any case, the national equilibrium is one that is continually changing and thus readjustment by regional labour markets often lags behind, creating further disruptions in succeeding time periods. Further, outmigration from an area of chronic unemployment may exacerbate rather than solve the imbalance in that region. Vanderkamp (1970) found that for every five unemployed persons leaving the Atlantic region an additional two persons became unemployed. In this case, continuous outmigration could have the effect of seriously depleting the local labour force and creating severe indirect effects not only on the viability of remaining industry but also on the financial resources of subnational governments within that region. On the other hand, the movement of industry into areas of high unemployment has not exactly been a characteristic of many developed countries without considerable incentives proffered by the national and local governments. The supposed cheaper labour existing in labour surplus regions may not have been a great enough differential to compensate for the additional costs of locating outside the 'core' areas of a nation.

The issue of labour costs over space is one that has received a good deal of debate. In Canada, in spite of considerable differences in unemployment rates between regions, the rate of change of money wages has not only been positive in some depressed regions but often as high as the rates of change in more prosperous areas. However, it should be conceded that existing levels of wages may be lower in less prosperous regions. Table 4.4. lists the rates of change of aggregate money wages for the Canadian regions during the period 1946 to 1969.

The experience in this period of each region is not remarkably different: in fact, it would be hard to identify regions as prosperous or depressed from a study of this table. At first glance, the data seem to provide insights which are counterintuitive (if we accept that intuition would lead us to believe in lower wage increases in depressed regions). If we assume that there exist differential disequilibrating 'states' in subnational labour markets (see Rees 1970; Tobin 1972):

1 An excess of vacancies over unemployed workers in one market may be sufficient to cause wages to rise in that market and hence for the average wage of all workers in all markets to rise. This will be an especially important influence if the market in question is a large prosperous metropolitan market.

2 In other markets, wages may rise more slowly reflecting an excess of unemployed over vacancies.

3 Even in markets where unemployed far outnumber the vacancies, average

Table 4.4 Annual rates of change of money wages for Canadian regions, 1946–1969

Year	Atlantic	Quebec	Ontario	Prairies	British Columbia
1946	4·82	6·15	7·09	6·29	5·60
1947	8·39	10·20	11·67	9·49	9·34
1948	6·84	8·39	8·73	8·28	8·22
1949	4·83	5·38	6·00	4·72	5·73
1950	7·15	7·20	7·87	6·36	7·63
1951	9·05	9·26	9·46	8·68	11·11
1952	8·32	7·13	7·07	7·44	8·98
1953	3·98	4·49	4·19	4·56	3·90
1954	1·28	3·43	3·17	2·83	1·86
1955	3·52	4·50	4·33	4·63	4·34
1956	6·00	5·33	5·29	5·42	5·43
1957	4·39	4·55	4·50	4·72	3·72
1958	2·59	4·00	4·00	4·05	4·17
1959	4·18	3·69	3·62	3·19	4·52
1960	3·78	3·44	3·06	3·18	3·06
1961	2·60	3·45	3·02	2·78	2·50
1962	3·25	3·40	2·94	2·47	2·93
1963	2·65	3·85	3·58	2·61	3·89
1964	4·03	4·52	4·56	3·42	5·64
1965	5·39	5·85	5·07	4·41	6·61
1966	6·21	6·61	5·76	5·86	6·42
1967	6·30	6·47	6·68	7·35	5·83
1968	6·84	6·06	6·91	7·62	6·15
1969	8·19	6·33	7·40	7·73	6·65

Note: The rates of change (W) are computed from first central differences, i.e.

$$W = \frac{W_{t+1} - W_{t-1}}{2W_t}$$

where t refers to the year.

Source: Statistics Canada, *Employment, Earnings and Hours*, 1946–1970 (monthly).

wages may rise more than expected because of the effects of national bargaining agreements.

4 Similar effects may be observed in cases where unemployed far outnumber vacancies, this time as a result of the differential skill requirements sought and available.

Situations 1–3 are self-explanatory. We may use Berman's (1965) model to assist the explanation of wage increases occurring in markets of type 4. Fig. 4.5 illustrates a short-run situation in a region in which, for the moment, we may assume that both the participation rates and the supply of labour are fixed. If labour is divided into unskilled (OM) and skilled (ON), we may trace the effect the short-run regional employment expansion path has on aggregate unemployment: such a path is denoted by ZZ. Successive increases in aggregate demand will result in an increased demand for both skilled and unskilled workers but with a bias toward the hiring of skilled labour. At point A, unemployment consists of AG skilled and GE unskilled. As aggregate demand increases, and as this is translated into the expansion of production and factor input requirements, labour will

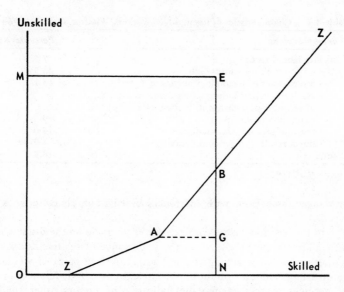

4.5   Regional disequilibrium in a two-sector skill classification model. *Source:* After Berman (1965).

continue to be hired up until the bottleneck point B where unemployment among skilled workers disappears although BE unskilled workers remain out of work. We may consider that as skilled labour becomes in short supply (e.g. from A to B), even though in aggregate the numbers unemployed may exceed vacancies, the number of skilled unemployed may be less than the vacancies for skilled persons. Thus, within a region of relatively high unemployment, there is a tight market for skilled labour and this may result in wage rates being forced upward in these occupations as the demand for this skilled labour intensifies. Thus, the effect will be to increase the rate of change of wages in the entire region.

In the long run, the ZZ curve may shift, reflecting a relaxation of hiring standards or attempts by firms or governments to retrain workers in the hope of shifting the skill endowment point E in the region to the right and down. The earlier discussion on changes in participation rates illustrated that in the long run we may not be certain that E will move in a favourable direction.

One further problem to which we have alluded concerns the causes of unemployment. The causes are obviously more varied than a simple classification into deficient demand and structural would suggest. Without making any inferences beyond the scope of the data, it is interesting to study the characteristics of a survey of unemployed in the Windsor labour market in 1964 (Horne *et al.* 1965).

It is quite obvious that the reasons for unemployment do not fit neatly into any specific category. What are needed are sets of comparable data across regions to provide insights into the various components of unemployment, although

Table 4.5   Characteristics of unemployed workers, Windsor, Ontario, 1964

'Cause' of unemployment	Percentage affected
New entrants into labour force	7·2
Unemployed – quit to look for another job	26·5
– direct result of technological change	15·1
– result of cyclical influctuations, indirect effects of technological change or indirect effects of business closedowns	9·5
– result of seasonal fluctuations	14·0
– direct results project completion	4·9
Cause unknown	14·9

Source: Horne *et al.* (1965).

there are dangers associated with inferences based upon characteristics of the unemployed.

Finally, in this section, some comments will be made on the discussions that have taken place in the literature on the importance of relative as opposed to absolute wage differences among regions both from the point of view of their influence on labour and on firm mobility. The existence of differences in money wages or earnings in regions may be indicative of factors other than those traditionally associated with these differences – higher concentration of industries which have grown at less than the national average, etc. One issue that has often been overlooked in these discussions is the difference that dealing with money as opposed to real wages can have upon the results of any analysis. For example, Foster (1972) concluded his discussion: 'it seems certain that the South (of the United States) is approaching parity with the nation in terms of *real income*, but still has a gap to bridge in terms of money income'. This conclusion is partially supported by Coelho and Ghali (1971). They tested the earlier propositions of Easterlin, Fuchs and Perlman and Galloway and suggested: 'in spite of observed money wage differentials, real wages are not different in the two regions (North and South of the United States) when due account is taken of differences in industry mix.'

When industry mix differences are ignored, the weighted average real wage (where the weights are the numbers of workers employed) is higher in the South than the North. Why? Unlike incomes of other factors of production, labour earnings are spent primarily in the region in which they are earned. If it is assumed that the cost of living in the two regions is different, then if money wages are equalized, real wages will be different. Thus labour market equilibrium in terms of wages should be one in which there is equality of real wages and where the differential in money wages is equal to the differences in cost of living. Coelho and Ghali (1971) conclude: 'arbitrary intervention to raise money wages in the South to North levels will result in a misallocation of resources as long as differentials in regional prices exist. Similarly distortive are the effects of minimum wage legislation'. However, the authors did not take into account the importance of wage drift – the ratio of earnings to minimum wage rates. Opportunity for higher earnings in real terms may be much greater in the North.

Conclusions

A number of issues have been raised here that are suggestive of their direct linkage to policy selection. In the next chapter, unemployment problems at a regional level will be placed in context of both aggregate regional and national policy, situations in which several goals are articulated as being desirable but resources for their attainment are limited.

5 Implementation of development: public policy issues

Introduction

In the preceding chapters, much more emphasis has been placed upon the development and understanding of various alternative frameworks for regional analysis than upon the application of techniques of regional analysis to actual regional development problems and their surrounding public policy issues. Although some new theoretical material will be introduced in this chapter, the main focus of interest will be upon application of techniques. Many of these techniques have received wide acceptance in North America: a recent bibliography on regional input–output studies listed almost 200 monographs, journal articles and unpublished material on regional and interregional input–output analysis in the United States alone (Hewings 1970a). However, while this represents, in a sense, an appreciation of the potential utility of input–output analysis, it should be pointed out that only a small percentage of these studies deals with the application of input–output analysis in the context of a problem-solving framework. Similar statements could be made about other techniques of regional analysis: the current interest in public policy issues is forcing greater attention on the applied utility of techniques rather than on the construction of the necessary analytical framework. Thus, one finds shift and share analysis being used for state employment projections (Brown 1969, James and Hughes 1973); the United States Department of Transportation's keen interest in the Polenske multi-region input–output model (MRIO) represented a recognition of MRIO in a planning context (Polenske, 1972a, 1972b); and current interest in fiscal federalism has encouraged new thinking in the context of national efficiency and interregional equity (Mera 1967, Oates 1972). Ecological interests have also been accommodated with attempts by Isard *et al.* (1972) and Cumberland (1966) among others to broaden the scope of traditional regional analysis from consideration only of the economic sector to embrace the complexity of interrelationships between economic and ecologic systems. Hence, the present trend is away from purely positive regional analysis and more toward a much more issue-oriented normative approach. A number of studies characterizing the latter approach will be discussed in this chapter.

Regional development: relationship with national development goals

In a study prepared for the United States Department of Commerce on the regional effects of government procurement programmes, the following general statement was made:

> The Federal Government's capability of – and responsibility for – assisting the American economy in achieving economic well-being and promoting employment growth has become a generally established and accepted concomitant of the nation's economic scene . . . . Unfortunately, many sectors of the economy have not participated fully in this growth. For these, the general affluence has served only to accentuate the differences between the lagging and prosperous regions . . . . Local government and market operations have been traditionally relied upon to provide these individual requirements, but the pervasiveness of current problems dictates a need for broader goals and more effective problem solving. (United States Department of Commerce 1967)

This general thesis, the need for integration of national and regional goals, has found a resonant response in a number of countries. It is now conceded that there is no longer a hard and fast distinction between national policies designed to achieve essentially national goals (for example, monetary policy, balance of payments decisions) and national policies designed to solve regional or mainly intranational problems. While the impact any one subset of policies will have upon the attainment of the whole set of goals or objectives will vary, the nature of economic relations in space requires us to look at the *whole* set of policies in the context of the total goals established for that society. The sheer magnitude of federal and national governments in terms of the quantity of goods and services they purchase and make requires us to go further and question the hegemony of government in an arena formerly occupied almost exclusively by free market operations.

In attempting to justify the incursion of government (at any level) into the operation of the free market, one should remember that tastes and preferences in not only the consumption of goods but also in the establishment of social equity and justice vary considerably from one country to another. While there may be some unifying or underlying principles involved, the degree to which these principles are adhered to will condition the nature of the response of various levels of government in the market operation. Oates (1972) suggests that Musgrave's (1959) discussion of this topic has considerable general validity. Musgrave contends that an economy without a government sector would tend to malfunction in three basic ways. First, there is the problem of *distribution*: even if a free market system were devised such that it operated at full employment with all resources allocated to their most efficient use, by itself this would not ensure an equitable distribution of income. Hence, there would be the need for a national authority to direct policies aimed toward the achievement of some measure of equity, especially in a spatial connotation. Secondly, there is no reason to believe that a market economy unfettered by a public sector will enable the nation as a whole to achieve a high and stable level of both output and employment. *Stabilization* policies, primarily enacted through monetary and fiscal controls, are needed to ensure some long-run stability in the economy. Thirdly, there is no guarantee that the free market operations will ensure efficient *allocation* of all resources among various alternative uses: one could envisage bottlenecks in some sectors or regions and oversupply in others. In many cases, certain goods or services may not be provided because of the expense involved (for example, national security considerations). Overriding all of these considerations is a desire for some commitment to be made to growth and development over time; Oates (1972) feels that the time aspect of government intervention is often overlooked but it is obvious that temporal considerations will weigh heavily in allocation decisions (conservation problems), stabilization policies (the degree and timing of tax cuts, subsidies, etc.) and in distribution problems (the effects inequities in the present time period will have on the possibilities for future redistribution).

While Musgrave's (1959) arguments provide substantive support for the introduction of regional development policies and programmes, it remains to be argued whether all of these programmes should be directed at the national or regional (or even subregional) level. Oates (1972) provides some fascinating arguments in favour of a federal system in which certain functions are centralized and others left to local, state or regional governments. These issues have not received the attention they warrant in the development literature, although recent consumer activism, and assertion of rights being demonstrated by certain racial minorities, have served to focus attention on the fact that consumer preferences are not uniform within a national economy. Oates contends that the limited fiscal policy alternatives open to regional and local governments preclude their providing significant input into a national stabilization programme. In addition, the absence of the ability to regulate monetary policy at the regional level further limits subnational control of employment and output levels.

The absence of monetary policy at the regional level should not be interpreted to mean that monetary policy is 'neutral' with respect to regional programmes and policies, as opposed to fiscal measures which can be, and often are, spatially discriminating in their impact. Comeau notes that the argument used to be that if governments must interfere with the economy

> . . . then monetary policy provided the type of interference which was least likely to upset the market-indicated preferences of the public and least likely to discriminate between segments, regions or groups in the satisfaction of those preferences. Monetary policy actions were thought to simply change the credit environment in which all parties and regions participated in much the same manner . . . . (Comeau 1973)

We will return to this question when policy decisions taken by a number of governments in furthering goals associated with regional development will be examined.

It has lately become common practice for each country, whether through a Council of Economic Advisers in the United States, the Economic Council of Canada or through the auspices of a National Plan (in Britain) to articulate several development objectives to assist in the allocation of resources. For example, in the *First Annual Review* (1964) of the Economic Council of Canada, five general goals were proposed for the Canadian economy: (1) a relatively high and stable rate of growth; (2) a viable balance of payments; (3) an equitable distribution of rising incomes; (4) a high level of employment, defined as a situation with a maximum of 3 per cent unemployment and (5) reasonable price stability, defined as a maximum increase of 2 per cent in the gross national expenditure price deflator (Economic Council of Canada 1964). Optimally, one would wish to achieve all five goals: problems of choice arise when, as is usual, all of these objectives may not be met simultaneously or when objectives conflict one with another.

In the regional development literature and, increasingly, in the work of welfare economists, attention is being focused on the problems of choice in selecting strategies for growth and development. An important side issue (in the present context, but of prime importance in general economic theory) concerns the method by which the choice is made – majority voting, federal decisions and so forth (see Arrow 1963; Oates 1972; Campbell 1972). It is unlikely, given the complexity of present-day economic systems, that there exists a unique strategy which, if followed, would result in the satisfying of all the five goals established for Canadian society. It is far more probable that a strategy focusing on the attainment of one or more of these goals tend to reduce the possibility of additional goals being reached. When such conflicts of choice arise in the attainment of goals, one can introduce the notion of a *trade-off*. A trade-off implies knowledge of the consequences involved in pursuing one goal and the 'costs' of not being able to achieve another goal. With five goals, there exists the possibility of many trade-offs – goal 1 with goals 2, 3, 4 and 5, etc. However, not all of these trade-offs may be relevant in the sense that the trade-off curve may not be negatively sloped (see fig. 5.1): if this is the case, then there would appear to be little conflict between the two goals in question. In fig. 5.1, some conflict is assumed to exist: complete attainment of goal 1 would result in something less than 50 per cent attainment of goal 2.

In recent years, considerable attention has been given to two trade-offs: that between the rate of change of money wages or prices and unemployment (the Phillips curve debate) and secondly, the national efficiency–interregional or regional equity debate. In the context of the Canadian goals, this would imply trade-offs between goals 1 and 3 (efficiency and equity) and between goals 5 and 4 (price stability and low unemployment). In the next section these two trade-offs will be examined in greater detail because they serve to focus attention on the usefulness of the integration of national and regional policy as well as providing considerable insights into the empirical verification of some received theory.

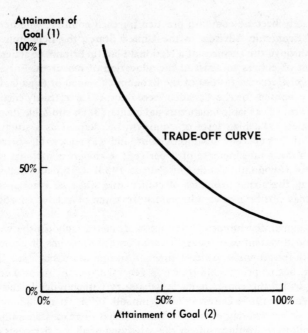

5.1 The concept of a trade-off between goals.

The trade-offs explored

If we may assume (after Mera 1967) that the market mechanism for the allo-cation of resources leads to the attainment of the maximum aggregate output in a national economy, a policy designed to improve interregional equity necess-arily curtails aggregate output unless the equity goal is achieved through some form of a non-market-oriented distribution policy that is carried out according to certain criteria of justice or equity established by the society. Thus, the equity goal could be achieved by lump-sum transfer payments in the form of negative income taxes, unemployment compensation and the like. This may be satisfactory if the equity goal relates solely to income, with a goal (say) of equal-izing real income *per capita* across all regions. However, given the prevailing 'work ethic' of most of Western society, it is unlikely that continued lump-sum transfer payments would be continued indefinitely, especially as incomes began to rise. One could foresee all sorts of problems arising! Thus, it is usual to think of the equity goal as embracing income considerations but not excluding pro-jects designed to increase the possibilities for expanding job opportunities in less developed regions.

As federal and provincial (or state) governments assume greater and greater control of the proportion of gross national expenditure that they are able to allocate, there exists considerable pressure upon these governments on the one hand to behave as though they were pure profit maximizers (if we may tentatively equate efficiency with profit maximization) and, on the other hand, to ignore efficiency criteria and attempt to allocate their resources in order to maximize social returns to society, some of which may be non-pecuniary. If we deal with the first pressure, the procedure is one of ranking various alternative projects (which we may assume to be neither interdependent nor mutually exclusive) competing for government funds according to their performance of efficiency. There has been a vast source of literature dealing with the problem of valuation of project benefits at market prices and the equally thorny issue of the appropriate rate at which the time stream of benefits should be discounted (see, for example, Mishan 1971). At this stage, we will assume that these issues have been resolved and that the size of project expenditures (the budget constraint) has been determined by allocating funds to successive projects such that the internal rate of return on the marginal project (the last one to be undertaken on the government's list) is equal to the social rate of return which should approximate the marginal rate of return on capital in the private sector. Irrespective of the method by which projects are selected, the main concern is that resources in both the public and private sector will be allocated in a manner that maximizes national product.

The equity issue has been ignored thus far: the assumptions and allocation rules discussed above rest on more traditional benefit-cost analysis in which it is assumed that distribution is irrelevant. In other words, in Canada, benefits to communities in the depressed areas of the Atlantic Provinces are assumed to be of equal value to benefits accruing to the more prosperous areas in southern Ontario and Quebec. Proponents of this line of argument continue that after the efficiency allocation has been made, the equity issues may be resolved through a costless transfer policy. This policy would not affect the pattern of production and thus the attainment of maximum efficiency. The separation of equity and efficiency criteria in allocation problems has come under severe criticism for a number of reasons (see Hetrich 1971):

1 Transfer payments are not costless: they involve both administrative and political costs.
2 There may be some maximal level, alluded to earlier, beyond which it would be contrary to the prevailing societal ethic to continue transfer payments.
3 Projects are rarely independent and often have pronounced sectoral and spatial feedbacks that will bear directly upon equity issues even though the initial allocation may have been premised on efficiency criteria alone.
4 Federal governments typically want to pursue both objectives in project selection especially in a democratic system where there exists considerable pressure to distribute the government pie to the various regions.
5 The latter concern has suggested to a number of authors that in a federal system there is no presumption that national product is the objective function to be maximized. It may be that the incomes of regions, states or provinces are of primary importance and, hence, in project selection, account must be taken of the regional incidence of benefits when projects

are ranked for selection. Mishan (1971) has been arguing similarly, in a more general sense, when he maintains that distribution should be decided first before one can discuss aggregate optimality.

If we accept the arguments in favour of considering both equity and efficiency criteria, the government, as a decision-maker, now faces a number of alternatives (not all of which may be admissible): (1) ignore distribution and finance projects in the most efficient manner until the budget is exhausted, (2) ignore efficiency and finance projects with the most desirable distributional or equity consequences, (3) establish a minimum level of efficiency and select according to equity criteria, (4) establish a minimum distributional requirement and select according to efficiency, or (5) develop an explicit preference function between equity and efficiency in order to rank projects. Alternative 1 has already been discussed: this is the case of pure efficiency allocation: similarly, alternative 2 is a purely equity-oriented policy. The remaining three alternatives involve some trade-off between the two criteria. Fig. 5.2 illustrates the possible trade-offs. Ignoring the *PP* curves for the moment, we may relate alternatives 1 and 2 to points *d* (maximum efficiency) and *a* (maximum equity). Efficiency may be expressed in terms of the rate of growth of gross national product[1] and equity in terms of some combination of weighted dispersion indices of income *per capita*, unemployment rates and the like. Alternative 3 specifies a minimum level of efficiency (say *b*) which we would be willing to accept (a growth rate of 2 per cent *per annum* in real terms?): thus, the trade-off in this situation is now restricted to points *b* and *d*, and points between *a* and *b* are thereby excluded. Projects may now be ranked on the basis of their contribution to the equity goal with the constraint that a level of efficiency no lower than *b* is achieved. Alternative 4 presents a constraint on efficiency allocation: in this case, a minimum level of equity is established (point *c*), and the trade-off becomes a choice of points between *c* and *a*. With both conditions – that is, a minimum level of both equity and efficiency – the trade-off will be between *b* and *c*. If we are able to introduce an explicit policy-makers' preference function, we may arrive at the optimal mix of policies between equity and efficiency: these preference functions, shown in fig. 5.2 as *PP*, *P'P'*, etc., will relate how much we would be willing to forego efficiency for distributional ends. The policy-maker will attempt to move to the concave function as far from the origin as is feasible, constrained by the realities of the trade-off curve. In fig. 5.2, alternative 5 may be satisfied with a mix of policies which would yield a point *e*, providing levels of both efficiency and equity that are in excess of the established minima in alternatives 3 and 4.

The development of the preference function presents familiar problems of empirical implementation. One alternative, suggested by McGuire and Garn (1969), suggests a procedure whereby we may discount benefits applied to more prosperous areas in relation to benefits in less prosperous regions. For example, let the net benefits to region *r* from each project be defined as

$$\lambda^r(p\beta^r - C^r) \tag{5.1}$$

[1] It should be noted that the first goal of the Economic Council of Canada considered not only the *level* of national growth but its *stability* over time.

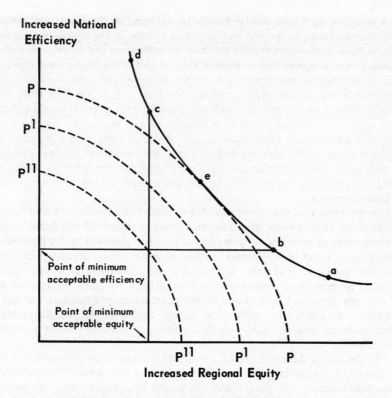

5.2   Trade-off between two goals with additional performance criteria.

where λ^r is the marginal utility of money in region r,
         β^r is the benefit to region r,
         p the market price of the benefits,
         C^r the costs of the project borne by region r.

When efficiency is the only objective, λ^r will be equal to one in all areas (this follows from the assumption that the spatial incidence of benefits is irrelevant in efficiency allocation); but when equity considerations are taken into account, we need to calculate the λ's. McGuire and Garn suggested a function of the form

$$\lambda^r = \lambda^r(E, Y) \qquad (5.2)$$

and they experimented with a specification of the form:

$$\lambda^r = a\left[\frac{\bar{E}}{E^r}\right]^\alpha + b\left[\frac{\bar{Y}}{Y^r}\right]^\beta \qquad (5.3)$$

where $\bar{E}$ United States average employment level,
         $\bar{Y}$ United States median income level,

and E^r, Y^r similarly for each region. Instead of employment levels, unemployment rates could be used with similar results on the value of the λ's. It was assumed here that additions to income and additions to jobs in the region had independent utilities and were therefore additive. In calibrating the model, the authors assumed that a region with a median income and employment level similar to that in the nation would have a $\lambda = 1 \cdot 00$. Regions with indicators that were higher than the national figures would thus have a λ of less than unity: conversely, regions which were less well off than the nation would have a λ greater than unity. In this fashion, project benefits in less prosperous regions would assume a greater real value than in the wealthier parts of the country. The McGuire–Garn model was applied to some data collected by the Economic Development Administration and they concluded that the selection of projects using the combined equity–efficiency measure improved performance in terms of both objectives.

One problem that they were not able to resolve was the issue of spill-overs or externalities. It is obvious from the discussions in chapters 2 and 3 that exogenous injections of spending by government in one region will have a pronounced impact upon other regions which are linked in an input–output sense through industrial purchases and sales. Given, also, the probability of a high regional marginal propensity to import on the part of local residents, the expenditures of incomes generated as a result of the government programmes will not be absorbed, black-box like, within the region. Incorporating the magnitude of these feedbacks into an equity–efficiency framework would present a considerable challenge!

The debate on the existence of a trade-off between unemployment and rates of change of consumer prices or money wages centres around the stability of these relationships over time. The expectations hypothesis school, whose most vocal proponents include Friedman (1968) and Phelps (1969), maintain that, in the long run, there is no trade-off between price stability and unemployment. The key argument in the theory is that the *expected* rate of increase of money wages is the main factor in determining the position of the Phillips curve. Thus, as Brechling (1969) comments, 'There is a unique rate of unemployment, U^*, at which actual wage increases equal expected wage increases.' Consequently, when the actual unemployment rate is below U^*, there will be ever-rising wage increases. Assuming some function, $\dot{P} = f(\dot{W})$, where $\dot{P}$ and $\dot{W}$ refer to rates of increase of prices and money wages, such a condition ($U < U^*$) would lead, *ceteris paribus*, to accelerating price inflation. The reverse will occur (i.e. accelerating price deflation) when the observed U is greater than U^*. With reference to a set of Phillips curves, we may, after Holt (1969), explain the process as follows. Assume that U^* is the equilibrium level of unemployment associated with a situation in which prices are constant (although similar reasoning could be applied to situations in which the rate of increases in prices was constant and greater than zero). At this point, it is assumed that any steady rate of inflation can be foreseen exactly and as a result unemployment would not be affected. The Phillips curve at this stage will then be the vertical line at U^*. If an unexpected increase in aggregate demand occurred, one greater than that required to maintain the stability of $\dot{W}$, then we could expect an increase in $\dot{W}$, to say, $\dot{W}_1$. The

unexpected increase in demand would allow expansion of production, employment (and, therefore, a reduction in unemployment if we may assume that the
growth of employment is greater than the growth of the labour force) and an
increase in prices. Assuming that the process could be described by curve I in
fig. 5.3, the economy would move from U^* to point A, where the rate of
increase of money wages would be $\dot{W}_1$ and unemployment U_1. Restoration of
the original equilibrium would take place as the economy became adjusted to
the new level of inflation rate (i.e. the new rate would gradually be accepted as
'the accepted rate of inflation'); this would cause the Phillips curve to move out
from the axes and the unemployment rate would rise until U^* was reached. Now
the equilibrium rate of unemployment would be associated with a higher rate of
increase of money wages. A similar analysis may be applied when there is an
unexpected fall in W. The existence of a natural rate of unemployment (U^*) has
been debated in the literature. Friedman (1968) comments that 'Unfortunately,
we have as yet devised no method to estimate accurately or readily the natural
rate of interest or unemployment.'

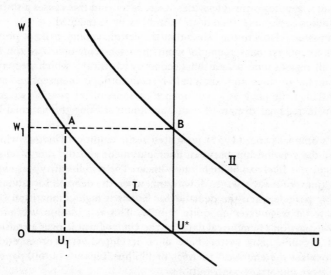

5.3   The 'natural rate' of unemployment. *Source*: After Holt (1969).

Friedman also noted that the natural rate itself changes from time to time
and thus suggested that adoption of a goal of say price stability or a controlled
rate of growth of inflation should replace primary concern with reduction of
unemployment. The outcome of this issue is not irrelevant at this point in that
the refutation of the existence of a medium-long-run Phillips curve would require
a re-evaluation of all policy strategies based on the assumed trade-off implied by
the Phillips curve. Note that the concern is with the longer run, for even
Friedman (1968) concedes a trade-off in the short run (this resulting from
unanticipated inflation of the type discussed above with reference to fig. 5.3).

However, it is not altogether clear whether the recent experience of high inflation rates and high unemployment represents (1) a stochastic departure from the long-run Phillips curve, (2) a shift in the curve away from the origin in unemployment – wage change/price change space, or (3) evidence of a need to restate the relationship in terms of a natural rate of unemployment with some other objective replacing more traditional concern with the unemployment/price change trade-off.

If we may assume that such a trade-off does exist in the longer run, what implications does this have for policies towards the constituent regional economies? For example, will a reduction in regional unemployment disparities shift the national Phillips curve towards the axes and thus provide either lower rates of inflation and unemployment or some other optimal combination of both. For example, in fig. 5.4, if curve *I* represents an initial condition, the optimal policy combination would be $\dot{W}_1$ and U_1. This policy would be chosen from what Lipsey (1965) calls the 'policy-makers' preference function', which would be represented by a set of concave indifference curves, *PP*, *P'P'*, etc. If we assume that regional unemployment disparities are reduced and this causes a shift in the national Phillips curve to *II*, then both $\dot{W}$ and *U* will be reduced.

A further issue relates to the effect that the national policy-makers' preference functions have on regional unemployment/inflation trade-offs. Are the Phillips curves for all regions within a national economy identical – which we may interpret in a number of ways, for example in respect to slope, intercept and stability over time? This issue obviously will determine some of the possible success that a reduction in regional disparities will have upon shifting the national Phillips curve.

Phillips's original paper (1958) presented some empirical findings which suggested that the relationship between unemployment and the rate of change of money wages was likely to be highly non-linear. The non-linearity was explained by the stickiness of *money* wages downwards when the demand for labour is low while during periods when the demand for labour is high competition (for this labour) may bid wage rates up quite rapidly. This relationship was presented from an investigation of empirical data for the UK as a whole over a considerable number of decades. Later writers have since developed various theoretical constructs to explain the empirical findings of Phillips, Lipsey's (1960) paper being one of the more important contributions.

In recent years, a number of authors have attempted to extend the theory (or what Tobin (1972) refers to as 'Phillips curve doctrine') to include other explanatory variables, such as labour market conditions (factors such as unemployment rates for different age–sex groups), change in participation rates, the rate of change of unemployment and prices, change in trade union membership and wage adjustment functions for subnational labour markets. The latter extension is of a relatively recent vintage and includes the work of Cowling and Metcalf (1967), Metcalf (1971), Thirlwall (1969, 1970) and Archibald (1969) for the UK and the studies of Kaliski (1964) and Thirsk (1973) of Canadian regions. What are the empirical and theoretical justifications for this extension?

Kaliski (1964) commented that this interest was primarily to attempt to

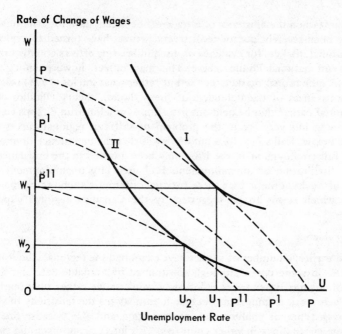

5.4 Shifts in the national Phillips curve associated with a reduction in the regional dispersion of unemployment rates.

avoid the disturbing effects that aggregation of labour markets at the national level might have on a pure adjustment mechanism in a single labour market. Obviously, disaggregation to regional levels by no means avoids this problem since subnational heterogeneity may be almost as marked as that existing in the national labour market. The theoretical importance of subnational disaggregation may be adduced to the interpretation of the concept of equilibrium in the national labour market. Tobin's (1972) paper noted the difficulty of precise definition and the relative importance of equilibrating and disequilibriating effects upon the labour market equilibrium (some of these issues were discussed in the section on factor mobility in chapter 4). Tobin (1972) has noted, and some casual empirical evidence would suggest, that disequilibriating effects are present all the time, although the regional sectoral distribution may shift over time. In addition, imperfect knowledge of the extraregional markets by those in regions r_i and of conditions in r_i by those in other regions, the friction of distance, and the costs involved in job search and long-distance moves, may provide both necessary and sufficient conditions for the existence of subnational disequilibria in regional labour markets. However, it should be conceded that changes in consumer preference functions over time and space, technological innovation and marketing practices of firms will also contribute to such disequilibria and their continued existence.

It is interesting to note that as a result of the experience of the last six or seven years (when the existence of a trade-off between 'inflation' and unemploy-ment has been severely questioned), several writers have turned to explorations of subnational markets for evidence of disequilibriating effects and distortions to the long-run national Phillips curve. This may reflect, however, not so much interest in subnational markets *per se* but rather what Phelps (1971) refers to as 'the inventiveness of the defenders of the orthodox theory (Phillips curves).' Phelps noted earlier that he held out little hope for a long-run Phillips curve that was anything but very steep; the problem of shifts in regional curves will be reviewed below. Hall's (1970) point of view is that the persistence of unemploy-ment at full employment in the USA may be attributed to the imbalance in the regional distribution of unemployment. Hall used city unemployment data in support of his hypothesis that these regional differentials tend to permanency – a point which seems to be suggested by the Canadian regional experience.

The UK evidence

As noted earlier, a number of studies have examined the regional labour markets of the UK in some detail although constrained by available data and the limi-tations of regional boundaries reflecting administrative rather than market div-isions. Their work is important because it emphasizes the sensitivity of the data to differing types of analysis and interpretation and also because one would expect similar findings in other countries. This latter proposition did not hold for Canada.

Simple Phillips curves for regions within the United Kingdom are shown in fig. 5.5. Although the slopes and location of these curves correspond to theory, imbalances within regional labour markets and the impact of earnings change in one region on other regions may influence the nature of the relationships between earnings changes and unemployment within any one given region. These issues are discussed below.

In his earlier paper, Thirlwall (1969) was concerned with the effect that dis-persion of market rates of unemployment might have on national wage rate changes and, subsequently, he examined a partial version of the earnings spread hypothesis.[1] Thirlwall defined a weighted standard deviation of industry (i) and regional (r) rates of unemployment:

$$v_i^* = \sqrt{\sum_{j=1}^{n} (\bar{u} - u_j)^2 w_j} \tag{5.4}$$

where $\bar{u}$ is the UK unemployment rate,

           u_j is the unemployment rate in the jth industry,

           w_j is the relative importance of the jth industry or rth region measured by proportion of total employees.

Similarly, using u_r, the unemployment rate in the rth region, he obtained a value for v_r^*: Thirlwall then tested two sets of relationships:

[1] This notation suggests that wage rate increases in markets where the demand for labour increases may spill over into other markets where there may be weak pressure of demand.

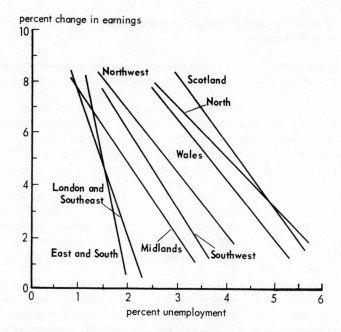

percent change in earnings

percent unemployment

5.5 Regional Phillips curves for the United Kingdom. *Note*: Estimating equation was $e_r = a \pm b_1 u_r$ where e_r is the rate of change of earnings in the regions, u_r is the percentage unemployed. *Source*: Thirlwall (1970).

$$\dot{W} = f(u, v_i^*): \quad W = f(u, v_r^*) \tag{5.5}$$

$$\dot{W} = f(u, v_r^*, v_i^*) \tag{5.6}$$

While the dispersion of industry rates of unemployment was a significant explanatory variable, the uneven regional distribution of the demand for labour was not an important independent influence on rate of change of money wage rates during the post-war period. The variable v_r^* was significantly intercorrelated with u and thus exerted its influence indirectly on $\dot{W}$ through the unemployment rate. When both industry and regional dispersion indices were used (equation (5.6)), the regional index again was not independently significant. Thirlwall thus concluded that lowering demand in the more prosperous south and raising it in the less prosperous north would not reduce wage inflation in the *aggregate* unless the aggregate pressure of demand is lowered or the dispersal of unemployment across industries is lowered at the same time.

Archibald (1969) included a regional dispersion index in his study of the UK economy: this index was the regional variance of unemployment each year. This variable, as well as a measure of the skewness of unemployment over the regions, was included in an equation of the form

$$\dot{W} = f(u^{-1}, \dot{P}, \dot{U}, \sigma^2, \gamma) \tag{5.7}$$

where σ^2 is the variance of regional unemployment
        γ is the skewness

The skewness variable was never significant – the nine observations each year may have been the main factor – but the 't' values for σ^2 were significant. This led Archibald (1969) to conclude that 'there is a Phillips curve, and that a reduction in the regional dispersion of unemployment in the UK would move the fiscal policy frontier in a favourable direction.' The apparent conflict with Thirlwall's conclusions may be attributed to: (1) Archibald's study covered the period 1950–66, whereas Thirlwall dealt with 1962–8 only, (2) Archibald used annual data whereas Thirlwall used consistent quarterly data, and (3) Archibald, following Lipsey, used U^{-1} (rather than U) and $\dot{U}$ (Lipsey considered this a proxy for dispersion); Thirlwall, however, used U. The result was that whereas r^2 for U and v_r^* was 0·437 (Thirlwall) the r^2 for U^{-1} and σ^2 was 0·213 (Archibald). Thus, transformation of U by Archibald enables the dispersion of regional unemployment to influence $\dot{W}$ directly and the explanatory power of Archibald's equations including σ^2 varied between 0·77–0·81, much higher than Thirlwall's (0·45–0·46).

Cowling and Metcalf (1967) tried to solve the limited regional data problems by grouping regions into areas of 'high' and 'low' demand. One of their conclusions was that a successful anti-inflationary policy should attempt to discriminate between these two types of regions, although it was recognized that intraregional differences in industrial structure in the areas of high and low demand would provide some strange and unusual effects. Secondly, they concluded that the rate of increase in *earnings* (not wages alone) in the London and Southeast region has been an important determinant of earnings increases in the low demand regions. This could account for the similarity of earnings rises in all regions over the time period under review (1960–5). Thirlwall (1970) suggests, however, that the notion of wage spread implies some time lag, and in his subsequent study he included a variable, $\dot{e}_{LSE-6}$, earnings increases six months earlier in London and Southeast region, in his regional wage adjustment equations. An unlagged version of $\dot{e}_{LSE}$ would imply a rapid regional reaction to national bargaining agreements (i.e. one less than six months). In fact the variable lagged by six months and, subsequently, one year gave no statistically significant results (lags shorter than six months were not possible because of data limitations). Thirlwall found that national wage rate increases were the major determinant of regional wage increases. By using vacancy data, Thirlwall developed a measure of imbalance (disequilibrium) in each regional market (e.g., for industries)

$$I_{ir} = \sqrt{\sum_{i=1}^{h} \left[\frac{\left(\dfrac{v-u}{u}\right)_i - \left(\dfrac{v-u}{u}\right)_r}{n} \right]^2} \; w_i \cdot 100 \qquad (5.8)$$

where $\left(\dfrac{v-u}{u}\right)_i$ is excess demand or supply in industry i,

$\left(\dfrac{v-u}{u}\right)_r$ is excess demand or supply in the region,

w_i is proportional importance of industry in the region as measured by share total employees.

A similar index was constructed for occupations across regions. The results suggested that in high demand regions, disequilibrium in the labour market would tend to produce a higher rate of earnings inflation than in low demand regions.

The UK regional evidence is, then, by no means conclusive, although there is a suggestion that regional *and* industries unemployment disparities do contribute to increases in the rate of earnings/wage increases.

The Canadian experience

Data problems beset any attempts to examine wage behaviour at the subnational level. In this section, the usual five standard Canadian regions will be used, although it is recognized that these do not represent an optimal spatial division of markets. The formulations reported here were devised to allow comparison with an earlier regional study by Kaliski (1964) and the national models reported in Bodkin *et al.* (1966). While this section was being completed, Thirsk's (1973) study on regional dimensions of inflation and unemployment was published; his analysis was broader than the one described here, but his conclusions reflect similar interpretations of the data.

Regional wage, price and unemployment data were utilized for the period 1946–70. Following suggestions of many authors, all rates of change variables were expressed as first central differences – for example, the rate of change of wages in time period t,

$$\dot{W}_t = \frac{W_{t+1} - W_{t-1}}{2W_t}. \qquad (5.9)$$

There has been some discussion in the literature about the validity of this formulation of rates of change, since it assumes that the wage in effect in time period t to be a function of wage levels in both time period $t-1$ and $t+1$ (on this point, see Bowen and Berry 1963). The main regional wage adjustment relations that were fitted were of the form:

$$\dot{W}_t = a \pm bU_t \pm e \qquad (5.10)$$

$$\dot{W}_t = a \pm bU_t^{-1} \pm e \qquad (5.11)$$

$$\dot{W}_t = a \pm b_1\dot{U}_t \pm b_2 U_t^{-1} \pm b_3\dot{P}_t \pm e \qquad (5.12)$$

where $\dot{W}_t$, $\dot{U}_t$ and $\dot{P}_t$ represent the rates of change of wages, unemployment and prices, U_t the observed annual unemployment rate and e a random disturbance term.

In table 5.1 and fig. 5.6 the results of application of equations 5.10 and 5.11 to Canadian regional data are shown. The nonlinear specification of equation 5.11 does not improve the degree of explanation of $\dot{W}$ substantially, except in

Table 5.1   Regional Wage Adjustment Relations, Canada, 1947–1969

	a	U^{-1}	U	R^2	SEE	DW
Atlantic	0·4940	34·4812 (3·4147)		0·36**	1·753	0·73++
	9·7723		− 0·5810 (3·3569)	0·36**	1·764	
Quebec	1·6550	19·6203 (6·5819)		0·67**	1·134	1·04+
	9·9574		− 0·7648 (5·8359)	0·62**	1·226	
Ontario	0·4162	14·8452 (5·7805)		0·61**	1·473	0·99++
	10·2089		− 1·4257 (4·7465)	0·49**	1·647	
Prairies	− 0·2593	14·0810 (4·8946)		0·53**	1·515	0·86++
	10·1734		− 1·7683 (4·4502)	0·49**	1·590	
British Columbia	0·9097	22·0125 (3·4553)		0·36**	1·919	0·78++
	10·0014		− 0·8543 (3·5677)	0·36**	1·896	

** Significant at the 1 per cent level.
 * Significant at the 5 per cent level.
   Numbers in parentheses refer to 't' values: critical values are 2·08 (5 per cent) and 2·82 (1 per cent).

++ Positive autocorrelation at the 1 per cent level.
 + Positive autocorrelation at the 5 per cent level.

Notes: SEE refers to standard error of the estimate.
       DW refers to the Durbin-Watson statistic.

the case of Ontario: the improvement in explanation here was something of the order of 12 per cent. In addition, the Durbin-Watson statistics reveal significant levels of autocorrelation present in the residuals, raising doubts about the validity of the simple relationships expressed in table 5.1. However, as one would have expected, *a priori*, the simple Phillips curves for the less prosperous region lie to the right and above those of the more prosperous regions. Thus, reductions of unemployment in the Atlantic region would be associated with much higher levels of wage changes than for a corresponding change in unemployment in Ontario or the Prairies.

Table 5.2 provides the wage adjustment relations which include additional explanatory variables (variables that may cause shifts in the simple relationship between rate of change of wages and unemployment expressed in equations 5.10 and 5.11). The inclusion of these additional explanatory variables resulted in significant improvements in the explanation of the regional $\dot{W}$'s both in terms of a higher coefficient of determination (R^2) and lower standard error (SEE). Transformation of U provided little or no reduction in the explanatory power of the equations. Note the poor explanatory power of the rate of change of unemployment variable; in none of the regional equations was the coefficient of $\dot{U}$ significantly different from zero. The influence of regional price changes ($\dot{P}$) may be

Table 5.2   Regional wage adjustment relations 1947–1969

	a	$\dot{U}$	U^{-1}	$\dot{P}$	R^2	SEE	DW
Atlantic	0·2480	− 0·0162	27·5349	0·4267	0·66**	1·342	1·10
		(0·8472)	(3·4781)	(3·6787)			
Quebec	2·2717	− 0·0137	12·5475	0·2808	0·81**	0·914	0·68++
		(1·0387)	(3·5573)	(2·7840)			
Ontario	1·4623	———	7·2369	0·5276	0·85**	0·965	1·13
			(3·2008)	(5·0932)			
Prairies	0·7911	0·0166	8·3365	0·4168	0·72**	1·251	1·12
		(0·9522)	(2·8638)	(3·4235)			
British Columbia	1·8396	− 0·0107	11·7663	0·4350	0·59**	1·617	0·91+
		(0·5574)	(1·8645)	(3·1902)			

** Significant at the 1 per cent level.
 * Significant at the 5 per cent level.
  Numbers in parentheses refer to '*t*' values: critical values are 2·09 (5 per cent) and 2·86 (1 per cent).

++ Positive autocorrelation at the 1 per cent level.
+ Positive autocorrelation at the 5 per cent level.

seen to exert a considerable impact upon $\dot{W}$; for British Columbia, this was the only significant explanatory variable.

The increasing, in magnitude, positive residuals of the last several years in the long run relationship of the type given by equation 5.12 (indicating under-prediction of wage rate increases in the period 1965 through 1969) suggested that recent experience may reflect a shift in the long-run relationships. To test this suggestion, the data were divided into two sets, one for the period 1947–65 and one for the whole period (1947–69). In addition, the data were divided into two subperiods, 1947–58, 1959–69, and equations of the form of 5.12 were run. The objective was to test whether the shorter-run subperiod relationships were significantly different from the longer-run relationship. These hypotheses were tested using Chow's Test (Chow 1960; Johnston 1972). The results are shown in table 5.3. None of the F levels revealed any significant change in the relationship in the two subperiods – i.e. the long-run Phillip curve has not changed significantly – in all regions except British Columbia. The equation for the first period was barely significant at the 10 per cent level, too high to accept. The behaviour of the adjustment relationship for that province reveals a behaviour different from other provinces. Whereas in the other four regions, the importance of U^{-1} declined in the second time period (in Ontario and the Prairies it had a negative although not statistically significant coefficient), in British Columbia the 't' value increased. In the other regions $\dot{P}$ became the most significant explanatory variable and, in the Prairies, $\dot{U}$ was significant in the second subperiod. The increasing importance of $\dot{P}$ and the decline of U^{-1} suggests that the trade-off between $\dot{W}$ and U may become less realistic as time goes on. The behaviour of the relationships over the last four years causes greater concern to adherents of Phillips curve doctrine. In the Atlantic and British Columbia regions, the F ratios comparing 1947–69 with 1947–64 and 1947–65 were not significant (i.e. the long-run Phillips-type curve described the whole period and departures from the curve were no more in recent years than those one would

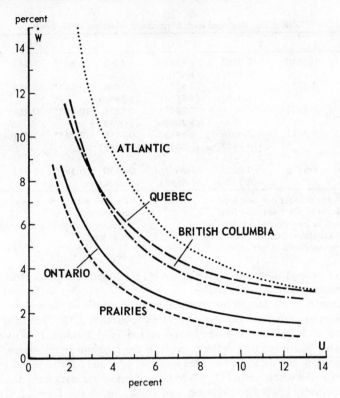

5.6   Phillips curves for Canadian regions, 1947–1969.

have expected by chance). However, in the other three regions, the F values for 1947–64 and 1947–65 compared to the longer-run curves were significant. Thus, recent experience in Quebec, Ontario and Prairies suggests, and the positive residuals indicate, a shift in the curves away from the origin, reflecting a trade-off that now sees reductions in regional unemployment associated with higher levels of wage rate increases.

An attempt at integration

During the discussion on the assumed trade-off between national efficiency and interregional equity, it was suggested that the trade-off curve was negatively sloped. Thus, increased equity could only be 'bought' at the cost of sacrificing national efficiency. McGuire and Garn (1969) suggested that simultaneous attention to both goals may make it possible to achieve, in effect, the shifting of the curve toward the origin, providing higher levels of equity and maintained or even improved levels of national efficiency. It was noted earlier that Archibald (1969) had presented evidence suggesting that a reduction in the dispersion of regional unemployment would yield positive benefits in price/wage–unemployment

Table 5.3 Regional wage adjustment relations (1) 1947–1958 (2) 1959–1969

		a	$\dot{U}$	U^{-1}	$\dot{P}$	R^2	SEE
Atlantic	(1)	− 2·3796	0·0008	38·8584	0·5132	0·75**	1·448
			(0·0278)	(3·0535)	(3·1837)		
	(2)	1·5410	− 0·0284	3·5646	1·4856	0·85**	0·807
			(0·5417)	(0·1678)	(2·5271)		
Quebec	(1)	2·3159	− 0·0413	14·4913	0·1400	0·91**	0·800
			(2·7096)	(3·8460)	(1·3952)		
	(2)	1·6490	0·0101	6·5968	1·0700	0·91**	0·490
			(0·5360)	(0·5650)	(2·4819)		
Ontario	(1)	1·3050	0·0245	9·3134	0·3672	0·92**	0·864
			(1·7553)	(3·6019)	(3·5379)		
	(2)	2·2951	0·0173	− 1·9354	1·3454	0·91**	0·586
			(1·1025)	(0·5040)	(4·9554)		
Prairies	(1)	0·9520	− 0·0382	9·6184	0·2242	0·82**	1·046
			(1·7606)	(2·7084)	(1·9863)		
	(2)	1·6628	0·0310	− 0·6577	1·4963	0·97**	0·394
			(2·9169)	(0·2319)	(7·3354)		
British Columbia	(1)	2·2170	− 0·0166	9·8872	0·4215	0·51**	2·287
			(0·5034)	(0·8210)	(2·1037)		
	(2)	− 0·3361	− 0·0017	23·8224	0·5887	0·91**	0·572
			(0·0916)	(3·3752)	(2·1765)		

Notes as for table 5.2

space; these benefits would be seen through a shift in the national Phillips curve closer to the axes, with lower unemployment rates now associated with lower rates of inflation or wage changes. It is therefore suggestive of the need to design policies that will reduce regional unemployment disparities; but the problem is not quite so straightforward, as Cameron reminds us: 'any attempt to lower the national rate of unemployment by general fiscal and monetary policies must simply result in faster growth for the oversize metropolitan areas and therefore even greater social costs' (Cameron 1971).

Furthermore, analysis of the Canadian data using a modified version of Archibald's model revealed rather different results. These are shown in table 5.4. Interpretation of the coefficient of σ would suggest that the rate of change in national (Canadian) wage rates would be reduced by *increasing* the disparities of regional unemployment! While the tests on the coefficient of σ in equations (2) and (3) in table 5.4 indicate that it is significant, the presence of positive auto-correlation in the residuals should caution unconditional acceptance of the results. The presence of serial correlation may reflect misspecification of the relationships between the dependent and independent variables or, more probably, the absence of a further explanatory variable. However, it is not clear that respecification of the relationships would result in the conversion of the sign of σ to positive, unless a larger number of regions was used thereby increasing the variance of σ and perhaps capturing more accurately the true variability of sub-national unemployment.

Given the divergence in results obtained using the British and Canadian data, one should be hesitant about drawing general conclusions on these issues. An

Table 5.4   National wage adjustment relations Canada 1947–1969

Equation number	a	$\dot{U}$	U^{-1}	$\dot{P}$	σ	R^2	DW
(1)	3·4654			0·6656* (7·0467)		0·75	
(2)	6·7690			0·5826* (9·2738)	− 1·8556* (4·5553)	0·88	
(3)	6·9637	− 0·0086 (0·7450)		0·0679* (8·3177)	− 1·9313* (4·5516)	0·88	
(4)	5·8564	− 0·0088 (0·7492)	2·5178 (0·4463)	0·5378* (5·8393)	− 1·5837** (1·7767)	0·88	0·21+

Notes: σ is defined each year as $\sqrt{\Sigma(U_n - U_r)^2 l_r}$ where U_n is the national unemployment rate, U_r is the regional unemployment rate ($r = 1 \ldots 5$), and l_r is the proportion of the labour force residing in the rth region.
DW is the Durbin-Watson statistic.
The numbers in brackets are the t statistics.
  * Coefficient significant at the 99 per cent level of confidence.
 ** Coefficient significant at the 90 per cent level of confidence.
  + Positive autocorrelation at the 99 per cent level.

observation of some generality that could be drawn may serve to amplify the view that regional dimensions of national issues are clearly important – even if they may work in different directions!

The evidence assembled by Higgins (1973) for a number of countries tends to support the earlier work of Archibald (1969). However, the trade-off curves shown in fig. 5.7 reveal that much more research is required into the relationship between aggregate national policies and regional disparities: for example, why is the curve for Australia so much closer to the origin than the one for Canada? Is it a function of regional imbalance in the distribution of unemployment? How important are subregional imbalances in countries, like Canada and Australia, where the size of the region used is very large? Notwithstanding these and many other unanswered questions, Higgins (1973) concluded:

> Measures to reduce regional gaps, far from being a 'luxury' to be afforded when things are otherwise going well in the country, are the essence of a policy to accelerate growth, reduce unemployment and maintain price stability. For developing countries, where efforts to accelerate growth are inhibited by fear of aggravating inflation, reduction of regional disparities may well be the *sine qua non* of a successful development policy.

On a number of points, it is agreed that the prospects for regional development even in developed countries are diminished without attention being paid to disaggregated monetary and fiscal policy. What is not clear is the nature of this policy, and, more importantly, the political ramifications that it would entail, in the context of the current decision-making structures in Western democratic societies.

However, with the exception of one or two minor modifications introduced in some of the analyses, none of the models deals explicitly with the spatial dimensions of economic change. This is not to suggest that the spatial dimension

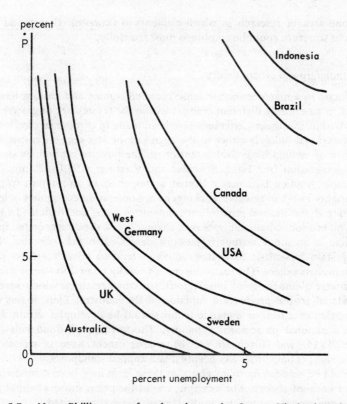

percent

P

Indonesia

Brazil

Canada

West
Germany

USA

5

UK

Sweden

Australia

0

0

5

percent unemployment

5.7   Macro Phillips curves for selected countries. *Source:* Higgins (1973).

will be in the more familiar distance-decay form. Pred's (1974) work on major job-providing organizations (discussed in chapter 3) provides enough evidence to caution us against such oversimplifications. Wage rate changes, expansion leads and lags and other economic impetuses may move through regions in a topological sense rather than moving from one contiguous region to another. The work of Bassett and Haggett (1971), King, Casetti and Jeffrey (1969), Casetti, King and Jeffrey (1971) and King and Forster (1973) has provided some initial guidance for modelling efforts designed to explore the way in which spatial dimensions influence economic activity. For example, Casetti, King and Jeffrey (1971) were able to suggest the importance of migration in the persistence of structural unemployment in the United States system of cities.

Goldstein (1973) in commenting on the work of King and Forster (1973) suggests that the modelling efforts, if they are indeed to incorporate the effects of labour market interrelationships, should include variables to explain how the effects are transmitted from one labour market to another. He suggests a set of simultaneous relationships comprising migration, unemployment and wage changes. Thirlwall (1975) has moved partially in this direction with a simultaneous equation system to forecast regional unemployment in Great Britain. Clearly, this is one area of research in which elements of economic theory and spatial hierarchial structure could be combined most fruitfully.

Growth pole/growth centre theory

The linkages in a macroeconomic sense between regions and nations have been explored in an entirely different context within the framework of growth centre theory. Within this theory attempts have been made to explore interregional and national–regional linkages either in the aggregate or at a very microspatial level. A number of writers have paid attention to the positive economies associated with agglomeration (see Isard, Schooler and Vietorisz, 1959): Chinitz (1961), for example, studied two major United States cities in an attempt to provide some insights into the possible workings of agglomeration economies in location decisions and the general growth environment of cities and regions. In the discussion on economic base multipliers in chapter 2 and the disaggregated industry multipliers in an input–output framework described in the following chapter, the suggestion was made that some activities tend to provide greater positive multipliers than others. The reasons were not totally related to size of the industry, but were a composite of intraregional structural relations which were themselves related to the production function of the industry. Thus, it was natural that a notion of a lead or dynamic sector should be developed within the context of a national or regional economy. The writings of Boudeville (1966), Perroux (1955) and Hirschman (1958), among others, have all stressed these sorts of concepts both from a conceptual and applied standpoint.

It would be misleading to suggest that these ideas have been synthesized into a unified body of theory. For example, one of the prime movers behind the diffusion of the growth centre idea in the United States commented:

> ... it must be admitted that we still do not have specific criteria for identifying relevant urban centres, determining how big they should be, or deciding what kinds of investments should be placed in them. Perhaps this reflects a fundamental need to be more specific about the nature of spatial resource allocation problems to which growth centres should be related. (Hansen 1972)

Growth pole[1] theory is attractive because it embraces, within one conceptual framework, a number of different theories and ideas that have been developed in regional analysis. At the same time, it should be cautioned that in the popularization of the theory distortions have arisen and many false claims made for the theory. The reader of the increasingly extensive literature is cautioned accordingly! Thomas (1972) commented recently in relating a number of deficiencies of growth pole theory:

> One deficiency is related to our lack of knowledge concerning the processes of growth within poles over time. The second deficiency is connected with

[1]The terms growth pole and growth centre have specific meanings: until these are defined, the term growth pole should be regarded as one embracing the whole growth pole/growth centre idea.

the paucity of information about the nature and significance of the spatial components of interindustry linkages that exist between various kinds of industries found within growth poles.

Growth pole theory has been described informally as an attempt to express the concept of an unbalanced growth strategy in a spatial context. Hirschman (1958), for example, has advocated a national growth strategy which emphasizes the need to bias investment in favour of one sector or another – in his model, between directly productive investment and social overhead capital. The idea here is that linkages between sectors are such that growth impulses will filter down through the national economic system. The *growth pole* idea is similarly structured, although one of the main problems of interpretation, as Lasuen (1969) reminds us, relates to the concept of space being discussed. Perroux (1955) was concerned to escape from the idea that space was a limiting force in economic development. He conceived of space as much in a topological as in a Euclidean sense. In the Perroux system, the critical element was the leading industry[1] and the way growth in this industry generated growth in other industries within the industrial complex through interindustry linkages. This complex could have a specific geographical location, although Perroux seemed to stress the sectoral characteristics of linkages rather than the geographical ones. The concept is well summarized by Thomas (1972):

> Perroux states that when a propulsive industry raises its output, it induces expansions in the outputs of other industries. In cases where the induced growth in outputs is much greater than the initial growth of the propulsive industry's output, such a propulsive industry is called a *key* industry. It should be noted that Perroux does not confine the notion of growth induced by a key firm or industry to a highly localized geographical area. He indicates that such induced growth may be traced throughout a national economy when considering the question of whether or not a propulsive industry is also a key industry.

The concept of growth poles, as described by Perroux, has been modified to conceptualize it within a much more explict spatial framework. The reworked concept is now generally known as a *growth centre*: it retains a number of characteristics associated with the growth pole idea but is explicitly conceived within Euclidean space. An operational definition, used by the United States Appalachian Regional Commision is reported by Hansen (1972):

> By a *growth centre* or *centres* is meant a complex consisting of one or more communities or places which, taken together, provide or are likely to provide, a range of cultural, social, employment, trade and service functions for itself and its associated rural hinterland. Though a centre may not be fully developed to provide all these functions, it should provide, or potentially provide, some elements of each, and presently provide a sufficient range and magnitude of these functions to be readily identifiable as the logical location for many

[1]Perroux (1955) considered that growth impulses would be generated through (1) a propulsive industry or firm and (2) a key firm or industry.

specialized services to people in the surrounding hinterland. A *growth area* is an extension of the growth centre itself. It is the adjoining area likely to experience residential and employment growth because of proximity to a centre or location between centres. The *hinterlands* are the surrounding rural areas which rely upon the growth centre and growth area for services and employment. The hinterlands contribute resources and manpower to the overall district economy.

The growth pole notion expressed in this more explict spatial framework has elements of the symbiotic relationship of a central place to its surrounding area, as conceived in central place theory, as well as elements of the unbalanced theory of economic growth and development which has been expounded in a spatial setting by Friedmann (1969) and has become known more generally as the core-periphery concept.

The development of the theoretical constructs of growth pole and growth centre theory is described in detail in Hansen (1972) and Kuklinski (1972). While there are many issues arising from these discussions that could be dealt with, a brief summary of some of the more critical ones follows. Identification of potential growth centres, while appearing relatively straightforward in a conceptual sense, may provide many intangible problems of applications to regional planning issues. Hansen (1972) has been somewhat critical of the allocation of investment in growth centres in the United States. He has suggested that while a number of potential centres may be identified, theories of urban growth, public locational preferences, and the types of externalities developed in Thompson's model in chapter 2, increase the potential success of a growth centre developed in a medium-sized city – one within the range 250,000 to 750,000. Hansen claims that it would be easier to accelerate growth in these centres than to accelerate growth in depressed regions. In addition, he proposes that the investment be broadened to include education and retraining programmes rather than being totally committed to visible fixed overhead capital. Politically, the latter is much more rewarding in the short run, but it is the longer-run equilibrium towards which the policy should be directed.

A related issue concerns the *development* of the growth centre over time. Paelinck (1972) has attempted to explore the general problem of (1) what industries should be attracted to a growth centre and (2) in what order should investment decisions be made such that the programme achieves some optimal rate of return. For example, one could envisage a situation in which some combination of industries would generate the greatest impact upon a growth centre and its surrounding hinterland. However, these linkages cannot be created overnight: for certain types of industrial investment, five or seven years' lag may occur before a plant is operational and working near optimal capacity. Thus, some ways must be found of examining the effects of a partial investment programme in the hope of developing a programme which is not only efficient in the long run but also provides a growth sequence which is, itself, the most efficient. The role of uncertainty, the effects of technological change and the diffusion of innovation will provide elements which may prohibit the estimation of the future structure of growth centres.

Furthermore, the degree of linkage between industries exhibited in some growth centres has been evaluated by Beyers (1973). He found that for the Puget Sound region of Washington state, the major impact of industrial growth, with one or two exceptions, would be through induced income effects. For the largest manufacturing industry in the state, aerospace, the interregional feedback effects were larger than the intraregional indirect effects; it was also unlikely that the degree of intraregional, interindustry linkages in this industry would increase over time. The importance of induced income effects should be considered as carefully as the nature and potential impact of the more traditionally oriented concerns with industry–industry linkages. A number of authors have attempted to examine regional interindustry structures in an attempt to identify key sectors. The results, to say the least, are discouraging. Hazari (1970) found that alternative methods of identifying key sectors provided a different set of industries each time! Hewings (1974) found that not only was the identification sensitive to the method used, but it was also sensitive to the level of aggregation in the input–output table.

From the preceding discussion, and the standard works on growth pole/growth centre theory, it is clear that while the notions have been articulated in a more rigorous conceptual framework, the utility of the theory in a planning framework is still below the potential that most authors claim it possesses. Part of the difficulty may lie in the rather loose way in which development objectives have been articulated, thus precluding careful evaluation of the contribution of not only this body of theory but virtually any theoretical construct to the attainment of these objectives.

Moseley (1974) has focused on another extremely important problem in growth centre analysis – the very pedantic issue of identification! In fig. 5.8 six of many ways of identifying growth centres are provided. In the first case (map 1), the higher order central places (those with the greatest number of functions) are identified as growth centres: such a procedure has been discussed by Parr (1973). However, as he points out, central place theory has been developed as a single state or static equilibrium model, whereas growth pole and growth centre theory both imply dynamic change in both a spatial and temporal sense. These and other difficulties with reference to the linkages of central place and growth centre theories are discussed in Parr (1973). Geographic interest in functional interaction has led to the application of graph theoretic concepts to the analysis of regions. Map 2 indicates the selection of centres on the basis of, say, indices of connectivity of the major transportation systems. Note that, already, we are beginning to notice that some cities identified by their central place functions as growth centres may not appear as such in terms of their importance as nodal locations.

A more traditional approach is found in map 3: in this case, the growth rate in employment in each city over a five or ten year period is used to identify growth centres. A similar procedure is found in map 4. In this case, the growth rates of each of the cities are 'compared' to surrounding cities. Semple *et al.* (1972) used trend analysis to identify those cities which were most prominent in terms of growth rates *vis-à-vis* surrounding cities. These cities were then

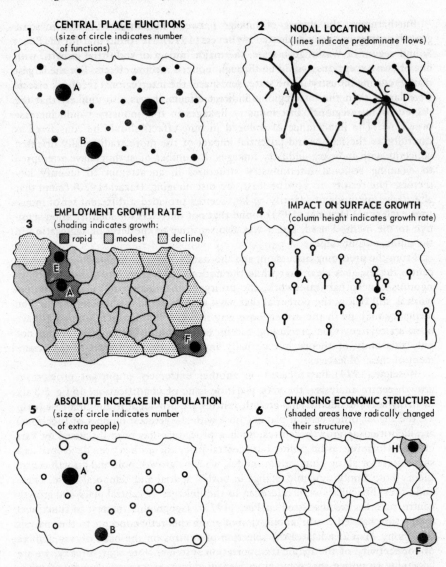

5.8 Alternative ways of identifying 'growth centres' in a hypothetical region (see text for discusion). *Source*: After Moseley (1974).

identified as growth centres. Map 5 provides the results of growth centre identification when absolute increases in population are used as the major criterion. Finally, map 6 provides a more subjective appraisal of growth centres: those cities whose economic structure has experienced some fundamental changes (e.g. become more diversified or less dependent upon one or two major 'exports') are designated growth centres. Obviously, the latter types of criteria are very difficult to quantify and evaluate but the underlying philosophy would appear to reflect the traditions of economic base theory embodied in Thompson's model (1965), which was discussed in chapter 4. In this case, one noted that the growth process was characterized by the eventual broadening of the base and a movement away from dependence upon a narrow range of economic activities.

Moseley's (1974) example, admittedly using a hypothetical region, does serve to illustrate the difficulties the regional analyst faces when trying to implement a very sound and intuitively appealing concept such as a growth centre.

A further difficulty, relating to the semantic issues surrounding growth pole–growth centre theory, has recently been reviewed by Campbell (1974). In essence, the main problem here has stemmed from the imprecise statements in Perroux's (1955) earlier writings. Campbell notes that the distinction between the notions of polarization (associated with growth poles) and concentration (associated with growth centres) has not been made clear enough. The former is conceived within economic or topological space: the latter vary definitely within geographic or real space. The confusion has led to assumptions to the effect that the impact of polarized growth would be localized in specific geographic centres. Beyers's (1973) comments, noted earlier, are especially applicable here; Campbell (1974) suggests that concentration on the technological interindustry aspects of growth pole and growth centre theory has limited their applicability. Growth centres may arise and function in a number of ways, stimulating local activity through employment and wage levels or through size and/or agglomerative economies which may be more attractive to new industry than any potential direct technological linkages.

Thus far, however, adequate testing of the utility of growth centre theory in the context of a regional planning strategy has not been accomplished. The experiments conducted in the United States (which will be discussed in the next section) leave much to be desired. It is becoming clear, however, that the concept is receiving increasing attention since it appears to offer demonstrable practicality with a not insubstantial theoretical base.

The impact of government on regional development: some case studies

Given that government expenditures now comprise such a large proportion of total expenditure in any society, are there ways in which this public purse could be controlled and reallocated to achieve some of the goals relating to regional development? A report prepared for the United States Department of Commerce (1967) commented:

> Federal procurement policies, with a few minor exceptions, do not reflect regional economic development goals as a major consideration . . . the traditional congressional criterion has been the procuring agency's own efficiency. However, a broader concept of efficiency exists – one that is concerned with the allocation of all resources and with optimizing the efficiency of the entire society.

This study considered the direct and indirect impacts of government expenditures and found that those states with a highly specialized industrial mix tended to attract a greater percentage of prime contract procurement expenditure, while those states with greater industrial mix had an advantage with subcontract and indirect effects. In a more extensive study of similar issues, it was found that the nature of subcontracting and indirect effects was such that redistributing the prime contracts would not change the total spatial impact: in other words, the leakages tended to 'leak' to the same areas, irrespective of where the initial contact was made (CONSAD 1967).

Bolton (1966) has studied a specific subset of total government expenditure, namely defence purchases, and attempted to indicate the impact these have on state growth and development in the United States. Map 5.1 indicates the percentage of exogenous income in each state which is composed of defence income, while map 5.2 looks at the contribution to state growth of defence expenditures during the period 1952 to 1962. The declines in the Midwest states of Wisconsin, Michigan and Indiana shown in map 5.2 may be a function of changing defence needs since the Department of Commerce study alluded to earlier showed Illinois, Indiana, Ohio and Michigan ranked fifth, eighth, fourth and sixth respectively in terms of the indirect impact of, admittedly, all types of government spending. Further, Bolton used a modified form of the economic base model and he may have underestimated the leakage effects which account for a high percentage of subcontracting work performed in the Midwest.

An alternative approach would be to use a modified shift and share model to analyse defence spending. In this case, the analysis was confined to the awards of prime military contracts worth at least $10,000 during the period 1962 to 1967. The results are summarized in table 5.5. During the period 1962 to 1965 (period A), total military awards declined 7·07 per cent, while increases were recorded in 1962 to 1967 (period B) and 1965 to 1967 (period C), these being 49·29 and 60·65 per cent. In considering the analysis, it should be remembered that indirect effects are not included, neither are the effects generated through changes in personal consumption expenditures. However, a number of results are worth commenting upon: for example, note that some states declined in period A very much more rapidly than would have been expected. In this sense, the share component of growth or decline is the amount that would have been expected to be placed (withdrawn) in each state if that state had grown (declined) at the national average. The states of New York, New Jersey, Ohio, Michigan and Massachusetts fared much worse than the national average decline. On the other hand, Missouri, Texas and Maryland recorded positive shifts which were well in excess of the expected decline. In period B, a negative shift would indicate that the state growth was less than the overall national average growth; again, New York and New Jersey and two very defence-dependent states, Colorado and Washington, recorded declines. In the latter state, the cancellation of the Dyna-Soar contract in 1963 was the cause of most of the decline in defence spending. In period C, very few states recorded negative total change, although the magnitude of some of the shifts varied appreciably.

An obvious question that could be raised from the data from table 5.5 and map 5.2 would relate to the importance of political representation. A student

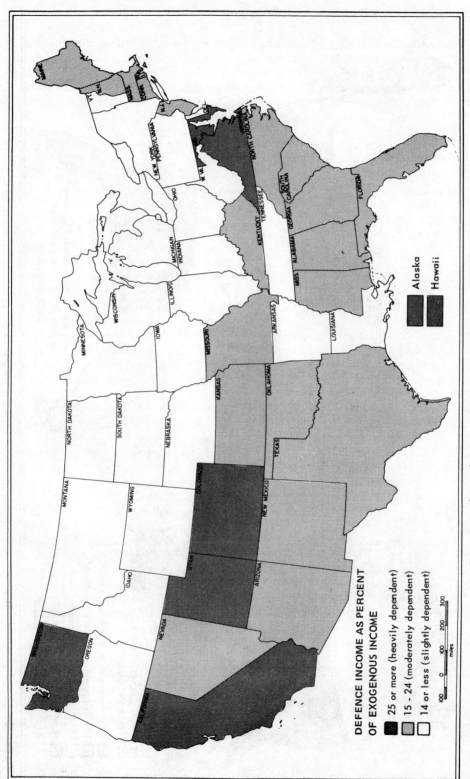

DEFENCE INCOME AS PERCENT
OF EXOGENOUS INCOME

25 or more (heavily dependent)

15 - 24 (moderately dependent)

14 or less (slightly dependent)

Alaska

Hawaii

MAINE

VT

N.H.

MASS

R.I.

CONN

NEW YORK

PENNSYLVANIA

N.J.

DEL.

MD.

W. VA.

OHIO

MICHIGAN

INDIANA

ILLINOIS

WISCONSIN

IOWA

MINNESOTA

NORTH DAKOTA

SOUTH DAKOTA

NEBRASKA

MONTANA

WYOMING

IDAHO

NEVADA

OREGON

WASHINGTON

CALIFORNIA

UTAH

ARIZONA

COLORADO

NEW MEXICO

KANSAS

OKLAHOMA

TEXAS

MISSOURI

ARKANSAS

LOUISIANA

MISS.

ALABAMA

GEORGIA

SOUTH CAROLINA

NORTH CAROLINA

TENNESSEE

KENTUCKY

VIRGINIA

FLORIDA

100 0 100 200 300
miles

Map 5.1   Dependence of states on defence income, 1962. *Source:* Bolton (1966).

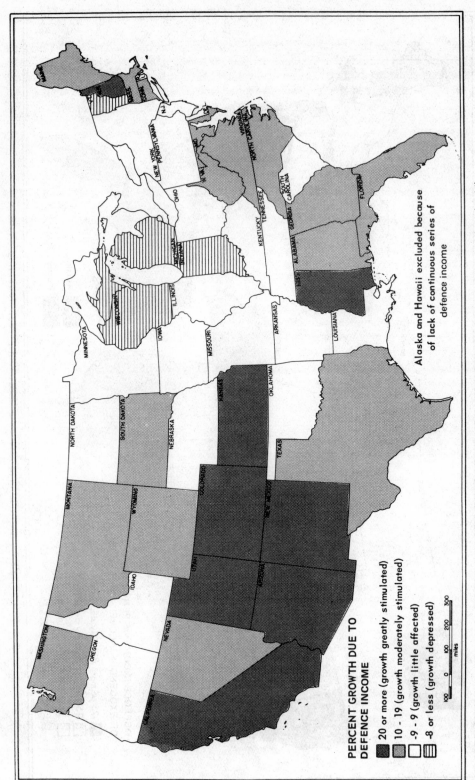

PERCENT GROWTH DUE TO
DEFENCE INCOME

■ 20 or more (growth greatly stimulated)
▨ 10 - 19 (growth moderately stimulated)
☐ -9 - 9 (growth little affected)
▥ -8 or less (growth depressed)

Alaska and Hawaii excluded because
of lack of continuous series of
defence income

100 0   100 200 300
       miles

Map 5.2   Contribution of defence income to growth, 1952–1962. *Source:* Bolton (1966).

Table 5.5 Shift and share analysis of growth in military prime contracts by state for selected periods, 1962–1967 (million dollars)

	1962–1965			1962–1967			1965–1967		
	Total change	Share	Shift	Total change	Share	Shift	Total change	Share	Shift
Maine	− 11	− 6	− 5	− 23	39	− 62	− 12	42	− 54
New Hamp.	− 6	− 4	− 2	103	29	74	109	32	77
Vermont	16	− 1	17	84	8	76	68	19	49
Mass.	− 131	− 93	− 38	112	646	− 534	243	715	− 472
Rhode Is.	28	− 4	32	140	29	111	112	52	60
Conn.	− 33	− 86	53	723	598	125	756	716	40
N.Y.	− 439	− 189	− 250	593	1316	− 723	1032	1353	− 321
N.J.	− 243	− 75	− 168	172	524	− 352	415	497	− 82
Penn.	37	− 67	104	697	469	228	660	600	60
Ohio	− 266	− 80	− 186	473	557	− 84	739	523	216
Indiana	34	− 40	74	327	281	46	293	367	− 74
Illinois	− 109	− 38	− 71	533	262	271	642	256	386
Michigan	− 145	− 48	− 97	356	334	22	501	323	178
Wisconsin	− 56	− 18	− 38	125	128	− 3	181	123	58
Minnesota	− 38	− 21	− 17	353	146	207	391	157	234
Iowa	− 145	− 20	− 125	0	138	− 138	145	81	64
Missouri	515	− 39	554	1732	269	1463	1217	644	573
N. Dak.	− 51	− 7	− 44	− 83	49	− 132	− 32	30	− 62
S. Dak.	− 92	− 8	− 84	− 104	56	− 160	− 12	13	− 25
Nebraska	− 10	− 4	− 6	51	26	25	61	26	35
Kansas	− 164	− 28	− 136	6	194	− 188	170	139	31
Delaware	1	− 3	4	15	18	− 3	14	23	− 9
Maryland	114	− 33	147	398	232	166	282	354	− 70
D.C.	66	− 13	79	176	90	86	110	150	− 40
Virginia	23	− 32	55	223	220	3	200	284	− 84
W. Virg.	− 54	− 10	− 44	− 2	71	− 73	52	55	− 3
N. Carol.	19	− 19	38	179	133	46	160	175	− 15
S. Carol.	17	− 5	22	116	32	84	99	50	49
Georgia	326	− 24	350	811	166	645	485	402	83
Florida	− 13	− 46	33	153	318	− 165	166	384	− 218
Kentucky	− 1	− 3	2	80	22	58	81	26	55
Tennessee	13	− 13	26	354	91	263	341	119	222
Alabama	11	− 11	22	143	76	67	132	100	32
Mississippi	52	− 7	59	15	49	− 34	− 37	92	− 129
Ark.	− 46	− 6	− 40	42	42	0	88	24	64
Louisiana	12	− 17	29	412	120	292	400	155	245
Oklahoma	− 16	− 10	− 6	22	67	− 45	38	73	− 35
Texas	441	− 71	512	2541	496	2045	2100	878	1222
Montana	38	− 2	40	47	15	32	9	42	− 33
Idaho	− 14	− 2	− 12	− 11	13	− 24	3	7	− 4
Wyoming	− 15	− 2	− 13	10	11	− 1	25	5	20
Colorado	− 316	− 40	− 276	− 355	279	− 634	− 39	151	− 190
Utah	− 108	− 21	− 87	− 120	147	− 267	− 12	116	− 128
Nevada	11	− 1	12	21	4	17	10	12	− 2
New Mex.	23	− 4	27	20	30	− 10	− 3	51	− 54
Arizona	24	− 11	35	97	75	22	73	107	− 34
Washington	− 376	− 65	− 311	− 315	454	− 769	61	331	− 270
Oregon	− 6	− 3	− 3	53	23	30	59	24	35
California	− 839	− 424	− 415	876	2954	− 2078	1715	3126	− 1411
Alaska	11	− 4	15	23	31	− 8	11	45	− 33
Hawaii	40	− 2	42	33	16	17	− 7	44	− 51

Source: Computations performed on data in *Military Prime Contract Awards by Region and State, Fiscal Year 1962–1967* (Office of Secretary of Defense, Washington, D.C., 1967).

Table 5.6 Percentage change in employment by region after a compensated 20 per cent cut in United States armament expenditures

Region	Total net change (%) (1)	Total gross increase (%) (2)	Total gross decrease (%) (3)
California	− 1·85	0·54	2·39
Colorado, New Mexico	− 1·40	0·67	2·07
Arizona, Nevada, Utah	− 1·35	0·69	2·04
Maryland, Virginia, Delaware, W. Virginia, D.C.	− 1·36	0·66	2·02
Texas	− 1·00	0·73	1·73
Oregon, Washington	− 0·81	0·91	1·72
Mississippi, Alabama	− 0·73	0·89	1·62
Georgia, Carolinas	− 0·57	1·02	1·59
Florida	− 0·43	1·12	1·55
New England	− 0·06	1·05	1·11
Arkansas, Louisiana, Oklahoma	0·21	1·26	1·05
Kansas, Iowa, Nebraska, Missouri	0·44	1·46	1·02
Kentucky, Tennessee	0·37	1·31	0·94
New York	0·66	1·44	0·78
New Jersey, Pennsylvania	0·53	1·26	0·73
Idaho, Montana, Wyoming	1·28	1·83	0·55
Michigan, Ohio	0·89	1·43	0·54
Indiana, Illinois, Wisconsin	0·93	1·46	0·53
Minnesota, Dakotas	1·54	1·96	0·42

Source: Leontief (1965).

of political science would have little trouble in recognizing those states whose members of the House or Senate serve on the military-related committees! In opposition to the political influences of state representatives and senators, there exists considerable pressure for the federal government to behave, as was noted earlier, as a cost minimizer/efficiency maximizer. As a consequence, it is often very difficult to measure the potential impact of government expenditures. Stellwagon (1967) concluded:

... there seems to be little relationship between a measure of net federal capital flows and measures of the overall economic performance because the allocation of most federal spending is not influenced by the relative economic prosperity of the individual states.

Stellwagon's analysis is interesting in that he attempts to examine the impact of reallocation of federal spending using a tax-sharing plan. This issue is receiving increasing attention (see Courchene and Beavis 1973).

It has often been stated that continued prosperity in most Western societies is a function of continued and increasing allocations for defence spending. Some years ago, Leontief (1961, 1965) examined the economic impact of a cut in defence spending: in the later paper, the analysis was extended to include not only the industrial effects but also the regional incidence of these reductions. The savings of 20 per cent of the military expenditures were reallocated to non-military components of final demand (investment, personal consumption and the like). Using a fifty-eight sector input–output table for 1958 and dividing the nation into nineteen regions, Leontief was able to show the uneven nature of the regional incidence of changes in final demand (the analysis represents a more detailed version of that conducted in chapter 3). Only ten of the fifty-eight sectors were estimated to experience a net decline in output and employment, but the regional experience was such that ten of the nineteen would have undergone a decline ranging from 1·85 per cent in California to as little as 0·06 per cent in New England (see table 5.6). On the other hand, the three Midwest regions, comprising Michigan, Ohio, Indiana, Illinois, Wisconsin, Minnesota and the Dakotas, would experience the largest positive gains. These results tend to amplify the earlier comments about the stability of the indirect effects that accrue to this area of the United States. The net figures do not completely provide an indication of the disruptive effects: the entries in columns 2 and 3 show the gross changes. Again these gross changes are largest in California, although a number of regions, while displaying low percentage net gains or declines, would experience considerable job changes. Of course, the aggregate nature of the model precluded considerations of labour quality and skill levels. It is not entirely clear, either, just how many industries could successfully adapt to the production of consumer as opposed to military-oriented goods – certainly not without some disruptive effects.

Analysis in the same tradition as that performed by Leontief addressed the issue of the energy savings that could accrue if federal highway trust funds in the United States were reinvested in five alternative federal programs (Bezdek and Hannon 1974). The alternative programs and the effects of the reallocation on employment and energy consumption are shown in table 5.7. The energy analysis was performed using the following equation:

$$e = [Q(I-A)^{-1} + T] \cdot Y \qquad (5.13)$$

where e is a $k \times 1$ vector of energy types (e.g. coal, petroleum),

           Q is a $k \times n$ matrix of energy sales of energy type i ($i = 1 \ldots k$) to industry section j ($j = 1 \ldots n$),

      $(I-A)^{-1}$ is an n by n Leontief inverse matrix,

           T is a $k \times n$ diagonal matrix of energy sales to final demand,

           Y is the $n \times 1$ expenditure vector of the particular final demand category under consideration.

Employment output coefficients are used to generate the employment impacts once the vector of output (associated with the change in final demand) has been calculated. The alternative programs involved four different construction programs (the first four listed in table 5.7), two more 'socially' oriented programs, one dealing with health, the other with justice, and a final program in which the savings from highway construction were reallocated as across-the-board tax decreases. These latter savings were applied to vector of consumption expenditures to generate the impact on the economy.

When the results of this analysis are interpreted, one should recall the assumptions inherent in input–output analysis, especially those dealing with linearity and absence of scale economies. However, the picture that emerges is one that

Table 5.7 The impact on energy consumption and employment of a $5 billion investment (1975 dollars) in seven federal programs

Federal program	Energy consumption			Employment demand		
	Requirement per 1963 dollar of program (Btu)	Total requirement (10⁹ Btu)	Decrease* (%)	Jobs per $100,000 of program (1975)	Total No. of jobs	Increase* (%)
Highway construction	112,200†	409·53		8·1	256,180	
Railroad and mass transit construction	43,100	157·32	+ 61·6	8·4	264,430	+ 3·2
Water and waste treatment facilities construction	65,400	238·71	+ 41·7	8·2	259,490	+ 1·3
Educational facilities construction	70,600	257·69	+ 37·1	8·5	268,980	+ 4·7
National health insurance	40,400	147·46	+ 64·0	13·4	423,220	+ 65·2
Criminal justice and civilian safety	118,500	432·53	− 3·4	12·4	393,520	+ 53·6
Personal consumption expenditures (tax relief)	86,000‡	313·90	+ 23·4	8·7	275,120	+ 7·4

*Per cent changes are relative to highway construction program. †As in all programs this number is for a technology of estimated efficiency. The actual energy intensity of all highway construction in 1963 was 98,000 Btu per dollar. ‡Includes direct energy purchases and the energy and labour required for trade and transportation margins.
Note: Five billion 1975 dollars are equal to $3·75 billion in 1963 and $3·165 billion in 1958. No attempt was made to correct for the technological impact on energy use efficiency between 1963 and 1975. It is generally expected that 1975 technology will be more energy intensive.
Source: Bezdek and Hannon (1974).

suggests significant savings in terms of energy requirements for all of the alternatives save the one dealing with civilian justice. As a basis for comparison it has been estimated that the cost of rebuilding the signalled track in the Northeastern and Midwest parts of the United States would be $8·1 billion. The complete system of 36,000 miles would be rebuilt including the subgrade and ballast, replacing the ties and rails and rehabilitating the signal systems (United States Department of Transportation 1974). Hence, a reallocation of $5 billion from highway construction to railroad rehabilitation could yield not only important benefits in terms of energy savings and employment gains, but would also serve to meet the needs of a transportation system that has been experiencing continuing problems over the last two decades.

Evaluating regional development policies

The critical test of regional policy comes at a time when some empirical evaluation may be made of its impact in moving the set of subnational economies closer to some prescribed goal of interregional equity. However, the evaluation must necessarily demonstrate some causal relationship between improvement in various selected indices of regional welfare and the policies that were designed to achieve such ends. In other words, the 'neutral' effects of general, national growth must be extracted and that which remains must be shown to have occurred through the influence of the regional policies. Casting this division into a shift–share framework, the objective here would be to account for the shift component of regional growth.

In recent months, several publications have been issued reporting the impacts of regional policies in the United Kingdom, Canada and the United States. In this section, an evaluation will be made of these findings with some further exploratory work pertaining to the Canadian experience.

The United Kingdom evaluation

Manners (1972), commenting upon British public policy related to the less prosperous regions, writes:

> Since it is impossible to judge what would have happened in these (less prosperous) areas without government assistance, however, it is equally impossible to spell out with any clarity the full implications of public policy intervention in their development. Yet the point cannot be evaded that in a number of important respects government policies in the less prosperous regions – policies which were frequently designed to cure the principal symptom of their economic stress, unemployment – left some of the fundamental causes of their long standing problems relatively untouched.

Both Manners (1972) and Brown (1972) agree that no one has yet come up with an acceptable figure on what the balance should be between the two alternatives of moving people and the movement of jobs. In this sense, too, both authors seem to feel that of the many policy alternatives that are open to planners, the main choice is between these two.

Manners does concede that while the less prosperous regions have a relative disadvantage in seeking and keeping a reasonable share of the new national economic growth, a fair measure of success has been achieved in providing the framework for facilitating new growth within these areas. His conclusions are supported in part by an evaluation of the effects of the regional employment premium (REP) made by Moore and Rhodes (1973). Choosing 1963 as the year indicative of the change from passive to active regional development policies, the authors tried to measure the impact that the active policy had on regional employment by the year 1971.

Moore and Rhodes contend that using employment criteria alone may provide a misleading impression of the total effect any one regional policy may have had. For example, the nature of the regional structure in depressed areas may be such that it includes a large percentage of industries which are everywhere declining in relative and absolute terms. The effects of release of labour through extensive lay-offs or business failure or closure will be exacerbated in the depressed areas.

As a result of factors such as these, one may discover that the net impact of a particular policy upon regional unemployment could be very small.[1] In addition, upturns in local activity (for example, new jobs created through the opening of new industries) can cause effects on the local labour force which may result in unemployment rates remaining constant or even rising. For instance, new jobs in an area may encourage some inmigration into the area or attract new entrants into the labour force; in both cases, the labour force will increase. If the supply of new jobs is less than the supply of new entrants into the labour force, local unemployment will rise. In notation, if U_t, E_t and L_t are the unemployed, employed and the labour force in time t in the region, the unemployment may be defined as

$$U_t/L_t = 1 - E_t/L_t.$$

Assume a change (positive) of E of ΔE, in U of ΔU and in L of ΔL. By definition,

$$\Delta U = \Delta L - \Delta E.$$

For ΔU to be $\leqslant 0$, $|\Delta E|$ must be $\geqslant |\Delta L|$. However, if the new entrants into the labour force (ΔL) outnumber the number of new jobs created, then ΔU will be positive; it is even conceivable to consider cases in which $\Delta U > \Delta E$ for a given change in ΔL, resulting in an increase in the unemployment rate (i.e., U_{t+1}/L_{t+1}). During the discussion of regional labour markets in chapter 4, it was reported that Miernyk (1971) found that it was extremely difficult to determine the precise effect upon unemployment of job creation programmes.

For these reasons, Moore and Rhodes decided to focus attention upon employment growth. In order to show that the observed differential growth rates in manufacturing in the development areas were the results of policy rather

[1] For example, in Nova Scotia in 1971, 700 new jobs were created in manufacturing: this gain was considerably reduced through the closing of several industries, two of which together employed 545 persons (*Globe and Mail* 1972). In 1970, in Canada as a whole, business failures rose 23 per cent and the thirty-five business failures reported in the less prosperous Atlantic Provinces represented some $20 million in liabilities and an unknown number of lost jobs (Dun and Bradstreet 1971).

than differences in industrial structure, it was necessary to extract from the growth rates, the rate of growth in each industry in these areas which would have occurred if the industry had grown at the same rate as the industry in the nation as a whole. In a sense, the authors provided a slightly modified version of the shift–share technique. Up to 1963, the structurally adjusted manufacturing employment series showed little difference between the growth expected (on the basis of national growth rates) and that observed. After 1963, the difference increased such that, by 1971, actual employment was 12 per cent above what would have been expected had a passive regional development policy been applied to these areas. As further confirming evidence, the authors applied a similar analysis to the more prosperous Midlands and Southeast regions and found that these regions' share of increased manufacturing employment actually fell – as one would have expected if the policy of attempting to divert manufacturing employment away from these (more prosperous) areas had been successful.

Part of the success of this movement of manufacturing jobs to less prosperous areas after 1967 has been attributed to the introduction of the regional employment premium. The premium amounted to a subsidy on all labour employed in manufacturing in the development areas and represented about 7 per cent of the average earnings for male workers in 1967. However, one disturbing feature of the policy was that it applied only to manufacturing industry. It is well known that, over time, the total percentage employed in manufacturing industry has declined both absolutely and relatively in most developed countries. Using a similar structural transformation of the service employment time series as that applied to manufacturing, Moore and Rhodes found that the actual employment growth in the service sectors (utilities, trade, personal and professional services and the like) was less than one would have expected from national movements, although the divergence stabilized after 1966. Although the authors did not do this, one would have expected that the main areas receiving greater than expected growth would have been the Midlands and the Southeast – the prosperous regions. In summary, there is little doubt that the shifts in the regional location of new manufacturing growth in the period 1963–71 were closely associated with the more active regional policy pursued by the Labour Government. It may well be that in the longer run, through multiplier effects, a certain amount of service activity will locate to serve the needs of the new manufacturing activities.

The Canadian experience

Courchene (1970) has recently written that:

> Problems relating to regional economic disparity are becoming the focal point of Canadian economic policy. Not only do these regional disparities evoke policy measures directed specifically toward regions, but their presence also impinges on the types of policies that can be prescribed for other economic ills.

Canadian interest in regional disparities accelerated after the severe recession of the late 1950s, although the total impact of federal programs was dissipated through independent schemes concerned with land utilization and low income in rural areas, the development of infrastructure in the Atlantic region and various forms of incentive schemes for industrial development. The first forms of industrial incentives tackled the problem of attracting industry to less prosperous areas through the use of tax concessions, providing, in designated areas, a three year exemption from federal income tax and various allowances for capital costs for the construction of new plants or extensions to existing facilities. In 1965, the incentives, administered by the Area Development Agency (ADA), were modified to take the form of cash grants rather than relief from taxation. By December 1972, it was estimated that the grants under the 1965 Area Development Incentives Act and the tax reliefs under the 1963 legislation had provided about 57,697 new jobs, almost one third of which were located in the Atlantic region.

In a study of the impacts of industrial incentives under the provisions of the 1965 Act, Yeates and Lloyd (1970) examined the response to these incentives by industrialists locating or expanding in the Southern Georgian Bay Region, an area that has until quite recently been bypassed by the general mainstream of economic progress in southern Ontario. A total of thirty-one plants made use of these incentives, eighteen of which were new to the area, representing some $80 million of direct and indirect investment in new buildings and plants. Using a 'from–to' input–output matrix of the type pioneered by Leven (1961) and Hansen and Tiebout (1963), the authors were able to estimate the impacts the grant-assisted industries had on non-assisted firms in the area. As one would have expected, in dealing with a small subregion, the interregional interindustry linkages were not well developed: the main impact of these new and expanding firms was in the form of wages and salaries paid to local residents and the spending impacts so generated by consumption expenditures (the induced multiplier effects introduced in chapter 3). The close proximity to the Toronto Metropolitan area was reflected in the intensity of the interregional linkages between Southern Georgian Bay and Toronto; thus, substantial benefits from each government incentive dollar were accruing to an already prosperous and expanding area as a result of import leakages from the Southern Georgian Bay Region.

The various regional efforts of a number of organizations were incorporated under one ministry in 1969 with the formation of the Department of Regional Economic Expansion (DREE). The Regional Development Incentives Act of 1969 established varying grants to firms establishing, modernizing or expanding business in parts of all ten provinces (see map 5.3): some 30 per cent of the labour force is contained within these areas. Table 5.8 details the incentives offered by area and type of project. There are several overriding considerations, for example, the total allocation to one firm cannot exceed $6 million and for new plants or new product expansions the grant must not exceed $30,000 per job created or one half of the total capital to be employed whichever is smaller (DREE 1973).

The incentives program of 1969 has recently come under a great deal of

Table 5.8   Regional industrial incentives to industry in Canada provided by the 1969 Regional Industrial Incentives Act

Region	Modernization or expansion	New plant or new produce expansion
Region A (Atlantic Provinces)	30% of eligible capital costs	35% of capital cost plus $7000 per eligible job created
Region B (see map)	20% of eligible capital costs	25% of capital cost plus $5000 per eligible job created
Region C (see map)	10% of eligible capital costs	10% of capital cost plus $2000 per eligible job created

Note: Jobs created refer only to *direct* job creation.

criticism. A number of politicians have claimed that firms in some parts of northern Ontario have ceased operations and relocated in regions where they could receive federal assistance. In defence, it may be claimed that without the incentives scheme, the plant may have gone out of business altogether, thus depriving society of at least some jobs. However, the impact such closures have on smaller communities in northern Ontario and Quebec has often been most severe, especially in instances when the plant was by far the largest employer.

A more serious criticism has been levelled at the incentives scheme from the point of view that the scheme fails to affect, in any significant manner, the location decisions of industry and is thus nothing more than a windfall to companies who would have located or expanded or modernized where they did. There is a certain element of the 'chicken and egg' argument here, in that it would be virtually impossible to differentiate a 'pure' location decision and one influenced by incentive grants. Springate (1972), however, conducted some in-depth interviews with executives of thirty-one companies of varying size, all of whom had received DREE assistance. His main substantive conclusion was that in only one third of the cases was the location of the plant significantly affected by the grant. Industrialists did claim, and this may be as useful a justification for the grants and the influence on location decisions, that the grants affected decisions about the timing and size of projects.

Springate's thesis unleashed an expected publication from DREE which claimed a much greater influence in plant location decisions than that claimed by Springate (1972) or an earlier study by George (1969). As of 31 December 1972, the DREE claims that the projected effect of the offers accepted thus far under the provisions of the 1969 Act would result in the allocation of $324·4 million in incentive grants to provide 81,752 jobs and capital investment of $1,616·3 million. Excluding region C (see map 5.1), the number of jobs would be just over 55,000. Analysis of the type and quality of job being supported provides some important insights into the possible workings of this program for it is far too early (1973) to judge authoritatively whether the success claimed will, in fact, be realized.

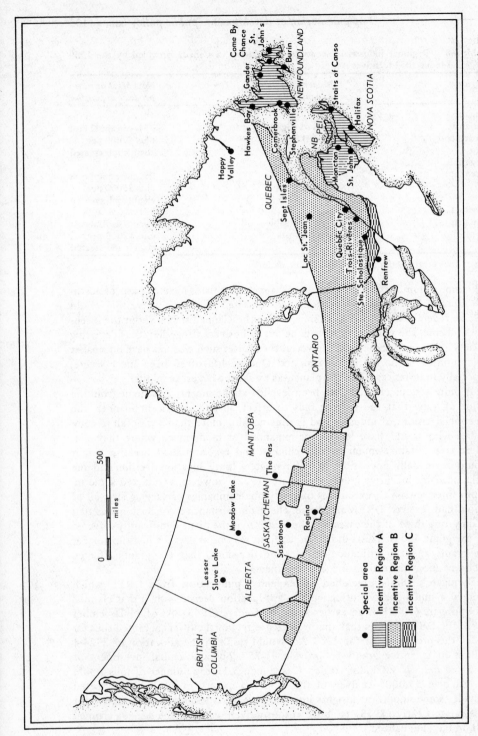

Map 5.3 Canadian designated regions and special areas, 1971–1972, *Source*: Department of Regional Economic Expansion (1972).

In the DREE report, the following statement is made.

> Capital intensive projects are frequently associated with high quality jobs. If it is true that more remunerative and skilled jobs are found in capital intensive industries, then it would appear that Alberta and Ontario have benefited somewhat more than other provinces in terms of the quality of job being supported. (DREE 1973)

This point serves to highlight a dilemma apparent in not only regional but international development theory. If the policy objective is reduction in unemployment, then it would appear that the policy adopted by the DREE is consistent since those provinces with the greatest surplus of labour are the ones receiving labour intensive projects. This policy would also be consistent with comparative advantage theory since the Atlantic Provinces have *vis-à-vis* the United States a relatively greater endowment of labour and since by far the greatest percentage of Atlantic Province's exports go to the United States (Atlantic Provinces Economic Council 1970) attracting labour intensive jobs would assist in (1) increasing employment opportunities and (2) assuring the possibilities of continued competitive exports.

However, the longer-run advisability of the program may be open to question. In earlier chapters, a number of comments were made about the cyclical sensitivity of some regions to changes in aggregate demand. Part of this sensitivity was attributed to the narrowness of the region's economic base and the particular demand characteristics associated with certain types of product. Thus, on the one hand, one would wish to see a development policy gain by any regional comparative advantage that may exist; on the other hand, the importance and need for diversification may claim greater priority if longer-run growth and development are given more consideration. The distribution of manufacturing employment as of 1969 and the distribution of employment to be created by incentive grant projects are shown in table 5.9. It would be very hard to justify an assertion that the projects will provide for diversification in, say, the Atlantic region and British Columbia; there would appear to be a greater tendency to support more traditional activities in each region (especially in British Columbia). The data could be misleading in the sense that it could be claimed that the grants would provide for new firms or the modernization of existing firms and thus provide a technological comparative advantage, not only over existing firms in the region but also an advantage over firms in other regions or countries. The role of the 'best practice' firm is one that has been discussed in great detail by Le Heron (1973).

Understandably, the DREE is somewhat defensive about whether its program should be attempting, in some normative fashion, to create a diversified industrial structure in less prosperous regions.

In attempting to refute the claims made by Springate, the DREE performed an in-house survey to try to determine the real impact of the incentives program. Four types of 'incrementality' of investment and job support were identified (DREE 1973).

1 *Location option* – without the grant, the firm would have located in another region: in this way, the jobs and investment may be considered incremental to the region.

Table 5.9 Percentage distribution of total manufacturing employment and RDIA activity by sector up to 31 December 1972

	Atlantic		Quebec		Ontario		Prairies		B.C.	
	1969 base	Expected jobs	1969 base	Expected jobs	1969 base	Expected jobs	1969 base	Expected jobs	1969 base	Expected jobs
	%	%	%	%	%	%	%	%	%	%
Wood	9·6	10·6	4·1	11·4	2·2	30·3	6·9	11·7	32·2	90·8
Transportation	10·3	8·4	7·0	12·1	12·2	3·0	7·5	19·1	5·0	1·1
Clothing	0·6	1·5	12·2	9·6	3·0	10·7	7·9	14·1	1·7	—
Textile	1·8	1·8	7·9	9·3	3·8	6·8	1·4	3·6	0·8	—
Food Mfg.	16·0	11·9	7·8	5·4	7·9	1·8	20·8	11·0	9·6	—
Electrical	5·1	10·8	6·9	7·2	10·0	3·4	2·3	3·3	2·1	—
Metal Fab.	4·9	2·9	6·9	7·4	10·0	1·6	11·2	5·1	7·4	4·7
Primary Metal	N/A	1·9	5·0	4·8	8·1	17·1	5·4	5·5	6·7	—
Knitting	1·9	3·1	2·9	6·4	1·0	2·6	N/A	1·7	N/A	2·6
Fish Processors	14·8	19·8	—	0·5	—	—	N/A	1·3	N/A	—
Furniture	0·7	3·7	3·3	3·6	2·6	7·8	2·9	2·0	1·9	—
Machinery	0·6	2·1	2·9	2·6	6·9	1·4	5·5	4·8	3·6	—
Paper–Allied	12·0	0·3	8·5	2·8	5·6	1·3	3·1	5·8	14·2	—
Chemical	1·6	1·1	5·5	1·4	5·2	9·9	3·4	2·3	2·5	—
Rubber	N/A	10·0	1·3	0·5	2·1	0·4	N/A	0·4	N/A	—
Non-Metallic	3·0	1·1	2·7	2·4	3·3	0·4	5·8	0·9	2·7	0·5
Printing–Publishing	4·3	1·0	4·4	2·2	5·4	0·5	8·7	2·1	4·9	—
Leather	N/A	0·3	3·0	2·3	1·7	1·9	0·9	0·3	0·2	—
Beverage	2·7	0·8	1·9	0·4	1·3	0·5	3·0	1·0	1·6	—
Tobacco	N/A	0·2	1·2	—	0·4	—	—	—	N/A	—
Petroleum	N/A	—	0·6	—	1·1	—	1·7	—	0·7	0·3
Other	1·5	6·7	4·0	7·7	6·2	3·6	1·6	4·0	2·2	0·3

Source: DREE (1973).

Table 5.10 Incrementality impact of regional development incentives in Canada, 1969–1972*

Type of incrementality	Capital costs ($ million)	Jobs	Grants ($ million)
1 Location options	720·2	22,688	147·0
2 Size change	9·6	829	2·5
3 Timing change	9·5	834	2·5
4 Elements of both timing and size	8·9	829	3·7
5 Viability threshold	143·3	9,427	37·7
6 No effect	0	0	0
7 Incrementality total	891·5	34,607	103·4
8 Sample total	1118·4	49,429	248·3
9 7 as a % of 8	79·7	70·0	77·9

*Excludes region C (see map 5.1). *Source*: DREE (1973).

2 *Size change* – the grant provided the necessary conditions for a firm to con-struct a larger plant than would have been the case without a grant: the additional jobs and investment resulting *only* from the increase in size became incremental to the region.

3 *Timing change* – in this case, the availability of a grant would facilitate the undertaking of the project now rather than some time in the future: the incrementality here corresponds to the benefits gained from earlier job creation.

4 *Viability threshold* – a grant, in this case, makes the rate of return on invest-ment attractive enough to warrant the undertaking of the project. In this case, it is claimed that the project's viability is suspect or tenuous without the grant.

Table 5.10 lists the results of this survey.

According to the calculations by the DREE, some 70 per cent of the new jobs created represented a form of incrementality. However, these data may under-estimate the total impact that the job-creating programs may have had on the region; some of the new firms would have purchased from local industries and, through the familiar multiplier effects, created additional income and local employment opportunities. On the other hand, a number of these firms will probably go out of business within a few years – reflecting, no doubt, the vicissi-tudes of the national economic climate and observed statistics which indicate that business failure is more probable in the early years of operation (see fig. 5.9).

A further attempt was made to examine the impact of DREE incentives upon regional unemployment rates (see table 5.11). The methodology used is perhaps of questionable validity but it does serve to suggest that the impacts of the incentives Act, if any, are at least greater in the regions with the higher unemployment rates, although the relative distribution of unemployment appears not to have been altered. An expected unemployment rate was calculated by assigning all new jobs attributable to the incentives program each year to the unemployment totals, maintaining observed participation rates and labour force totals. The results indicate that, by 1972, the effects were of an order of one

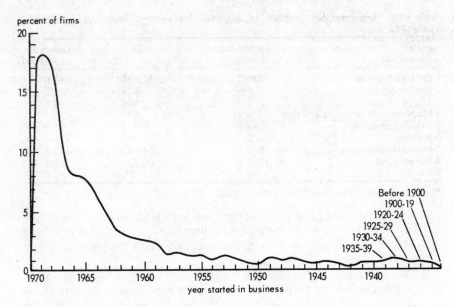

percent of firms

5.9 Business failures in Canada, 1970. Graph shows the age distribution of firms which went out of business in 1970. *Source*: Dun and Bradstreet (1971).

percentage point in Quebec and almost as high in the Atlantic region. Obviously, because the labour force is much smaller in the Atlantic region, the effects of small changes will be much greater in percentage terms: correspondingly, the incremental additions to employment totals in Ontario (mainly through job creation in region C on map 5.3) would cause only minor changes in the total unemployment rates for this region.

A more penetrating criticism of the DREE program has been levelled by Woodward (1974). He claims that subsidies offered by the DREE are inconsistent with the Department's primary objective – that of increasing employment in depressed regions. Woodward notes:

> The problem with attempting to increase employment by 'stimulating private investment' (or financing part of the plant and machinery expenses) is that most firms can substitute such capital for labour in their productive process. In particular, most firms which find that they will be eligible for a larger grant if they increase their capital–labour ratio are likely to include a larger than necessary amount of capital in their application. Further, most firms which have their machinery costs reduced substantially more than their labour costs are likely to expand their output by purchasing a proportionately greater increment of machinery and equipment than of labour. (Woodward 1974)

Where a firm's elasticity of substitution (of capital for labour) is large, a capital-biased subsidy may cause a reduction in the firm's absolute level of employment. Woodward claims that the employment creation is less than if the incentives had

Table 5.11 Hypothetical impact of DREE industrial incentives program on Canadian regional and national unemployment rates 1969–1972

	1969		1970		1971		1972	
	Expected	Observed	Expected	Observed	Expected	Observed	Expected	Observed
Atlantic	7·64	7·49	7·98	7·60	9·28	8·58	9·86	9·02
Quebec	6·93	6·89	8·09	7·86	8·96	8·22	9·32	8·28
Ontario	3·13	3·13	4·32	4·28	5·30	5·23	4·85	4·80
Prairies	2·90	2·88	4·62	4·42	4·77	4·50	4·70	4·45
British Columbia	5·02	5·02	7·65	7·63	7·09	7·02	7·61	7·57
Canada	4·70	4·68	6·05	5·91	6·73	6·39	6·75	6·32

Note: The expected unemployment rate was computed by assigning all new jobs attributable to the incentives program to unemployment totals: participation rates and labour force totals were held constant at the levels *observed* each year.
Source: Computations on data from DREE and Statistics Canada, *Labour Force* (monthly).

been neutral or labour biased. In fact, more substitution may reduce labour required through output expansion. As a consequence, job creation per dollar of government investment is reduced and the capital bias could lead to increased purchases of capital and equipment from the more industrial areas of Canada, causing positive impacts upon employment in these areas. However, Woodward did not include the impact that these capital biased incentives may have upon (1) other activity in the region (through expenditures on raw materials, payments of salaries, consumption of municipal services and so forth) or (2) the impact the location of capital-biased firms in depressed areas may have upon the viability of the regional economy in the longer run. In the discussion of table 5.9, it was noted that there had been a tendency for the new employment activity that has been created to reflect closely the existing distribution of manufacturing activity in the less prosperous areas. If the new activity brings to the area the 'best practice' technology, then it would also seem to be bringing a greater probability for its continued existence. Given the small size of the industrial and consumer markets in the less prosperous regions, many of these firms would be forced to sell their products in competition with firms in southern Ontario and Quebec. Unless it can be demonstrated that a clear comparative advantage would accrue from using a more labour-intensive production process (implying that more than one profitable production process exists), there would appear to be little advantage to adopting other than the technology that would yield the greatest returns. Furthermore, leakages from a regional economy are unavoidable: *a priori*, one would expect that the *total* impact on a less prosperous region of two firms exercising technology biased towards capital and labour respectively may not be radically different. The impact upon *specific* sectors of the regional economy would vary according to the degree of interdependence that characterizes the industrial and industrial-consumption sectors within the region.

The United States experience

In the earlier sections of this chapter, the issues of fiscal federalism were discussed in general terms. Basically, these issues relate to the disaggregation of decision-making in a federal structure and the perceived or real need for federal intervention in aiding local economies. In the United States, this has proven to be one of the most contentious battles in the broad area of national–regional development. The battle lines are drawn roughly between those who look upon regional poverty as a transient phase in the context of the perturbations of the national business cycle; a more extreme position on this side of the fence would contend that regional unemployment is a *necessary* condition for national prosperity. On the other side are those who claim that the market clearing process (whereby the presence of unemployment would attract new investment or where unemployed workers would migrate to areas of better employment opportunity: on this issue see Parr 1966) has consistently failed to do its job. In addition, the geographical incidence of these less prosperous areas seems not to have been randomly chosen: on the contrary, several areas have been experiencing evidence of economic stress for many decades.

The approach to regional development problems in the United States has been varied: Cumberland (1971) has produced a very good guide to these various programs and has contributed some useful insights into their success or lack of it in the last several decades. The reader is encouraged to read this book for an appreciation of the programs especially as they relate to the structure of political organization within the United States. One of the many programs that has been undertaken will be discussed here, the Economic Development Administration's Growth Centre Strategy (Economic Development Administration (EDA) 1972). It should be borne in mind that this is but one of many policies dedicated to regional development at either the federal or state level.

The Growth Centre Strategy program grew out of earlier criticism with the predecessor of the EDA, the Area Redevelopment Administration, and (1) its policy orientation to single-county problems and (2) its concentration on areas with substantial and persistent unemployment or low median family income. In other words, the potential for development of less prosperous areas was not given due consideration and the focusing of attention upon single administrative units precluded the development of joint multi-county ventures. A change in emphasis took place in 1965 with the creation of the EDA and its emphasis on selecting only those areas which exhibited potential for development. In this case, an area need not be distressed to receive aid, provided it would generate some impact upon nearby communities and rural areas that were experiencing varying degrees of economic poverty. Further, the goals were expanded to include an objective of stemming outmigration from these less prosperous areas. In August 1965 the growth centre strategy became law as part of a broader Public Works and Economic Development Act.

The provisions of the legislation empowered the Secretary of Commerce to designate areas for federal assistance. Several criteria were adopted: (1) these places must exhibit potential for development and (2) their designation would allow the program of the local district to be carried out effectively. It was felt that the cities designated as growth centres should normally be less than 250,000 but that the local centres should have a relatively large labour force which would be capable of facilitating economic growth. Table 5.12 shows the geographic breakdown of expenditures as of March 1971. By the middle of 1970 it was felt within the EDA that some attempt should be made to evaluate the performance of these designated centres. Accordingly, a sample of growth centres was chosen together with some nondesignated areas for the purposes of comparison. These evaluations revealed that, to date, the growth centre strategy has not been yielding very substantial positive results; it appears that growth centre projects have resulted in no greater job impact than similar projects placed in economically depressed counties. Employees in the growth centre projects revealed that they would have remained in the county irrespective of their success or lack of success in obtaining a job. The EDA suggested that this factor provided little encouragement for continuing success for the objective related to migration. Further statistics were used to show that the growth centres had really not outperformed non growth centre areas. While one may take these statistics at their face value, several criticisms should be directed at the evaluation since it casts the utility of

Table 5.12   EDA assistance to economic development centers (31 March 1971)

Region	EDA obligations in economic development centres			
	Public works	Business development	Technical assistance	District planning grants *
Atlantic (Conn., Del., Me., Md., Mass., N.H., N.J., N.Y., Pa., P.R., R.I., Vt.)	$6,768,000	$4,775,000	$301,920	1,563,000
Mideastern (Ky., N.C., Ohio, Va., W.Va.)	$7,487,000	$2,452,000	$38,435	1,737,000
Southeastern (Ala., Fal., Ga., Miss., S.C., Tenn.)	$27,469,000	$10,902,000	$335,721	4,584,000
Midwestern (Ill., Ind., Iowa, Mich., Minn., Mo. Ned., N.D., S.D., Wis.)	$7,329,000		$267,854	2,603,000
Southwestern (Ariz., Ark., Colo., Kan., La., N.M., Nev., Okla., Tex., Utah, Wyo.)	$29,181,000	$5,701,000	$427,891	5,686,000
Western (Alas., Cal., Haw., Idaho, Mont., Ore., Wash.)	$1,057,000			780,000
Totals	$79,201,000	$23,830,000	$1,371,821	$16,953,000

*As of 28 February, 1971. *Source*: Economic Development Administration 1972

the growth centre strategy in a rather unfavourable and somewhat unfair light. First of all, designating an area as a growth centres does not automatically make it different from any other area. During the discussion of growth pole and growth centre theory, it was noted that some confusion exists between the two terms. It would seem that the EDA is expecting to see, within only a few years, some polarizing influence concentrated in geographic space! As has been noted earlier, the development of technological and other pecuniary and nonpecuniary linkages takes considerable time. A growth centre will not become one just because the federal government designates it! Secondly, it may well be that the greatest returns from federal investment would be realized in intermediate growth centres rather than in those with populations of 25,000 to, say, 100,000. The economies of city size, the concept of a threshold or ratchet, would appear to be relevant in this context. Furthermore, it is unlikely that *any* federal policy will be able to successfully stem outmigration from a larger number of rural areas and small urban centres. By providing intermediate, intervening opportunities in medium-sized (say 200,000 to 750,000) cities, as Hansen (1972) has advocated, one may be able to stem the migration flow from the less prosperous areas to the larger, northern metropolises.

The basic issue here is that the evaluation may be premature – as an evaluation of growth centre strategy – although, as an appraisal of the EDA policy, it may have provided some useful feedback about the misapplication of federal funds in a spatial sense. One has to be careful here to balance political pragmatism with economic theory: the old problem of making all regions equal while treating all regions equally of necessity will result in a less than optimal (from an economic theoretic point of view) allocation of public funds.

Cumberland (1971) has crystallized the dilemma faced by regional development agencies in the United States as one of trying to be invisible and not disrupting the operation of market place decisions to any great extent and, at the same time, trying to influence the location of economic activity and promote development in less prosperous areas. The dangers of such compromise action are that, in attempting to appease proponents of both the interventionist and free-market schools, the policies that are often developed succeed only rarely. A more comprehensive approach to regional development was initiated under the auspices of the Appalachian Regional Commission, created by the Appalachian Regional Development Act of 1965. Provisions were made under this act for development of a wide variety of programs in states from Alabama northeastward to Pennsylvania, although appropriations for highway expenditures dwarfed allocations to programs such as health improvements, timber development, sewage treatment and other community and social endeavours. One of the more interesting aspects of the Regional Commission was the fact that federal monies were appropriated for the Commission and a great deal of latitude was given (within broadly defined areas) to the Commission in the allocation of these funds throughout the region. Both Newman (1972) and Rothblatt (1971) have commented on the problems that this caused: states vying for an 'appropriate share' of the funds while at the same time trying to be receptive to the notion of equity with the Appalachian region (for example, although thirteen states are represented, the Appalachian portion of Pennsylvania contains almost three and one-half times as many people as West Virginia which is wholly contained within the region). Rothblatt (1971) proposes, on the basis of the Appalachian experience, a model for the allocation of funds for multifunctional and multijurisdictional planning programmes:

First, Congress should authorize and appropriate block grants, perhaps constrained for reasons of national interest (such as civil rights). Then, some equitable means (e.g. · population, *per capita* income) should be used to apportion the regional grant into participant block grants. Again, only in cases and programs which have a broader regional or national impact (such as a major highway system) should constraints be placed on the use of funds. Finally, some mechanism for bilateral trading should be provided to accommodate the varying priorities or absorptive capacities of each participant.

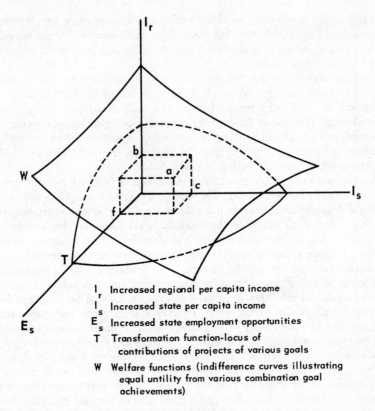

I_r Increased regional per capita income
I_s Increased state per capita income
E_s Increased state employment opportunities
T   Transformation function-locus of contributions of projects of various goals

W   Welfare functions (indifference curves illustrating equal untility from various combination goal achievements)

5.10 Trade-offs for a regional development programme with more than two goals. *Source*: Rothblatt (1971).

An elementary idea of this type of formulation is shown in fig. 5.10. Regional goals (i.e. for Appalachia) are articulated subject to certain minimum levels of achievement in the constituent states. The trade-off space will thus be greater than three-dimensional but the basic ideas will be the same. In fig. 5.10, the main goal is to maximize I_r but subject to $I_s \geqslant c$ and $E_s \geqslant f$. In other words, minimum conditions are established for the other goals.

The increased interest in problems of fiscal federalism, revenue sharing, tax equalization schemes and the like has created a new dimension in areas of regional economic development. The goals and policies designed to meet those goals have not always been consistent. Schramm (1972) has shown, for example, the problem of establishing minimum national standards and then allocating funds to maximize the attainment of other goals at the regional level. With reference to fig. 5.11, this difficulty can be demonstrated. The curve A through K represents the trade-off curve for a project yielding benefits to the region and the nation (note that these are *net* benefits). National net benefits increase to a maximum at C and remain at that level until D and then decline until they reach

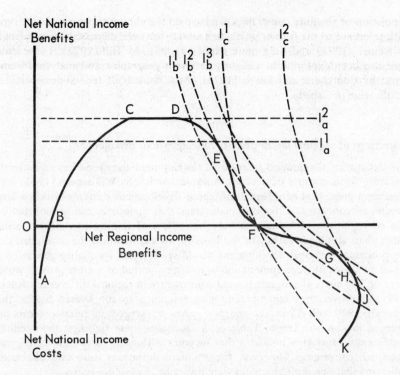

5.11 Comparison of national and regional income benefits. *Source*: Schramm (1972).

zero at *F*. Beyond that point, the benefit cost ratio is less than one while, up to point *J*, net benefits are still positive at the regional level. The sets of curves I_a, I_b and I_c represent various social welfare functions: the former, being horizontal imply no trade-off between national efficiency and regional equity, whereas the last set (I_c) imply substantial trade-offs. The middle set comprises a function that would envisage moderate trade-offs.

Schramm (1972) discussed the issues as follows. The trade-off curve between *A* and *D* and *J* and *K* may be ignored since there are other portions of the curve which will yield at least as high a level on one axis and a greater level on the other. Dealing with a social welfare function of the type I_a, point *D* will be chosen.[1] If a restriction is imposed that net national benefits must be ≥ 1, the trade-off curve is further limited to the portion *B* through *F*. With a more elastic social welfare function (curves I_b), the policy maker will choose point *E*. In the absence of the restriction, he would choose *G*. Finally, if the social welfare function were of the type I_c, point *F* would be chosen with the restriction and *H* without the restriction. Two main points arise from this discussion: (1) the importance of the nature of social welfare functions and (2) the influence the

[1] This is because although point *C* and *D* yield equal national benefits, regional equity is greater at *D* with no loss of national benefits.

imposition of absolute constraints can have on the choice of project size or type. With reference to the former point, this matter has been discussed at some length by Reiner (1971) and, in a more explicit fashion, by Hill (1973). These issues have also been explored, in a slightly different geographic and analytical framework, by Courchene and Beavis (1973) in the context of federal-provincial tax equalization in Canada.

Projections of regional development: convergence or divergence?

The debate on the process of regional development over time has raged in the literature for a number of decades. A seminal article by Williamson (1965) drew together a great deal of information about development patterns within a large number of countries. Williamson maintained that the proper measure of the process of regional development should be indices of relative income *per capita* rather than absolute values. On the basis of his examination, he concluded that the process of regional development would see regional inequality generated in the early stages of development and only after a period of mature growth would there be any signs of progress toward convergence in regional differences. Kuehn (1971), however, has commented, with reference to the United States, that between 1929 and 1968 income *per capita* converged in relative terms but diverged in absolute terms. Table 5.13 illustrates these findings; the declining coefficient of variation indicates that incomes within the forty-eight contiguous states are converging. However, the standard deviations were also increasing, indicating that *per capita* incomes were diverging in absolute terms.

More recently, some estimates of regional *per capita* incomes were made for various sets of regions within the United States (Obers 1972). Using the twenty water resources regions, the indices of regional income *per capita* have been plotted in fig. 5.12. The indices are based on the use of constant 1967 constant dollars, with the national average *per capita* income represented by the value 100 each year. Data for the years to 1969 are observations, those beyond are projections. These were made using a trend extrapolated shift–share technique to provide estimates of regional industrial activity and various other models to project agricultural activities, population growth, employment growth. From these projections, estimates of regional income *per capita* were obtained.

It is quite obvious from the data presented in fig. 5.12 that relative regional *per capita* incomes are converging and are projected to continue in this fashion through the end of the projection period. However, what they do not indicate is the difference in *real per capita* incomes. It was noted at the end of chapter 4 that considerable debate has ensued on the issue of differences in wages between the south and north of the United States. It was shown that measures using real and measures using money wages provided differing contributions to the debate on regional convergence or divergence. Few authors would claim that differences in real costs of living do not exist within the United States; the problem becomes one of trying to decide how much of the difference in money incomes is a reflection of cheaper costs of living and how much reflects lower standards of

Table 5.13 Frequency distribution measures of *per capita* personal income for the forty-eight contiguous states*

| Year | Current dollars | | | | Constant dollars† | | |
	Mean	Range	SD	Coeff. of var.	Mean	Range	SD
1929	617	889	223	0·361	1033	1489	374
1930	545	840	208	0·380	937	1443	357
1931	457	712	183	0·401	862	1343	346
1932	349	555	145	0·414	734	1166	305
1933	329	505	133	0·405	730	1120	296
1934	374	519	141	0·377	802	1114	303
1935	427	548	145	0·340	893	1146	304
1936	481	628	175	0·364	996	1300	363
1937	513	709	177	0·344	1027	1418	354
1938	477	592	161	0·338	972	1206	329
1939	505	711	178	0·351	1044	1469	367
1940	540	786	191	0·352	1107	1611	391
1941	664	829	215	0·323	1295	1616	419
1942	868	1107	256	0·295	1528	1949	451
1943	1035	1062	277	0·267	1717	1761	460
1944	1108	974	262	0·236	1808	1589	428
1945	1146	1017	253	0·220	1827	1622	403
1946	1162	1112	268	0·230	1709	1635	393
1947	1240	1070	282	0·227	1594	1375	362
1948	1351	1026	282	0·209	1613	1224	337
1949	1294	1163	283	0·218	1559	1401	341
1950	1401	1376	325	0·231	1672	1642	387
1951	1554	1420	349	0·224	1717	1569	386
1952	1625	1545	365	0·224	1757	1670	395
1953	1673	1539	376	0·225	1795	1651	404
1954	1654	1529	364	0·219	1768	1634	389
1955	1733	1529	379	0·218	1857	1639	406
1956	1820	1729	396	0·217	1922	1826	419
1957	1889	1672	396	0·209	1927	1706	404
1958	1933	1523	377	0·194	1920	1512	374
1959	2002	1564	399	0·199	1972	1541	393
1960	2058	1651	408	0·198	1997	1601	396
1961	2102	1660	417	0·198	2017	1593	400
1962	2222	1932	431	0·194	2108	1833	409
1963	2288	1808	435	0·190	2144	1694	408
1964	2394	1760	448	0·187	2215	1628	415
1965	2575	1838	458	0·177	2343	1672	417
1966	2776	1945	474	0·170	2455	1720	419
1967	2938	2116	496	0·168	2526	1819	427
1968	3175	2175	530	0·166	2620	1795	437

*Calculated from data for forty-eight states. *1929–47 source*: Schwartz and Graham (1956), pp. 142–43. *1948–68 source*: Office of Business Economics, *Survey of Current Business*, (August, 1969), p. 15.
†Consumer price index 1957–9 = 100.
Source: Kuehn (1971).

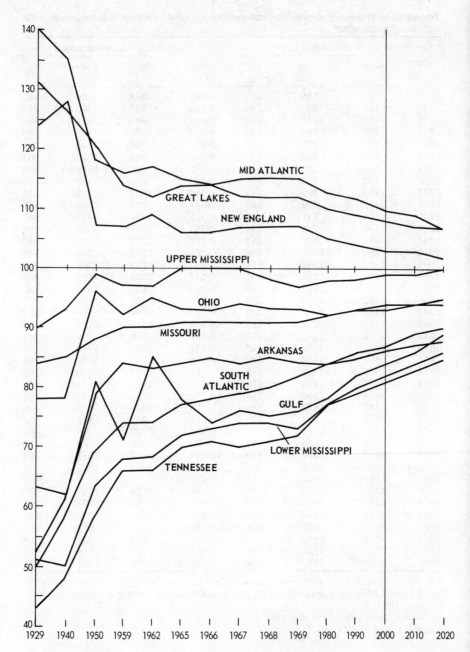

5.12 Indices of regional income *per capita* in the United States, 1929–2020 (constant 1967 dollars). *Source*: United States Water Resources Council (1972).

prosperity. The problem is further compounded by the fact that regional differences in tastes, living styles, the influence of environmental factors and the like combine to make comparison difficult. Hence, there can be no absolute statement made about the progress of regional development and its future prospects in the United States. Richardson (1969b) experienced similar difficulties with reference to the United Kingdom data:

> The percentage gap between the poorest and the richest region narrowed steadily. Nevertheless, the convergence hypothesis is not supported. Perhaps the period 1949–50 to 1964–5 is too short to reveal the trend. Another difficulty is that the data refer to money incomes, and we have no regional cost-of-living data to show whether the variation in *real* incomes has the same distribution.

He further noted that the convergence tendencies in Britain may be weak because of the small gap between the low and high income regions. While this gap is definitely smaller in more prosperous countries, it is still significant within the United States. If county data were utilized rather than larger regions, the differences would become much more marked.

Regional development and environmental issues

Given the present general interest in environmental matters, it is only natural that regional development issues should have been broadened to include concern with quality allocations in society. The literature in this field is growing very rapidly: in this section, a selection of two of many approaches will be made from this vast literature. A more comprehensive approach is contained in Isard *et al.* (1972).

The Cumberland model

In an earlier paper, Cumberland (1966) expounded on a modified input–output model which would be able to accommodate the impacts of economic activities (associated with development objectives) on the environment. Subsequent research by Cumberland, Isard (1969) and Isard *et al.* (1972) has focused on the implementation of various models for small areas. Recently, Cumberland and Korbach (1973) reported on the expanded Maryland model and its empirical implementation. Their concerns are those shared by a number of regional scientists: are the net benefits from development positive in any meaningful fashion? For example, they write,

> Only under very restrictive conditions will any proposed development satisfy generalized regional Pareto-optimality conditions which leave no one worse off with respect to private sector *per capita* income, public sector net revenues and environmental quality.

The model was designed to examine the impact of alternative regional development programs and comprises three components: (1) the familiar inverse of the interindustry model discussed in chapter 3, together with coefficients relating changes in output to changes in value added and employment; (2) a state revenue model; and (3) a waste-loading model. The equations are listed below.

$$[1 - A]^{-1}[\Delta Y] = [\Delta X] \tag{5.14}$$

$$[\Delta X]g = [\Delta VA] \tag{5.15}$$

$$[\dot{\Delta X}]e = [\Delta E] \tag{5.16}$$

$$[\Delta VA]ft = [\Delta SR] \tag{5.17}$$

$$[\Delta VA]g = [\Delta SG] \tag{5.18}$$

$$[\Delta X]p = [\Delta GR] \tag{5.19}$$

The first equation relates changes in final demand to changes in total output. Given these changes (ΔX), estimates are then made (equations 5.15 and 5.16) of changes in value added (ΔVA) and employment (ΔE). Obviously, a linear relationship between these changes is assumed. From the estimated changes in value added, changes in state revenue (equation 5.17) and state expenditure (5.18) are made. The former is obtained by applying a matrix of tax revenue to value added coefficients (f) to the vector of changes in value added and multiplying this product by the relevant tax rates (t). A similar matrix of state expenditure to value-added coefficients (q) was used to generate the changes in state expenditure (ΔSG). Finally, the changes in total output were used for the compilation of changes in initial waste loadings (ΔGR) by applying a matrix of waste loading to output coefficients to the column vector of changes in total output. These last data do not include the effects of recycling and other treatment processes. The model was recently used to examine the claims made by proponents of a Disneyland type of complex that the construction of such a complex would yield considerable benefit to the state of Maryland through its impacts on sales, local investment and generation of increased local spending. The project was compared with several other alternative ventures; the comparisons are summarized in table 5.14. Note that the development project ranked second in terms of contributions to total output but first in terms of gross wastes. Herein lies the crux of the problem for regional development analysts in the future: How much is an additional job created worth in terms of environmental degradation? How much is an additional dollar of tax revenue worth in the same terms? There are other issues which clearly focus in on this problem: How reliable are the economic-ecologic coefficients? Are the relationships linear? What impact can recycling and better management of environmental resources have in shifting the trade-off curve between economic gains and environmental 'losses'? As Cumberland and Korbach (1973) readily admit, these problems are not easily soluble given our present-day limitations in terms of data sources. However, models such as this one do focus again on the unity of the physical and human systems – something geographers long ago propounded but somehow seem to have ignored in recent decades (see Bunge 1974).

Table 5.14 Maryland state impacts of alternative development projects

Project	Amusement and recreation		Electronic components		Printing and publishing		Household appliances		Instruments clocks		Photographic optical	
	Amount	Rank	Amount	Rank	Amount	Rank	Amount	Rank	Amount	Rank	Amount	Rank
Annual impact from increases in deliveries to final demand												
Change output*	158,589	2	148,261	5	52,757	3	160,464	1	148,836	4	142,567	6
Change in value* added	89,255	1	78,693	3	77,559	5	70,212	6	78,678	4	82,229	2
Change employment**	6,784	3	7,717	1	6,002	5	6,236	4	5,885	6	7,569	2
Change in tax revenue	10,487	3	12,864	1	10,719	2	7,429	6	8,972	4	7,489	5
Change in gross waste†	119·640	1	86·550	4	93·960	3	98·711	2	82·320	5	80·880	6
Change output/emp.	23·380	4	19·212	5	24·450	3	25·731	1	25·293	2	18·835	6
Change value added/emp.	13·160	2	10·197	6	12·922	3	11·259	4	13·370	1	10·863	5
Change tax revenue/emp.	1·547	2	1·667	3	1·786	1	1·191	5	1·525	4	0·989	6
Change gross waste/emp.	0·018	1	0·011	5	0·016	2	0·016	2	0·014	4	0·011	5

Notes: *In $1000
**In actual numbers
†In 1000 tons
Deliveries in final demand were equalized at $59·446 million for each development alternative.

Source: Cumberland and Korbach (1973).

Beyers' model

To hard-line environmentalists, it may be nothing short of sacrilegious to consider a national park as an economic concern and then to attempt to formulate its contribution to the local and national community. On the other hand, there exists considerable pressure on resources and there are many who point to the supposed high opportunity costs involved in keeping resources of lumber or minerals locked up for posterity. For example, one attitude was well expressed during hearings before the United States House Committee on Insular and Interior Affairs on Bill H.R. 8970, a bill to establish the North Cascades National Park in Washington state. The writer, an executive vice president of the Industrial Forestry Association, writes in opposition of proposals to allocate federal timber lands to the proposed national park:

> You won't find much clamor for or acceptance of further dismemberment of the Mt Baker, Wenatchee and Okanagan National Forests in the North Cascade counties because the people there know their jobs, their homes, their private investments in their businesses and their public investments in school and roads depend on a continuing timber supply from both the national forests and the state and private lands which make up their resource and economic base. (United States House Committee 1968)

These arguments make sound reading in one sense: jobs lost through the creation of a regional park may indeed wreak havoc on the economic base of local communities. On the other hand, national parks are enjoyed by a varied clientele, whose enjoyment usually involves consumption of a variety of goods and services. While avoiding the trap of viewing a national park as a commodity in a purely economic sense, it is important to realize that the park may provide jobs and generate activity locally and nationally as well as providing benefits of a psychic kind. Beyers (1970), at the behest of the United States National Park Service, attempted to quantify these benefits using case studies of the Olympic and Mt Rainier National Parks. Visitors' expenditures were treated as components of final demand and their impact on Washington State and United States economic activity was measured using an input–output model. It was found that 85 per cent of Park visitors' and operations' expenditures were made in Washington state: however, because of the relatively open nature of the Washington economy, only 25 per cent of the income impacts were noted in Washington state (Beyers 1970). Table 5.15 shows the allocations of expenditures between the visitors' home community, on the way to and from the park and in the vicinity of the park. From these estimates, Beyers was able to provide a measure of the impact visitors' expenditures to all the park systems would have on the national economy – a figure in the range of $1·5 to $2·5 billion. Thus the impact is considerable. However, the local impact may vary. In some instances, the local employment and income generated may more than compensate for any lost jobs and revenues from the closures of mining operations or timber production. In other instances, severe dislocation may take place, especially when the visitation is on a highly seasonal basis.

Table 5.15   Comparisons of regions of national park visitor expenditures

Region of expenditure	Groceries and beverages	Restaurants and drive-ins	Lodging	Gasoline and auto service	Other
In home community					
Clawson-Knetsch	15%	0%	0%	10%	10%
Rainier visitors	60%	11%	0%	53%	68%
Olympic visitors	51%	6%	0%	32%	47%
On way to and from the park					
Clawson-Knetsch	50%	60%	55%	60%	45%
Rainier visitors	19%	47%	55%	32%	10%
Olympic visitors	21%	54%	53%	43%	28%
In and near park					
Clawson-Knetsch	35%	40%	45%	30%	45% (est.)
Rainier visitors	13%	43%	45%	15%	22%
Olympic visitors	28%	40%	47%	25%	26%

Notes: 1 Figures add down the column within estimates.
  2 Rainier and Olympic visitors data drawn from Beyers (1970). The estimates referred to as Clawson-Knetsch are from: Clawson and Knetsch (1969), p. 237.

Summary

Readers interested in this particular aspect of regional analysis would do well to look at the materials balance approach of Kneese *et al.* (1970), Victor's (1972) model using Canadian economic and ecologic data and the Isard *et al.* (1972) model. Each of these models is constructed on the fundamental premise that no longer can we assign externalities associated with production to some nonmarket influencing subset of the model. Integrated within the main framework of the model, knowledge of the potential impacts of economic activities on the environment provides a further dimension (and, perhaps, an additional complication) to the analysis of regional development alternatives.

Regional industrial analysis and development

It was noted in the introduction that only a limited number of methods of regional analysis would be discussed in this book, partially because of space limitations and partially the reasoning that many of the methods not discussed here are derivatives of economic base or input–output analysis. The greatest challenge facing the regional analyst is not necessarily the development of new models but rather the functioning of existing modelling efforts within a policy oriented framework. Some examples of these efforts from the Illinois Regional Science and Economics Group will serve to illustrate the direction in which these endeavours are likely to be moving in the years ahead.

Located within the boundaries of the state of Illinois are some 14 per cent of the United States coal reserves. For a long time these reserves were thought to represent an energy source of dubious value. Environmental legislation had placed severe restrictions on the use of coal in its more traditional forms. However, the energy crisis of the early 1970s and political pressures to move towards

Energy Independence have created a completely different environment. At the present time (1976) two pilot coal gasification plants are being built in the southern part of the state – precursors to a more intensive use of these coal reserves. A logical question to raise would be: what impact will these developments have upon the state? To this end, the development of an input–output model is proceeding. Such a model, as we have discussed in earlier chapters, will enable the calculation of direct, indirect and induced impacts upon the state economy. Through the addition of tax vectors, an estimate may be made of the contribution of coal gasification plants to the state tax revenues. However, the two other important impacts are in need of estimation: (1) the impact upon economic development of the local communities in which the coal gasification plants are located and (2) the impact upon the local communities in terms of their ability to provide the necessary infrastructure to house new workers, new children in the local schools and so forth.

In connection with the first set of impacts, the work of Czamanski (1973, 1976) will assume considerable importance. Czamanski has been attempting to integrate the idea of an industrial complex with the notion of spatial association. Whether new industry will be attracted to the area in which the coal gasification plants are located will depend in part upon the type of gas that is to be produced. For example, if the gas is to be high btu, then it is capable of being shipped via existing pipelines to any other location in the United States. On the other hand, if the gas is to be low btu, then the maximum radius for shipment will be much reduced (probably to less than 100 miles). In that case, there may be some incentive for industry, if only power generation plants, to locate within the vicinity of the coal gasification plant.

The impact of energy resource development upon local communities has been the subject of a number of analyses (see, for example, Gilmore 1976). Many of these communities have an infrastructure (sewage, water treatment plants, school systems) which may not be capable of rapid adjustment to the influx of many hundreds of new employees over a short period of time. As a consequence, a great deal of tension and conflict arises between local residents, local entrepreneurs and landowners, city officials and the owners of the coal gasification plants. In addition, the development of these new plants will create differential impacts on the local communities over time; this results from the fact that the construction and operating phases of the plant may not only employ vastly different numbers of workers but the job skills may vary as well. Consequently, the community may experience another turnover as the construction phase ends and the production phase commences. The local community decision-makers are thus faced with the dilemma of how to improve local services and when to improve them (on this issue, see Hewings 1975).

This brief summary to the mainly *economic* issues surrounding coal gasification development suggests that the regional analyst has a great deal to contribute to the provision of methodologies to assist the resolution of conflicts and the provision of development strategies. In addition, there will be interaction with other aspects of the development process including impacts on mobility, and the technology of the gasification process.

In 1975 the Illinois legislature passed a law requiring consideration of the macroeconomic impacts of all proposed environmental legislation prior to that legislation becoming law. For example, a bill before the legislature would require the use of returnable bottles and containers in the dispensing of beverages. What impact would this have upon the state in terms of jobs, income, community development and state and local taxes? To assist in answering these questions, an Illinois input–output model is being developed. Industry consultants will provide inputs on the nature of the changes that the legislation is likely to induce in the production function, the proportion of inputs purchased from Illinois suppliers, and the additional capital investments that may be necessary. Furthermore, an estimate is made of the temporal nature of these impacts. The data are then put into the input–output model and estimates of the state-wide impacts on each industry are documented. In a preliminary analysis, it was found that the net job impact was positive – although the impacts on specific industries varied from positive to negative. The job skills required were also estimated: with returnable bottles, more truck delivery drivers and retail sales clerks would be required.

Periodically, the armed forces go through a period of evaluating the efficiency of their operations. Efforts to save money often point to closing down bases in some parts of the country and combining functions previously allocated to several bases to just one or two. In some communities, however, the base may represent the major source of employment and income to the civilian residents. A county-based economic base model has been developed to provide estimates of the impacts of base closing following procedures suggested in Isserman (1975). This technique provides a bracketing approach to the multiplier – in a sense, providing an upper and lower estimate of the impact.

The analyses described above provide a small sample of the variety of issues that geographers, economists and regional scientists are investigating. They are attempting to offer avenues of solution for some problems and attempting to develop a critical awareness of the way the spatial perspectives can provide insights hitherto unappreciated. Perhaps, as Dziewonski (1973) has commented, the next major challenge for regional analysts will be to provide prognostications of the future patterns of regional development. The problems involved here are of a different order and complexity and involve dimensions of experience indicating a need for awareness of ethics of behaviour and procedure and the responsibilities of the analyst to the community of which he is a part.

References

AIROV, J. (1963) The construction of interregional business cycle models. *J. Reg. Sci.* 5, 1–20.

AIROV, J. (1967) Fiscal policy theory in an interregional economy: general interregional multipliers and their application. *Pap. Reg. Sci. Assoc.* 19, 83–108.

ALEXANDER, J. W. (1954) The basic–nonbasic concept of urban economic functions. *Econ. Geogr.* 30, 246–61.

ALMON, C. (1966) *The American economy to 1975.* New York.

ANDREWS, R. B. (1953–6) Mechanics of the urban economic base. *Ld Econ.* 29–31.

ARCHIBALD, G. C. (1967) Regional multiplier effects in the UK. *Oxford Econ. Pap.* 19, 22–45.

ARCHIBALD, G. C. (1969) The Phillips curve and the distribution of unemployment. *Am. Econ. Rev.* 59, 124–34.

ARCHIBALD, G. C. (1972) On regional economic policy in the United Kingdom. In PRESTON, M. and CORRY, B. (eds) *Essays in honour of Lord Robbins.* London.

ARROW, K. J. (1963) *Social choice and individual values.* New Haven, Conn.

ASHBY, L. D. (1970) Changes in regional industrial structure: a comment. *Urb. Stud.* 7, 298–304.

BACHARACH, M. (1970) *Bi-proportional matrices and input–output change.* Cambridge.

BASSETT, K. A. and HAGGETT, P. (1971) Towards short-term forecasting for cyclical behaviour in a regional system of cities. In CHISHOLM, M., FREY, A. E. and HAGGETT, P. (eds) *Regional forecasting*, 389–413. London.

BAUMOL, W. J. (1970) *Economic dynamics.* New York.

BELL, F. W. (1967) An econometric forecasting model for a region. *J. Reg. Sci.* 7, 109–27.

BENOIT, E. and BOULDING, K. (eds) (1965) *Disarmament and the economy.* New York.

BERMAN, B. R. (1965) Alternative measures of structural unemployment. In ROSS, A. M. (ed.) *Employment policy and the labor market*, 256–68. Berkeley, Calif.

BEYERS, W. B. (1970) *An economic impact study of Mt Rainier and Olympic National Parks.* Seattle.

BEYERS, W. B. (1972) On the stability of regional interindustry models: the Washington data for 1963 and 1967. *J. Reg. Sci.* 12, 363–74.

BEYERS, W. B. (1973) Growth centers and interindustry linkages. *Proc. Assoc. Am. Geogr.* 5.

BEZDEK, R. and HANNON, B. (1974) Energy, manpower and the Highway Trust Fund. *Sci.* 185 (4152), 669–75.

BLUMENFELD, H. (1955) The economic base of the metropolis. *J. Am. Inst. Planners* 21, 114–32.

BODKIN, R. G. *et al.* (1966) *Price stability and high unemployment.* Econ. Counc. of Canada Spec. Stud. 5. Ottawa.

BOLTON, R. E. (1966) *Defense purchases and regional growth.* Washington, D.C.

BORTS, G. H. and STEIN, J. L. (1964) *Economic growth in a free market.* New York.

BOUDEVILLE, J. (1966) *Problems of regional economic planning.* Edinburgh.

BOURQUE, P. J. *et al.* (1967) *The Washington economy: an input–output analysis.* Seattle.

BOURQUE, P. J. and COX, M. (1970) *An inventory of regional input–output studies in the US.* Seattle.

BOURQUE, P. J. and HANSEN, W. (1967) *An inventory of regional input–output studies in the US.* Seattle.

BOWEN, W. G. and BERRY, R. A. (1963) Unemployment conditions and movements of money wage levels. *Rev. Econ. & Stat.* 45, 163–72.

BRECHLING, F. (1969) Discussion. *Am. Econ. Rev. Pap. & Proc.* 59, 161–7.

BREWIS, T. N. (1969) *Regional economic policies in Canada.* Toronto.

BRITTON, J. N. H. (1967) *Regional analysis and economic geography.* London.

BROWN, A. J. (1967) The 'Green Paper' on the development areas. *Nat. Inst. Econ. Rev.* 40, 26–33.

BROWN, A. J. (1972) *The framework of regional economics in the United Kingdom.* Cambridge.

BROWN, H. J. (1969) Shift and share projections of regional economic growth: an empirical test. *J. Reg. Sci.* 9, 1–18.

BUNGE, W. (1974) 'Footnote to the geography'. *Prof. Geogr.* 26, 104–5.

CAMERON, G. C. (1971) *Regional economic development: the federal role.* Baltimore, Md.

CAMPBELL, D. F. (1972) Theory and applications of a collective choice rule. Inst. Quant. Anal. Soc. Econ. Policy Working Pap. 7206. Toronto.

CAMPBELL, J. (1974) A note on growth poles. *Growth and Change* 5, 43–5.

CANADIAN PRICES AND INCOMES COMMISSION (1972) *Inflation, unemployment and incomes policy.* Ottawa.

CARTER, A. P. (1966) The economics of technological change. *Sci. Am.* April, 25–31.

CARTER, A. P. (1967) Changes in the structure of the American economy, 1947 to 1958 and 1962. *Rev. Econ. & Stat.* 49, 209–24.

CARTER, A. P. (1970) *Structural change in the American economy*. Cambridge, Mass.

CARTER, A. P. and BRODY, A. (eds) (1970) *Contributions to input–output analysis*.

CARTER, A. P. and BRODY, A. (eds) (1972) *Input–output techniques*.

CASETTI, E., KING, L. and JEFFREY, D. (1971) Structural imbalances in the US urban-economic system 1960–5. *Geogr. Anal.* 3, 239–55.

CHALMERS, J. A. (1971) Measuring changes in regional industrial structure: a comment on Stillwell and Ashby. *Urb. Stud.* 8, 289–92.

CHALMERS, J. A. and BECKHELM, T. (1974) *Shift and share and the theory of industrial location*. Univ. Arizona Fac. Working Pap. 74-18. Tucson.

CHINITZ, B. (1961) Contrasts in agglomeration: New York and Pittsburgh. *Am. Econ. Rev. Pap. & Proc.* 51, 279–89.

CHISHOLM, M. and MANNERS, G. (eds) (1971) *Spatial policy problems of the British economy*. Cambridge.

CHOW, G. C. (1960) Tests of equality between sets of coefficients in two linear regressions. *Econometrica* 28, 591–605.

CHRIST, C. F. (1966) *Econometric models and methods*. New York.

CLARK, C. (1957) *Conditions of economic progress*. London.

CLAWSON, M. and KNETSCH, J. L. (1969) *The economics of outdoor recreation*. Baltimore, Md.

COELHO, P. R. P. and GHALI, M. A. (1971) The end of the north–south wage differential. *Am. Econ. Rev.* 61, 932–4.

CONSAD (1967) *Regional federal procurement study*. Washington, D.C.

COMEAU, R. L. (1973) Little chance for a regional monetary policy: fiscal policy, moral suasion are better bets. *Atlantic Provinces Econ. Counc. Newsletter* 17, 1–4.

COURCHENE, T. J. (1970) Interprovincial migration and economic adjustment. *Can. J. Econ.* 3, 550–76.

COURCHENE, T. J. and BEAVIS, D. A. (1973) Federal–provincial tax equalization: an evaluation. *Can. J. Econ.* 4, 483–502.

COWLING, K. and METCALF, D. (1967) Wage–unemployment relationships: a regional analysis for the United Kingdom 1960–5. *Oxford Univ. Bull. Econ. & Stat.* 29, 31–9.

CUMBERLAND, J. H. (1966) A regional interindustry model for analysis of development objectives. *Pap. Reg. Sci. Assoc.* 17, 65–94.

CUMBERLAND, J. H. (1971) *Regional development: experiences and prospects in the USA*. Paris.

CUMBERLAND, J. H. and KORBACH, R. J. (1973) A regional interindustry environmental model. *Pap. Reg. Sci. Assoc.* 30, 61–75.

CZAMANSKI, S. (1973) Linkages between industries in urban-regional complexes. In JUDGE, G. G. and TAKAYAMA, T. (eds) *Studies in economic planning over space and time*, 180–204.

CZAMANSKI, S. (1976) *Study of formation of spatial complexes.* Inst. Public Aff., Dalhousie Univ.

CZAMANSKI, S. and MALIZIA, E. E. (1969) Applications and limitations in the use of national input–output tables for regional studies. *Pap. Reg. Sci. Assoc.* 23, 65–78.

DALY, M. C. (1940) An approximation to a geographical multiplier. *Econ. J.* 50, 248–58.

DAVIS, N. H. W. (1971) *Cycles and trends in labour force participation: 1953–68.* Spec. Lab. Force Stud. Ser. B, J. Ottawa.

DENTON, F. T. (1966) *An analysis of interregional differences in manpower utilization and earnings.* Econ. Counc. of Canada Staff Stud. 15. Ottawa.

DEPARTMENT OF REGIONAL ECONOMIC EXPANSION (1973) *Assessment of the regional development incentives program.* Ottawa.

DOMAR, E. (1957) *Essays in the theory of economic growth.* Oxford.

DUN & BRADSTREET (1971) *The failure record through 1970.* Toronto.

DUNN, E. S. (1960) A statistical and analytical technique for regional analysis. *Pap. Reg. Sci. Assoc.* 6, 97–112.

DZIEWONSKI, K. (1973) Presidential address. *Pap. Reg. Sci. Assoc.* 30, 7–13.

ECONOMIC COUNCIL OF CANADA (1964) *First annual review.* Ottawa.

ECONOMIC DEVELOPMENT ADMINISTRATION (1972) *Program evaluation: the Economic Development Administration growth center strategy.* Washington, D.C.

ESTEBAN-MARQUILLAS, J. M. (1972) A reinterpretation of shift–share analysis. *Reg. & Urb. Econ.* 2, 577–81.

ESTLE, E. F. (1967) A more conclusive regional test of the Hecksher-Ohlin hypothesis. *J. Pol. Econ.* 75, 886–8.

FERGUSON, C. E. (1960) The relationship of business size to stability: an empirical approach. *J. Indust. Econ.* 9, 43–62.

FISHER, A. G. B. (1933) Capital and the growth of knowledge. *Econ. J.* 43, 374–89.

FLOYD, C. F. and SIRMANS, C. F. (1973) Shift and share projection revisited. *J. Reg. Sci.* 13, 115–20.

FLOYD, C. F. and SIRMANS, C. F. (1975) The stability of the regional share component: some further evidence. *Ann. Reg. Sci.* 9, 72–82.

FOSTER, M. I. (1972) Is the south still a backward region, and why? *Am. Econ. Rev. Pap. & Proc.* 62, 195–203.

FRIEDMAN, M. (1968) The role of monetary policy. *Am. Econ. Rev.* 58, 1–17.

FRIEDMANN, J. (1969) The future of urbanization in Latin America: some observations on the role of the periphery. *Pap. Reg. Sci. Assoc.* 23, 161–74.

FRIEDMANN, J. and ALONSO, W. (eds) (1975) *Regional policy.* Cambridge, Mass.

GALLAWAY, L. (1963) The north–south wage differential. *Rev. Econ. & Stat.* 45, 264–72.

GEORGE, R. E. (1969) *A leader and a laggard.* Toronto.

GIGANTES, T. (1970) The representation of technology in input–output systems. In CARTER, A. P. and BRODY, A. (eds) *Contributions to input–output analysis*, 270–90.

GILLEN, W. J. and GUCCIONE, A. (1970) The estimation of postwar regional consumption functions in Canada. *Can. J. Econ.* 3, 276–90.

GILLEN, W. J. and GUCCIONE, A. (1972) A simple disaggregation of a neo-classical investment function. *J. Reg. Sci.* 12, 279–94.

GILMORE, J. S. (1976) Boom towns may hinder energy resource development. *Sci.* 191 (4227), 535–40.

GOLDMAN, M. R. (1969) Comments on Czamanski and Malizia. *Pap. Reg. Sci. Assoc.* 23, 79–80.

GOLDSTEIN, G. S. (1973) Comments on paper by King and Forster. *Pap. Reg. Sci. Assoc.* 30, 197–8.

HALL, R. E. (1970) Why is the unemployment rate so high at full employment? *Brookings Pap. on Econ. Activity* 3, 369–402.

HANSEN, N. M. (ed.) (1972) *Growth centers in regional economic development.* New York.

HANSEN, N. M. (ed.) (1974) *Public policy and regional economic development.* Cambridge, Mass.

HANSEN, W. L. and TIEBOUT, C. M. (1963) An intersectoral flows analysis of the California economy. *Rev. Econ. & Stat.* 45, 409–18.

HARROD, R. F. (1949) *Towards a dynamic economics.* New York.

HARTMAN, L. M. and SECKLER, D. (1967) Toward the application of dynamic growth theory to regions. *J. Reg. Sci.* 7, 167–74.

HAZARI, R. B. (1970) Empirical identification of key sectors in the Indian economy. *Rev. Econ. & Stat.* 52, 301–5.

HENDERSON, J. M. and KRUEGER, A. O. (1965) *Economic growth and economic change in the Upper Midwest.* Minneapolis.

HETRICH, W. (1971) *Why distribution is important: an examination of equity and efficiency criteria in benefit–cost analysis.* Econ. Counc. Canada Spec. Stud. 19. Ottawa.

HEWINGS, G. J. D. (1969) Regional input–output models using national data: the structure of the West Midlands economy. *Ann. Reg. Sci.* 3, 179–91.

HEWINGS, G. J. D. (1970a) Regional planning: problems in the application of interregional input–output analysis to state planning and program activities. *Ann. Reg. Sci.* 4, 114–22.

HEWINGS, G. J. D. (1970b) *Regional input–output analysis in the United States: a bibliography.* SE Kent Input–Output Stud. Discussion Pap. 3. Canterbury.

HEWINGS, G. J. D. (1971a) *Some thoughts on regional forecasting using input–output models.* Centre Env. Stud. Conf. Pap. CP 1, 71–97. London.

HEWINGS, G. J. D. (1971b) Regional input–output models in the United Kingdom: some problems and prospects for the use of nonsurvey techniques. *Reg. Stud.* 5, 11–22.

HEWINGS, G. J. D. (1974) The effect of aggregation on the empirical identification of key sectors in a regional economy: a partial evaluation of alternative techniques. *Env. & Planning* 6, 439–53.

HEWINGS, G. J. D. (1975) Threshold analysis and urban development: an evaluation. *Ann. Reg. Sci.* 9, 21–31.

HEWINGS, G. J. D. (1976) On the accuracy of alternative models for stepping down multicounty employment estimates to counties. *Econ. Geogr.* 52, 206–17.

HEWINGS, G. J. D. and SCHRANZ, N. (1976) *The effects of spatial aggregation on the detection of spatial autocorrelation in economic projections.* Unpub. pap. read at Midcontinent Reg. Sci. Assoc. meeting. Bowling Green, Ohio.

HIGGINS, B. (1973) Trade-off curves and regional gaps. In BHAGWATI, J. N. and ECKAUS, R. S. (eds) *Development and planning*, 152–77. Cambridge, Mass.

HILDEBRAND, G. H. and MACE, A. (1950) The employment multiplier in an expanding industrial market: Los Angeles county 1940–7. *Rev. Econ. & Stat.* 32, 241–9.

HILL, M. I. (1973) *Planning for multiple objectives.* Reg. Sci. Res. Inst. Monog. ser. 5, Philadelphia.

HIRSCHMAN, A. O. (1958) *The strategy of economic development.* New Haven, Conn.

HOOVER, E. M. (1948) *The location of economic activity.* New York.

HOOVER, E. M. (1969) *An introduction to regional economics.* New York.

HOLT, G. C. (1969) Improving the labor market trade-off between inflation and unemployment. *Am. Econ. Rev.* 59, 135–46.

HORNE, G. R. *et al.* (1965) *A survey of labour market conditions, Windsor, Ontario.* Econ. Counc. Can. Spec. Stud. 2. Ottawa.

HOUSTON, D. (1967) The shift and share analysis of regional growth. *S. Econ. J.* 33, 577–81.

INNIS, H. (1933) *Problems of staple production in Canada.* Toronto.

ISARD, W. (1951) Interregional and regional input–output analysis: a model of a space economy. *Rev. Econ. & Stat.* 33, 318–28.

ISARD, W. (1960) *Methods of regional analysis.* Cambridge, Mass.

ISARD, W. (1969) Some notes on the linkages of the ecologic and economic systems. *Pap. Reg. Sci. Assoc.* 22, 85–96.

ISARD, W., SCHOOLER, E. and VIETORISZ, T. (1959) *Industrial complex analysis and regional development.* Cambridge, Mass.

ISARD, W. and ROMANOFF, E. (1968) *The printing and publishing industries of Boston SMSA, 1963, and a comparison with the corresponding Philadelphia industries.* Reg. Sci. Res. Inst. Tech. Pap. 7. Cambridge, Mass.

ISARD, W. *et al.* (1969) *General theory: social, political, economic and regional, with particular reference to decision-making analysis.* Cambridge, Mass.

ISARD, W. *et al.* (1972) *Ecological economic analysis for regional development.* New York.

ISSERMAN, A. M. (1975) Regional employment multiplier: a new approach. *Ld Econ.* 51, 290–3.

ISSERMAN, A. M. (1976) *Effective use of location quotients in estimating regional economic impacts.* Univ. Illinois Dept. Urb. Plan. Pap. 75-14. Urbana, Ill.

JAMES, F. J. and HUGHES, J. (1973) A test of shift and share analysis as a predictive device. *J. Reg. Sci.* 13, 223–31.

JOHNSTON, J. (1972) *Econometric methods.* New York.

KAIN, J. F. and MEYER, J. R. (eds) (1971) *Essays in regional economics.* Cambridge, Mass.

KALISKI, S. F. (1964) The relation between unemployment and the rate of change of money wages in Canada. *Internat. Econ. Rev.* 5, 1–33.

KATOUZIAN, M. A. (1970) The development of the service sector: a new approach. *Oxford Econ. Pap.* 22, 362–82.

KENNEDY, C. M. (1966a) Keynesian theory in an open economy. *Soc. & Econ. Stud.* 15, 1–21.

KENNEDY, C. M. (1966b) Domar-type theory in an open economy. *Soc. & Econ. Stud.* 15, 22.

KING, L. J., CASETTI, E. and JEFFREY, D. (1969) Economic impulses in a regional system of cities: a study of spatial interaction. *Reg. Stud.* 3, 213–18.

KING, L. J., CASETTI, E., JEFFREY, D. and ODLAND, J. (1972) Classifying US cities: spatial-temporal patterns in employment growth. *Growth & Change* 3, 37–42.

KING, L. J. and FORSTER, J. J. H. (1973) Wage-rate change in urban labor markets and intermarket linkages. *Pap. Reg. Sci. Assoc.* 30, 183–96.

KLASSEN, L. H. and PAELINCK, J. H. P. (1972) Asymmetry in shift-and-share analysis. *Reg. & Urb. Econ.* 2, 256–61.

KLEIN, L. R. (1968) The specification of regional econometric models. *Pap. Reg. Sci. Assoc.* 23, 105–15.

KNEESE, A. V. *et al.* (1970) *Economics and the environment.* Baltimore, Md.

KUEHN, J. (1971) Income convergence: a delusion. *Rev. Reg. Stud.* 2, 41–51.

KUKLINSKI, A. (ed.) (1972) *Regional planning.* Netherlands.

KUZNETS, S. (1959) *Six lectures on economic growth.* New York.

LASUEN, J. R. (1969) On growth poles. *Urb. Stud.* 6, 137–61.

LAURENT, E. A. and HITE, J. C. (1972) *Environmental planning: an economic analysis.* New York.

LE HERON, R. B. (1973) *Productivity change and regional economic development. The role of best practice forms in the Pacific Northwest plywood and veneer industry, 1960–72.* Unpub. PhD dissertation, Univ. Washington. Seattle.

LEONTIEF, W. W. (1953) Domestic production and foreign trade: the American capital position re-examined. *Proc. Am. Phil. Soc.* 97, 332–49.

LEONTIEF, W. W. (1956) Factor proportions and the structure of American trade: further theoretical and empirical analysis. *Rev. Econ. & Stat.* 38, 386–407.

LEONTIEF, W. W. (1961) The economic effects of disarmament. In *Input–output economics,* 167–83. Oxford.

LEONTIEF, W. W. (1965) The economic impact – industrial and regional – of an arms cut. In *Input–output economics,* 184–222. Oxford.

LEONTIEF, W. W. and STROUT, A. (1963) Multiregional input–output analysis. In BARNA, T. (ed.) *Structural interdependence and economic development*, 119–49. London. (Also in *Input–output economics*, 223–59. Oxford.)

LEVEN, C. L. (1961) Regional income and product accounts: construction and applications. In HOCHWALD, W. (ed.) *Design of regional accounts*, 148–95. Baltimore, Md.

LEVEN, C. L. (1964) Regional and interregional accounts in perspective. *Pap. Reg. Sci. Assoc.* 13, 127–44.

LIPSEY, R. G. (1960) The relation between unemployment and the rate of change of money wage rates in the United Kingdom 1862–1957: a further analysis. *Economica* 27, 1–31.

LIPSEY, R. G. (1965) Structural and deficient demand unemployment reconsidered. In ROSS, A. M. (ed.) *Employment policy and the labor market*, 210–55. Berkeley, Calif.

LIPSEY, R. G. (1969) *An introduction to positive economics*. London.

MCGUIRE, M. C. and GARN, H. A. (1969) The integration of equity and efficiency criteria in public project selection. *Econ. J.* 79, 882–93.

MACKAY, D. I. (1968) Industrial structure and regional growth: a methodological problem. *Scot. J. Pol. Econ.* 15, 129–43.

MCKEE, D. L., DEAN, R. D. and LEAHY, W. H. (eds) (1970) *Regional economics*. New York.

MCKEE, L. (1967) *Income and employment in the Southeast: a study in cyclical behavior*. Lexington, Ky.

MANNERS, G. *et al.* (1972) *Regional development in Britain*. London.

MANNERS, G. (1972) National perspectives. In MANNERS *et al.* (1972), 1–69.

MATHUR, V. J. and ROSEN, H. S. (1974) Regional employment multiplier: a new approach. *Ld Econ.* 50, 93–6.

MATUSZEWSKI, T., PITTS, P. R. and SAWYER, J. A. (1964) Linear programming estimates of changes in input coefficients. *Can. J. Econ. & Pol. Sci.* 30, 203–10.

MATUSZEWSKI, T. *et al.* (1967) *Rapport intérimaire sur le système de comptabilité économique du Québec*, vol. 1. Quebec.

MERA, K. (1967) Trade-off between aggregate efficiency and interregional equity: a static analysis. *Q. J. Econ.* 81, 658–74.

METCALF, D. (1971) The determinants of earnings changes: a regional analysis for the United Kingdom 1960–8. *Internat. Econ. Rev.* 12, 273–82.

METZLER, L. A. (1950) A multiple region theory of income and trade. *Econometrica* 18, 329–54.

MEYER, J. (1963) Regional economics: a survey. *Amer. Econ. Rev.* 53, 19–54. (Also reprinted in NEEDLEMAN 1968.)

MIERNYK, W. H. (1965) *The elements of input–output analysis*. New York.

MIERNYK, W. H. *et al.* (1969) *Simulating regional economic development*. Morgantown, W. Virginia.

MIERNYK, W. H. (1971) Local labor market effects of new plant locations. In KAIN, J. F. and MEYER, J. R. (eds) *Essays in regional economics*, 161–85. Cambridge, Mass.

MIERNYK, W. H. and SEARS, J. T. (1974) *Air pollution abatement and regional economic development.* Lexington, Ky.

MILLER, R. E. (1966) Interregional feedback effects in input–output models: some preliminary results. *Pap. Reg. Sci. Assoc.* 17, 105–25.

MILLER, R. E. (1969) Interregional feedbacks in input–output models: some experimental results. *W. Econ. J.* 7, 57–70.

MISHAN, E. J. (1971) *Cost-benefit analysis.* London.

MOORE, B. and RHODES, J. (1973) Evaluating the effects of British regional economic policy. *Econ. J.* 83, 87–110.

MORONEY, J. R. (1970) Factor prices, factor proportions and regional factor endowments. *J. Pol. Econ.* 87, 158–64.

MORONEY, J. R. and WALKER, J. M. (1966) A regional test of the Heckscher-Ohlin hypothesis. *J. Pol. Econ.* 74, 573–86.

MOSELEY, M. J. (1974) *Growth centres in spatial planning.* Oxford.

MOSES, L. (1955) The stability of interregional trading patterns and input–output analysis. *Am. Econ. Rev.* 45, 803–32.

MUSGRAVE, R. A. (1959) *The theory of public finance.* London.

MYRDAL, G. (1957) *Economic theory and underdeveloped regions.* London.

NBER (1957) *Problems of capital formation.* Princeton, N.J.

NEEDLEMAN, L. (ed.) (1968) *Regional analysis.* London.

NEVIN, E. T., ROE, A. R. and ROUND, J. I. (1966) *The structure of the Welsh economy.* Cardiff.

NEWMAN, M. (1972) *The political economy of Appalachia.* Lexington, Ky.

NORTH, D. C. (1955) Location theory and regional economic growth. *J. Pol. Econ.* 63, 243–58.

NORTH, D. C. (1956) A reply. *J. Pol. Econ.* 64, 165–8.

NOURSE, H. O. (1968) *Regional economics.* New York.

OATES, W. (1972) *Fiscal federalism.* New York.

OBERS (1972) *Projections of regional economic activity in the United States,* vol. 1: *Concepts, methodology and summary data.* Washington, D.C.

O'DONNELL, J. L. *et al.* (1960) *Economic and population base study of the Lansing Tri-County Area.* Detroit.

OFFICE OF BUSINESS ECONOMICS (1969) *Survey of current business* (August).

OFFICE OF SECRETARY OF DEFENSE (1967) *Military prime contract awards by region and state, fiscal years 1962–7.* Washington, D.C.

OFFICER, L. H. and ANDERSON, P. R. (1969) Labour force participation in Canada. *Can. J. Econ.* 2, 278–87.

OSTRY, S. (1968) *Unemployment in Canada.* Ottawa.

OSTRY, S. and ZAIDI, M. (1972) *Labour economics in Canada.* Toronto.

PAELINCK, J. (1972) Programming a viable minimal investment industrial complex for a growth center. In HANSEN, N. M. (ed.) *Growth centers in regional economic development,* 139–59. New York.

PARASKEVOPOULOS, C. C. (1974) Patterns of regional economic growth. *Reg. & Urb. Econ.* 4, 77–105.

PARR, J. B. (1966) Outmigration and the depressed area problem. *Ld Econ.* 42, 149–59.

PARR, J. B. (1973) Growth poles, regional development and central place theory. *Pap. Reg. Sci. Assoc.* 31, 173–212.

PEACOCK, A. T. and DOSSER, D. G. M. (1959) Regional input–output analysis and government spending. *Scot. J. Pol. Econ.* 6, 229–36.

PERLOFF, H. *et al.* (1960) *Regions, resources and economic growth.* Lincoln, Neb.

PERROUX, F. (1955) Note sur la notion de 'pole de croissance'. *Economie Appliquée* 307–20.

PFISTER, R. L. (1961) The terms of trade as a tool of regional analysis. *J. Reg. Sci.* 3, 57–65.

PFISTER, R. L. (1963) External trade and regional growth: a case study of the Pacific Northwest. *Econ. Dev. & Cult. Change* 11, 134–51.

PHELPS, E. S. (1969) The new microeconomics in inflation and employment theory. *Am. Econ. Rev.* 59, 147–60.

PHELPS, E. S. (1971) Inflation, expectations and economic theory. In SWAN, N. and WILTON, D. (eds) *Inflation and the Canadian experience*, 31–47. Kingston, Ontario.

PHILLIPS, A. W. (1958) The relation between unemployment and the rate of change of money wages in the United Kingdom 1862–1957. *Economica* 25, 283–99.

POLENSKE, K. R. (1966) *A case study of transportation models used in multi-regional analysis.* Unpub. PhD dissertation, Harvard Univ. Cambridge, Mass.

POLENSKE, K. R. (1969) Empirical implementation of a multiregional input–output gravity trade model. In CARTER and BRODY (1970).

POLENSKE, K. R. (1970a) An empirical test of interregional input–output models: estimation of 1963 Japanese production. *Am. Econ. Rev.* 60, 76–82.

POLENSKE, K. R. (1970b) *The implementation of a multiregional input–output model for the United States.* Mimeo.

POLENSKE, K. R. (1970c) *A multiregional input–output model for the United States.* Econ. Devel. Admin. Rep. 22. Washington, D.C.

POLENSKE, K. R. (1972a) *A guide for users of the United States multiregional input–output model.* Washington, D.C.

POLENSKE, K. R. (1972b) The implementation of a multiregional input–output model for the United States. In CARTER and BRODY (1972), 171–89.

PRATT, R. T. (1968) An appraisal of the minimum requirements technique. *Econ. Geogr.* 44, 117–24.

PRED, A. R. (1974) *Major job-providing organizations and systems of cities.* Assoc. Amer. Geogr. Res. Pap. 27. Washington, D.C.

REES, A. (1970) The Phillips curve as a menu for policy choice. *Economica* 37, 227–38.

REINER, T. A. (1971) A multiple goals framework for regional planning. *Pap. Reg. Sci. Assoc.* 26, 207–39.

RICHARDSON, H. W. (1969a) *Regional economics.* London.

RICHARDSON, H. W. (1969b) *The elements of regional economics.* London.

RICHARDSON, H. W. (1971) *Urban economics.* London.

RICHARDSON, H. W. (1972) Theory of the distribution of city sizes: review and prospects. *Reg. Stud.* 7, 239–51.

RICHARDSON, H. W. (1973) *Regional growth theory.* London.

RICHARDSON, H. W. (1973) *Input–output and regional economics.* London.

RIEFLER, R. and TIEBOUT, C. M. (1970) Interregional input–output: an empirical California–Washington model. *J. Reg. Sci.* 10, 135–52.

ROSENBLUTH, G. (1968a) *The Canadian economy and disarmament.* New York.

ROSENBLUTH, G. (1968b) *Input–output analysis.* Unpub. pap. read at AUTE conf.

ROSTOW, W. W. (1960) *The stages of economic growth.* Cambridge.

ROTHBLATT, D. N. (1971) *Regional planning: the Appalachian experience.* Lexington, Ky.

ROUND, J. I. (1972) Regional input–output models in the United Kingdom: a reappraisal of some techniques. *Reg. Stud.* 6, 1–9.

ROWAN, D. C. (1969) *Output, inflation and growth.* London.

SAKASHITA, N. (1973) An axiomatic approach to shift-and-share analysis. *Reg. & Urb. Econ.* 3, 263–72.

SAMUELSON, P. A. (1976) *Economics.* New York.

SCHAFFER, W. A. and CHU, K. (1969) Nonsurvey techniques for constructing regional interindustry models. *Pap. Reg. Sci. Assoc.* 23, 83–101.

SCHRAMM, G. (1972) Regional benefits in federal project evaluations. *Ann. Reg. Sci.* 6, 84–95.

SCHWARTZ, C. F. and GRAHAM, R. E. (1956) *Personal income by states since 1929.* Washington, D.C.

SEMPLE, R. K. *et al.* (1972) Growth poles in Sao Paulo, Brazil. *Ann. Assoc. Am. Geogr.* 62, 591–8.

SIEBERT, H. (1969) *Regional economic growth.* Scranton, Pa.

SIEGAL, R. A. (1966–7) Do regional business cycles exist? *W. Econ. J.* 5, 44–57.

SMILEY, M. A. (1973) *Employment trends in Ontario 1961–72.* Ontario Min. Labour Res. Branch Employment Inf. Ser. 1. Toronto.

SPRINGATE, D. (1972) *Regional development incentive grants and private investment in Canada.* Unpub. PhD dissertation, Harvard Univ. Cambridge, Mass.

STEELE, D. B. (1969) Regional multipliers in Great Britain. *Oxford Econ. Pap.* 21, 268–92.

STELLWAGON, M. A. (1967) *An analysis of the spatial impact of federal revenues and expenditures 1950 and 1960.* Unpub. PhD dissertation, Univ. Washington. Seattle.

STILWELL, F. J. B. (1969) Regional growth and structural adaptation. *Urb. Stud.* 6, 162–98.

STONE, R. *et al.* (1963) *A programme for growth.* Cambridge.

SU, T. T. (1970) A note on regional input–output models. *S. Econ. J.* 37, 325–7.

TANDAN, N. K. (1969) *Underutilization of manpower in Canada.* Spec. Lab. Force Stud. 8. Ottawa.

THEIL, H. (1967) *Economics and information theory.* Chicago.

THIRLWALL, A. P. (1966) Regional unemployment as a cyclical phenomenon. *Scot. J. Pol. Econ.* 13, 205–19.

THIRLWALL, A. P. (1967) A measure of the proper distribution of industry. *Oxford Econ. Pap.* 19, 46–58.

THIRLWALL, A. P. (1969) Demand disequilibrium in the labour market and wage inflation in the United Kingdom. *Yorks Bull.* 66–76.

THIRLWALL, A. P. (1970) Regional Phillips curves. *Oxford Univ. Bull. Econ. & Stat.* 32, 18–32.

THIRLWALL, A. P. (1975) Forecasting regional unemployment in Great Britain. *Reg. Sci. & Urb. Econ.* 5, 357–74.

THIRSK, W. (1973) *Regional dimensions of inflation and unemployment.* Prices & Incomes Commiss. Rep. Ottawa.

THOMAS, M. D. (1964) The export base and development stages theories of regional economic growth: an appraisal. *Ld Econ.* 40, 421–32.

THOMAS, M. D. (1969) Regional economic growth: some conceptual aspects. *Ld Econ.* 46, 43–51.

THOMAS, M. D. (1972) Growth pole theory: an examination of some of its basic concepts. In HANSEN, N. M. (ed.) *Growth centers in regional economic development,* 50–81. New York.

THOMPSON, G. E. (1959) An investigation of the local employment multiplier. *Rev. Econ. & Stat.* 41, 61–7.

THOMPSON, W. (1965) *A preface to urban economics.* Baltimore, Md.

THOMPSON, W. (1966) Urban economic development. In HIRSCH, W. Z. (ed.) *Regional accounts for policy decisions,* 81–121. Baltimore, Md.

THOMPSON, W. (1968) Internal and external factors in the development of urban economies. In PERLOFF, H. S. and WINGO, L. (eds) *Issues in urban economics,* 43–62. Baltimore, Md.

TIEBOUT, C. M. (1956) Exports and regional economic growth (and) rejoinder. *J. Pol. Econ.* 64, 160–4, 169.

TIEBOUT, C. M. (1962) *The community economic base study.* New York.

TIEBOUT, C. M. (ed.) (1965) Symposium: the regional impact of defense expenditures. *W. Econ. J.* 3, 125–51.

TIEBOUT, C. M. (1968) *Economic study of Puget Sound and adjacent waters: projections 1980, 2000, 2020.* Seattle.

TIEBOUT, C. M. (1969) An empirical regional input–output projection model: the State of Washington 1980. *Rev. Econ. & Stat.* 51, 334–40.

TIEBOUT, C. M. and LANE, T. (1966) The local service sector in relation to economic growth. In *Research and education for regional and area development,* 95–109. Ames, Iowa.

TILANUS, C. B. (1966) *Input–output experiments.* Rotterdam.

TOBIN, J. (1972) Inflation and unemployment. *Am. Econ. Rev.* 62, 1–18.

TORONTO GLOBE AND MAIL (1972) *Business review.* 12 January, B5.

ULLMAN, E. L. (1968) Minimum requirements after a decade: a critique and an appraisal. *Econ. Geogr.* 44, 364–9.

ULLMAN, E. L. and DACEY, M. F. (1960) The minimum requirements approach to the urban economic base. *Pap. Reg. Sci. Assoc.* 6, 175–94.

ULLMAN, E. L., DACEY, M. F. and BRODSKY, H. (1969) *The economic base of American cities.* Seattle.

UNITED STATES BUREAU OF LABOR STATISTICS (1966) *Projections 1970.* Bull. 1536. Washington, D.C.

UNITED STATES DEPT OF COMMERCE (1967) *Regional effects of governmental procurement and related policies.* Washington, D.C.

UNITED STATES DEPT OF TRANSPORTATION (1974) *Rail service in the Midwest and Northeast region.* Washington, D.C.

UNITED STATES HOUSE COMMITTEE ON INSULAR AND INTERNAL AFFAIRS (1968) *Hearings before subcommittee on national parks and recreation.* Ser. No. 90-24. Washington, D.C.

VANDERKAMP, J. (1970) The effects of outmigration on regional employment. *Can. J. Econ.* 3, 541–9.

VICTOR, P. A. (1972) *Pollution: economy and environment.* Toronto.

WACHTER, M. L. (1972) A labor supply model for secondary workers. *Rev. Econ. & Stat.* 54, 141–51.

WHITE, D. A. (1970) *Business cycles in Canada.* Econ. Counc. of Canada Staff Stud. 17. Ottawa.

WILLIAMSON, J. I. (1965) Regional inequality and the process of national development: a description of the patterns. *Econ. Dev. & Cult. Change* 13, 3–45.

WILSON, T. (1968) The regional multiplier-critique. *Oxford Econ. Pap.* 20, 374–93.

WOODWARD, R. S. (1974) The capital bias of DREE incentives. *Can. J. Econ.* 7, 161–73.

YEATES, M. H. and LLOYD, P. E. (1970) *Impact of industrial incentives: southern Georgian Bay region.* Ottawa.

ZIMMERMAN, R. (1975) A variant of the shift and share projection formulation. *J. Reg. Sci.* 15, 29–38.

Appendix

Guide to major journals publishing articles in the area of regional industrial analysis.

Papers of the Regional Science Association
Published by the Regional Science Association, two volumes yearly containing papers presented at annual North American and European Meetings. Available from Regional Science Association, University of Pennsylvania, Philadelphia, PA 19174, USA.

Journal of Regional Science
Three numbers per volume containing refereed papers on a variety of topics, usually of a theoretical nature. Available from the Regional Science Research Institute, Box 8776, Philadelphia, PA 19101, USA.

Regional Science and Urban Economics
Four numbers per volume with article content similar to the *Journal of Regional Science*. Published by Elsevier/North-Holland, P.O. Box 211, Amsterdam, The Netherlands.

International Regional Science Review
A new journal with a planned two issues per volume. Contains articles with a broader appeal than the *Journal of Regional Science*, particularly stressing applications of theory and policy analysis. Available from the Regional Science Association (see first listing).

Annals of Regional Science
Three numbers per volume. Published by the Western Regional Science Association and contains both unsolicited papers and those presented at the annual meeting. Available from: Department of Economics, Western Washington State College, Bellingham, WA 98225, USA.

Review of Regional Studies

A similar type of journal to the *Annals of Regional Science*, published by the Southern Regional Science Association with three numbers per volume. Available from J. C. Hite, Clemson University, Clemson, SC 29631, USA.

Regional Science Perspectives

The Journal of the Midcontinent Regional Science Association, containing papers presented at the annual meeting. Available from Department of Economics, Kansas State University, Manhattan, KS 66506, USA.

Northeast Regional Science Review

Contains papers given at the annual Northeast Regional Science Conference. Available from Manas Chatterji, School of Management, SUNY, Binghampton, NY 13901, USA.

Environment and Planning series A

Eight numbers per volume with articles covering a broad spectrum of theoretical and applied urban and regional research. Available from Pion Ltd, 207 Brondesbury Park, London NW2, England.

Journal of Urban Economics

The US counterpart to *Urban Studies*, but with a more theoretical bias in the traditions of economic theory. Available from Academic Press, III, Fifth Avenue, NY, NY 1003, USA

Regional Studies

The journal of the British Regional Studies Association, four numbers per volume. Contributions emphasize application and policy analysis. Available from Pergamon Press, Headington Hill Hall, Oxford, England.

Growth and Change

Published four times a year and contains shorter articles designed to appeal to a wide audience of academics and nonacademics in government and the private sector. Available from University of Kentucky, Lexington, KY 40506, USA.

Economic Geography

Four numbers per volume with articles reflecting a wide range of topical interests in economic analysis, transportation, diffusion, industrial location, etc. Available from Clark University, Worcester, MA 01610, USA.

Land Economics

Four numbers per volume, with a wide range of articles from a variety of social science perspectives. One of the first journals to publish articles in this field. Available from University of Wisconsin, Madison, WI 53701, USA.

Urban Studies
The first journal to devote some attention to urban analysis. Three numbers per volume with contributions from economists, sociologists, geographers and planners predominantly. Available from Longman Journals, 43–45 Annandale Street, Edinburgh, Scotland.

Indexes

Author index

Subject Index